Stanley Lane-Poole

A History of Egypt

Second Edition

Stanley Lane-Poole

A History of Egypt
Second Edition

ISBN/EAN: 9783337324353

Printed in Europe, USA, Canada, Australia, Japan

Cover: Foto ©ninafisch / pixelio.de

More available books at **www.hansebooks.com**

A
HISTORY OF EGYPT

UNDER ROMAN RULE

BY

J. GRAFTON MILNE, M.A.
SOMETIME SCHOLAR OF C.C.C., OXFORD

WITH NUMEROUS ILLUSTRATIONS

SECOND EDITION

METHUEN & CO. LTD.
36 ESSEX STREET W.C.
LONDON

PREFACE

It may seem somewhat premature to issue a History of Roman Egypt, when there are masses of papyri, belonging to the period under consideration, waiting for publication in half a dozen different museums. But the additions to our knowledge made by the documents already published are so considerable, that it will be of service to students to have them briefly summarised.

It must be recognised that the story of Egypt during the centuries of Roman rule is not, and probably never will be, anything like a connected narrative. From time to time a chance notice by some writer throws a momentary light on the state of the country; but, for the most part, events in Egypt were too monotonously uninteresting for the historians of the Roman Empire to pay any attention to them. Egypt supplied corn, not men, to Rome.

There is one point on which I should like to forestall criticism. In the spelling of proper names and titles, I have found it impossible to be consistent when dealing with the mixture of Egyptian, Greek, and Latin which prevailed during the period. And so I have used whatever form was most familiar to me, as it seemed better even to write the Latinized "drachmae" beside the Greek "arourai," than to fall into the pedantry of such a style as "Thebai"; the more so, when it is necessary to deal with such compound names as Ælius Eudæmon or Aurelius Didymus.

I have to thank Professor Petrie for continual help and advice throughout the time that I have been preparing this book, both in Egypt and in England. Mr. F. G. Kenyon and Mr. B. P. Grenfell have most kindly put at my disposal the proof-sheets of their publications of papyri, and the latter has also made a number of valuable suggestions; while Mr. F. Ll. Griffith has given me information on various points connected with Egyptian religion. I have tried to acknowledge in the references all facts and ideas which I have drawn from other writers, but I feel that I owe a special debt to Professor Mommsen and Professor J. B. Bury in a wider sense than can be stated there. And I must also thank Mr. D. S. Crichton for much careful work in preparing the index; and my wife, for constant clerical assistance.

LONDON, 13*th September* 1898.

CONTENTS

	PAGE
PREFACE	v
LIST OF ILLUSTRATIONS	ix
LIST OF ABBREVIATIONS	xiii

CHAP.
- I. THE ORGANISATION OF EGYPT UNDER THE ROMANS . 1
- II. THE FIRST CENTURY OF ROMAN RULE IN EGYPT, 30 B.C.–68 A.D. 15
- III. A CENTURY OF PROSPERITY, 68–192 A.D. . . . 39
- IV. THE DECAY OF THE PROVINCIAL SYSTEM, 193–283 A.D. 67
- V. THE STRUGGLE BETWEEN THE STATE AND THE CHURCH, 284–379 A.D. 84
- VI. ESTABLISHMENT OF THE SUPREMACY OF THE CHRISTIAN CHURCH, 379–527 A.D. 96
- VII. UNION OF TEMPORAL AND RELIGIOUS POWER, 527–642 A.D. 106
- VIII. THE REVENUES AND TAXATION OF EGYPT . . 118
- IX. RELIGIOUS INSTITUTIONS 128
- X. LIFE IN THE TOWNS AND VILLAGES OF EGYPT 159

APP.
- I. THE ROMAN GARRISON IN EGYPT . 169
- II. PREFECTS OF EGYPT 176
- III. INSCRIPTIONS IN THE GHIZEH MUSEUM . 183
- IV. NOTES 196
- V. REFERENCES . . . 231

INDEX 249

LIST OF ILLUSTRATIONS

FIG.		PAGE
1.	Augustus: Temple K, Philæ	16
2.	Augustus adoring Isis: Tentyra	17
3.	Philæ: Temple of Hathor	17
4.	Khnum forming Augustus, and Hekt giving him life: Tentyra	18
5.	Talmis: Front of Temple	18
6.	Tentyra: Temple from the south	19
7.	Augustus: Talmis	20
8.	Augustus: Debôt	20
9.	Talmis: Temple from behind	21
10.	Dendur: Temple	22
11.	Pselkis: Temple and Pylon	22
12.	Hiera Sykaminos: Temple	23
13.	Tiberius: Philæ	25
14.	Philæ: West side of Great Court . . .	25
15.	Tentyra: Portico of Temple. (Photo. by W. M. F. Petrie.).	26
16.	Tiberius: Philæ	27
17.	Stele of Tiberius adoring Isis and Horus, in Ghizeh Museum. (Photo by J. G. M.)	27
18.	Tiberius: Philæ	28
19.	Caligula: Tentyra	29
20.	Alexandria: Ruins of the Gymnasium. (Ainslie, Views in Egypt.)	30
21.	Claudius: Philæ	32
22.	Latopolis: Capitals of columns. (Photo. by W. M. F. Petrie.)	32
23.	Hermopolis Magna: Temple. (Description de l'Égypte.)	33
24.	Nero: Tentyra	35
25.	Karanis: Interior of Temple of Pnepherôs and Petesouchos. (Photo. by J. G. M.)	35
26.	Nero: Ombos	36
27.	Karanis: Gateway of Nero in Temple of Pnepherôs and Petesouchos. (Photo. by J. G. M.) . . .	37

LIST OF ILLUSTRATIONS

FIG.		PAGE
28.	Galley of Nero. (Bodleian.)	38
29.	Galba: Thebes	39
30.	Otho: Thebes	40
31.	Karanis: Gateway of Vespasian in Temple of Pnepheros and Petesouchos. (Photo. by J. G. M.)	43
32.	Alexandria: "Cleopatra's Needle" and Roman tower. (Description de l'Egypte.)	44
33.	Roman Stele: in Ghizeh Museum. (Photo. by J. G. M.)	45
34.	Titus: Latopolis	46
35.	Domitian: Latopolis	47
36.	Nerva: Latopolis	49
37.	Trajan: Latopolis	49
38.	Philæ: Temple of Trajan	50
39.	Trajan dancing: Tentyra	51
40.	Tentyra: Gateway of Trajan	51
41.	Trajan: Philæ	52
42.	Roman fortress of Babylon. (Description de l'Egypte.)	53
43.	Hadrian: Philæ	55
44.	Mummy portrait: from Hawara	56
45.	Statue of Antinous? (Vatican.)	57
46.	Antinoopolis: Arch of Triumph. (Description de l'Egypte.)	57
47.	Antinoopolis. (Description de l'Egypte.)	58
48.	Cartouche of Sabina	59
49.	Hadrian approaching Alexandria. (British Museum.)	60
50.	Hadrian greeted by Alexandria. (British Museum.)	60
51.	Antoninus Pius: Tentyra	61
52.	Phœnix: Coin of Antoninus Pius. (Bodleian.)	62
53.	Aurelius: Latopolis	63
54.	Antæopolis: Temple. (Description de l'Egypte.)	64
55.	Commodus: Latopolis	65
56.	Roman tombstones from Abydos: in Ghizeh Museum. (Photo. by J. G. M.)	68
57.	Severus: Latopolis	69
58.	Severus and Julia: Latopolis	70
59.	Caracalla and Geta: Latopolis	71
60.	Geta: Latopolis	71
61.	Colossal head of Caracalla: from Koptos. (Photo. by W. M. F. Petrie.)	71
62.	Caracalla: Latopolis	72
63.	Statue, face recut to likeness of Caracalla: in Ghizeh Museum. (Photo. by J. G. M.)	72
64.	Wady Khardassy: Greek tablets	74
65.	Roman lamp in form of a boat. (Petrie Collection.)	74
66.	Decius: Latopolis	76
67.	Inscription of Quietus: from Koptos. (Petrie Collection.)	77
68.	Coin of M. Iulius Æmilianus. (British Museum.)	78
69.	Miniature altar. (Petrie Collection.)	79

LIST OF ILLUSTRATIONS

FIG.		PAGE
70.	Altar of M. Aurelius Belakabos: from Koptos. (Photo. by W. M. F. Petrie.)	79
71.	Roman terra-cotta figures (Petrie Collection.)	81
72.	Philæ: Arch of Diocletian	85
73.	Roman lamps and handles. (Petrie Collection.)	85
74.	Coin of Domitius Domitianus. (British Museum.)	86
75.	Column of Diocletian at Alexandria	87
76.	Roman lamp in form of a gateway. (Petrie Collection.)	88
77.	The Red Monastery: Interior looking west. (Photo. by J. G. M.)	98
78.	The White Monastery: North door. (Photo. by J. G. M.)	101
79.	The White Monastery: South wall. (Photo. by J. G. M.)	104
80.	Byzantine sculptures: from Ahnas. (E.E.F. Report.)	106
81.	Byzantine capital: from Ahnas. (E.E.F. Report.)	108
82.	Coptic tombstones: in Ghizeh Museum. (Photo. by W. M. F. Petrie.)	109
83.	Coptic tombstones: in Ghizeh Museum. (Photo. by W. M. F. Petrie.)	111
84.	Designs from fragments of Coptic pottery. (Petrie Collection.)	113
85.	Coptic painted pottery. (Petrie Collection.)	114
86.	Tariff-Stele of Koptos: in Ghizeh Museum. (Photo. by J. G. M.)	123
87.	Stele from Soknopaiou Nesos: in Ghizeh Museum. (Photo by J. G. M.)	129
88.	Column with figures of priests: at Rome. (Photo. by W. M. F. Petrie.)	130
89.	Figure of Bes: Tentyra. (Photo. by W. M. F. Petrie.)	132
90.	Phthah: Coin of Hadrian. (British Museum.)	132
91.	Zeus Ammon: Coin of Hadrian. (British Museum.)	133
92.	Pantheistic Zeus Sarapis: Coin of Hadrian. (British Museum.)	134
93.	Temple of Zeus: Coin of Trajan. (British Museum.)	134
94.	Zeus: Coin of Trajan. (British Museum.)	135
95.	Hera: Coin of Nero. (British Museum.)	135
96.	Poseidon: Coin of Claudius II. (British Museum.)	135
97.	Kybele: Coin of Julia Domna. (British Museum.)	135
98.	Apollo: Coin of Nero. (British Museum.)	136
99.	Helios: Coin of Hadrian. (Bodleian.)	136
100.	Artemis: Coin of Antoninus Pius. (British Museum.)	136
101.	Selene: Coin of Julia Paula. (British Museum.)	136
102.	Athene: Coin of Gallienus. (British Museum.)	137
103.	Temple of Athene: Coin of Antoninus Pius. (British Museum.)	137
104.	Ares: Coin of Hadrian. (Bodleian.)	137
105.	Dionysos: Coin of Trajan. (British Museum.)	138
106.	Pan: Coin of Hadrian. (British Museum.)	138

LIST OF ILLUSTRATIONS

FIG. | PAGE
107. Hermes: Coin of Claudius II. (British Museum.) . 138
108. Demeter: Coin of Antoninus Pius. (British Museum.) 138
109. Rape of Persephone: Coin of Trajan. (British Museum.) 138
110. Triptolemos: Coin of Hadrian. (British Museum.) . 139
111. Dioskouroi: Coin of Trajan. (British Museum.) . 139
112. Herakles: Coin of Trajan. (Bodleian.) . . . 139
113. Asklepios: Coin of Severus Alexander. (British Museum.) 140
114. Hygieia: Coin of Severus Alexander. (British Museum.) 140
115. Sarapis: Coin of Hadrian. (Bodleian.) . . . 140
116. Head of Sarapis. (Plaque in Petrie Collection.) . . 141
117. Temple of Sarapis: Coin of M. Aurelius. (British Museum.) 141
118. Sarapeion and Hadrianon. (British Museum.) . . 141
119. Sarapis: Coin of Hadrian. (British Museum.) . . 142
120. Isis and Sarapis. (Vatican Museum.) . . . 142
121. Temple of Isis: Coin of Trajan. (British Museum.) . 143
122. Isis Pharia: Coin of Antoninus Pius. (British Museum.) 143
123. Isis Sothis: Coin of Faustina II. (British Museum.) . 143
124. Isis: Coin of Nerva. (Bodleian.) 144
125. Isis suckling Horus: Coin of M. Aurelius. (Bodleian.) 144
126. Bronze Sistrum: at Naples. (Photo. by W. M. F. Petrie.) 144
127. Horus as a child in military dress. (Terra-cotta in Petrie Collection.) 145
128. Harpokrates: Coin of Trajan. (British Museum.) . 145
129. Osiris with stars: from Koptos. (Photo. by W. M. F. Petrie.) 146
130. Hermanubis: Coin of Hadrian. (British Museum.) . 147
131. Temple of Hermanubis: Coin of Antoninus Pius. (British Museum.) 147
132. Temple of Nilus: Coin of Hadrian. (British Museum.) 148
133. Nilus: Coin of Nero. (Bodleian.) 148
134. Nilus: Coin of Trajan. (British Museum.) . . 148
135. Euthenia: Coin of Livia. (British Museum.) . . 148
136. Temple of Tyche: Coin of Antoninus Pius. (British Museum.) 150
137. Tyche: Coin of Hadrian. (British Museum.) . . 150
138. Tyche of Alexandria: Coin of Antoninus Pius. (British Museum.) 150
139. Alexandria: Coin of Hadrian. (British Museum.) . 150
140. Roma: Coin of Antoninus Pius. (British Museum.) . 150
141. Roma: Coin of Antoninus Pius. (Bodleian.) . . 150
142. The White Monastery: Old nave of church, now the courtyard. (Photo. by J. G. M.) 156
143. The White Monastery: Walled-in columns of nave. (Photo. by J. G. M.) 157

LIST OF ABBREVIATIONS USED

B.C.H.	Bulletin de Correspondance Hellénique.
B.G.U.	Griechische Urkunden aus den Kgl. Museen zu Berlin.
B.M.	British Museum.
C.I.G.	Corpus Inscriptionum Graecarum.
C.I.L.	,, ,, Latinarum.
C.P.R.	,, Papyrorum Raineri.
E.E.F.	Egypt Exploration Fund.
G.G.P. i.	Grenfell, an Alexandrian Erotic Fragment and other papyri.
G.G.P. ii.	Grenfell and Hunt, Greek Papyri ii.
G.O.P.	,, ,, Oxyrhynchus Papyri.
M.A.	Musée d'Alexandrie.
M.G.	Musée de Ghîzeh.
N. et E.	Notices et Extraits des MSS. du Louvre.
Pap. Gen.	Papyrus de Genève, ed. J. Nicole.
P.S.B.A.	Proceedings of the Society of Biblical Archæology.
R.A.	Revue Archéologique.
R.E.	,, Egyptologique.
R.E.G.	,, des Études Grecques.

A HISTORY OF EGYPT

ROMAN EGYPT

CHAPTER I

The Organisation of Egypt under the Romans

1. The conquest of Egypt by the Romans produced little change in the internal organisation of the country. It was always the policy of Roman statesmen, when a country possessing a fully developed system of government was added to their empire, to interfere as little as possible with existing institutions; and there was a special reason in the case of Egypt for adopting this course. The country was, in a sense, the personal spoil of Augustus; while the older provinces of the Roman Empire had been won from foreign kings for the Republic by its generals and with its armies, Egypt was the fruit of his victory over a Roman rival, albeit a recreant to Roman ideas; and, as the personal property of that rival's wife, was confiscated for the private benefit of the victor.

2. The elaborate system of government which had gradually been developed by the native and Greek kings was therefore taken over bodily by the Roman emperors. In all probability the lower grades of officials were left to complete their terms of office: even in so high a position as that of epistrategos there

is found a Greek, Ptolemaios, the son of Herakleides, thirteen years after the conquest;[1] and as in later times that post was always held by a Roman, it may be presumed that he had continued in his place undisturbed by the change of dynasty. For, indeed, the Roman conquest of Egypt was practically nothing more than a change of dynasty, and was attended by far less disturbance than had many times been caused by the transference of power in the time of the native kings.

3. In the course which Augustus chose to follow with regard to the government of Egypt, he was guided partly by his personal claim explained above, and partly by considerations of prudence:[2] the country was rich, and could easily furnish the materials for supporting a revolt; while, at the same time, anyone who held Egypt could cause great inconvenience to the population of Rome without any further hostile measures than simply stopping the export of corn from Alexandria, and could thus practically starve Rome to his side, as Vespasian proposed to do.[3] Moreover, Egypt was difficult of access, especially from Rome: there was only one harbour on the Mediterranean coast available for large vessels, at Alexandria;[4] and the approaches by land across the deserts, either from east or west, were dangerous for a body of any large number of men. The Egyptians, too, were always ready for a disturbance; the most trivial question would raise faction-fights among the crowds of various nations and beliefs who inhabited Alexandria,[5] while the inhabitants of the upper country from time to time took up arms to settle their local grievances;[6] and from such small beginnings there might arise serious troubles, unless prompt and vigorous measures were taken. In all these reasons lay a great argument for autocratic rule, which could act on such an occasion without the danger of delay which might arise from the necessity of consulting the senate, purely formal as the consultation might be, to get consent to measures which seemed good to the emperor.

4. Egypt was therefore treated as the personal domain

of the Roman emperor; and from him, directly or indirectly, all the Egyptian officials held their posts. To guard against any possibility of senatorial interference, no member of the senate was allowed to take office, or even to set foot, without the special leave of the emperor, in the country.[7] The highest position—that of prefect —was usually filled by a Roman of equestrian rank;[8] on one occasion at least a freedman,[9] and on one an Alexandrian,[10] who had obtained the Roman citizenship, were placed in this office. The prefect, nominally a procurator of the emperor, was really a viceroy, taking almost the whole part played in the system of government by the Greek kings. His power was limited only by the right of appeal to the emperor; and he was head of every branch of the administration, financial, judicial, and military.[11] The sum-total that was to be raised by taxation was determined by the emperor; but the prefect was responsible to him for the collection and transmission of the money to Rome,[12] and consequently was particularly concerned to supervise the collectors and other subordinate officials, with a view of keeping in check their exactions, which tended to diminish the revenues of the state;[13] and also had to decide upon claims of exemption from taxation made by communities or individuals.[14] The judicial duties of the prefect, which theoretically embraced all cases, both civil and criminal, were lightened by the delegation of authority to lower officials;[15] but large numbers of legal questions came before him for settlement, as petitions for the redress of injuries could be addressed directly to him,[16] and he received appeals or references from the inferior courts.[17] He went on circuit throughout the country, probably every year, to try such causes.[18] He was also specially concerned to inquire into the efficiency of the police of the various districts.[19] The nominations to subordinate offices and liturgies, and appeals against them, also came before him;[20] and from him emanated the orders for official inquiries and returns, such as the census lists of persons and property of all kinds which were constantly required, and for the safe keeping of these and other records.(21) All the troops in Egypt were under his control, and their complaints and disputes were specially referred to him for decision.(22) He held office at the will of the emperor, and was not, apparently, appointed for any definite period ; (23) the longest recorded tenure of the office being that of Vitrasius Pollio, who was in Egypt for upwards of sixteen years : (24) and he was assisted by a council of Romans, who sat in the prætorium.(25)

5. In judicial matters, the immediate subordinate of the prefect was the dikaiodotes,(26) who went on circuit with him, and in his absence acted for him.(27) His work lay chiefly in hearing and deciding cases which had already been investigated by lower magistrates, and referred by them to his jurisdiction.(28) The majority of the prefects of Egypt would not be acquainted with legal procedure, and would require an assessor to help them in their judicial work. And the dikaiodotes was such an assessor : he filled the place taken by *legati juridici* in other provinces. He was, like the prefect, appointed by the emperor himself, and was usually a Roman knight.

6. The only other purely judicial officer was the archidikastes,(29) who was, according to Strabo, a local Alexandrian judge.(30) His court usually sat at Alexandria ; but he had competence in civil cases from all parts of the country,(31) and on one occasion is recorded to have tried a case at Memphis.(32) He appears to have had special charge of the archives at Alexandria, and to have been the ordinary judge before whom civil cases were brought which involved reference to the documents preserved in those archives. He, too, was usually a Roman citizen.

7. Immediately subordinate to the prefect there were, ultimately, three epistrategoi,(33) appointed respectively for the Thebais, the Heptanomis and Arsinoite nome, and the Delta. In Upper Egypt such an official had existed in Ptolemaic times ; but no evidence for the

appointment of an epistrategos either in Middle or Lower Egypt is found before the second century of the Empire. With one exception, to which reference has already been made, under Augustus, the epistrategoi were always, so far as is known, Romans; they were the lowest of the imperial officials appointed from Rome, and as such were the usual delegates for the exercise of many of the powers nominally fulfilled by the prefect. They held no military authority, except in so far as the soldiers were employed for police duties; but they frequently appear as competent judges in cases arising in their dioceses, through which they went on circuit.[34] They were also charged with the task of choosing on behalf of the government, from names submitted to them by the local scribes, men to hold the unpaid offices, such as that of strategos or gymnasiarch.[35] A considerable part of their work, however, was that of intermediaries for the transmission to the authorities of the nomes of the orders of the prefect, and the obtaining for the central government of returns of taxation, population, and the like.[36]

8. Below the epistrategos came the strategos,[37] who occupied the next step for the transmission to and fro of orders and returns. The unit of government for the strategoi was the nome; though occasionally two nomes were temporarily united under one strategos,[38] or one nome was divided between two strategoi.[39] In judicial affairs, they were the usual recipients of complaints, where proceedings were to be taken under the civil law: [40] and for the purpose of hearing such they made circuits of their nomes, probably every month; [41] but, except when the power was specially delegated to them by the prefect, dikaiodotes, or archidikastes, they had no competence to deliver judgment: [42] complaints, when received, were filed to await the visit of the prefect on circuit. In such cases, however, it is probable that the strategos made a preliminary investigation, to satisfy himself that there was a *primâ facie* grievance; and he certainly took evidence on oath, copies of which were filed like the complaints.[43]

Copies of all census returns, whether of land, persons, or animals, were addressed to him, as well as to the census officers and scribes.[44] In financial matters, the strategos was responsible for the collection of the taxes in his nome, and consequently had to supervise the assessments of the districts into which it was divided, and to take steps to recover debts due for taxes;[45] he was also required to arrange the incidence of the various liturgies, such as the *corvée* for the maintenance of the dykes and canals.[46] Strategoi were appointed for a period of three years, presumably from the inhabitants or property-holders of the nomes for which they were to hold office, by the epistrategoi, the nominations being confirmed by the prefect.[47] They were chosen indifferently from Romans, Greeks, and Egyptians; and were required, upon entry into their office, to give up all other work, and to provide security for the proper observance of their duties, besides taking an oath to act according to law;[48] while, at the close of their term, their accounts were subjected to an official audit before the prefect.[49]

9. With the strategos was habitually associated the royal scribe, who was his assistant in all departments of his work, especially in receiving returns [50] and collecting evidence for legal proceedings;[51] and, on occasion, could act on his behalf.[52] The royal scribe, to judge from the records preserved, served for about the same period as the strategos, though, in one case at least, a scribe, Herakleides, was in office for over five years.[53] He was probably also appointed in the same manner. Instances of the appointment of Romans to this post are rarer than to that of strategos.

10. The nomarchs,[54] who had originally filled the chief positions in each nome, had been deposed from most of their functions by the strategoi; but they were still retained under the latter as financial officers, and also appear to have had some special duties in connection with the transport of goods.[55] They exercised some supervision over the collection of the taxes,[56]

and the payment of the money to the local treasury.(57) They were responsible for the performance of these duties to the government, and were liable, in default of raising the due amount of revenue, to have their property confiscated.(58) In connection with their position of supervisors of taxation, they were apparently ranked as the financial authorities for the various trades and occupations of the nome.(59)

11. The records of the nome were kept by the bibliophylakes, with whom copies of all official documents were deposited,(60) and who received notice of all changes in the ownership of land,(61) together with periodical returns from the landholders of the nome describing their property.(62) They were divided into two departments, the one concerned with the work of land-registry,(63) the other with the financial statements of the district.(64) The staff of the former at Arsinoe numbered two.

12. The local government of the villages was in the hands of a number of officials, whose precise relationship to each other is hard to determine. The elders were probably responsible for the general management of affairs; they were a body of men known in one instance to have numbered about ten, and in another four, and to have been of no very substantial position, possessing, in the first case, incomes of four or five hundred drachmæ, and in the second eight hundred.(65) They acted as intermediaries for the payment of taxes on behalf of their village;(66) and were held liable to the authorities of the nome for the peace of its inhabitants; which liability carried with it the duty of assisting to present malefactors for trial, and of collecting evidence when required.(67)

13. The elders probably formed the village council, which is only known from a single instance, in which its president appears as hiring two dancing-girls for the service of the village, doubtless to dance at a festival.(68)

14. The village scribe was the person ultimately responsible for the supply of all the various items of

information required by the central government: it was he who drew up lists of the inhabitants of the village, their several holdings of land, the extent to, and manner in, which each holding was cultivated; and generally gave all particulars necessary for the assessment of the taxes upon each individual. In connection with this duty, he had also to supply the names of men suitable to be appointed to the liturgies of the village.[69]

15. In his work of cataloguing the inhabitants, the village scribe was assisted by the laographoi, who were appointed in each village for the sole purpose of collecting census returns.[70]

16. The agoranomoi[71] were village officials who were chiefly, if not entirely, occupied with the execution and registration of contracts, wills, and other legal documents. The parties to the contract attended before an agoranomos, and, after it was drawn up, probably by the clerk, and signed, it was registered, and a copy deposited in the local archives.[72] If the contract was not drawn up at the agoranomeion, notice had to be given there of its completion.[73] In the Arsinoite nome, contracts appear habitually to have been made at the grapheion;[74] or, if completed privately, to have been registered there:[75] but it does not seem clear whether the grapheion was under the control of the agoranomos.

17. The police administration of the nome[76] was under the general supervision of the two eirenarchai:[77] subordinate to them there were in each village one or two archephodoi, who were the officials responsible for the custody and production of offenders in court;[78] in which duty the elders or others were sometimes associated with them.[79] The euschemones and cirenophylakes appear to have held about the same rank, and to have performed similar duties to those of the archephodoi.[80] The actual work of arrest was done by the lestopiastai or phylakes,[81] the latter of whom were paid officers, and were divided into classes according to their work. In the maintenance of order, however,

FINANCIAL ADMINISTRATION

the assistance of the military was constantly summoned; and the centurions of the Roman army were empowered to receive complaints, in the same manner as the strategoi, with the addition that they could order the summary arrest of offenders.[82]

18. There were also a number of officials in the towns and villages whose precise functions it is at present impossible to determine: the exegetai,[83] euschemones,[84] kosmetai,[85] and gymnasiarchs.[86] These were probably all offices which were imposed as liturgies upon the wealthier members of the community; and the holders of them shared with the elders the general management of the affairs of their town or village. In this capacity they could be called upon by the higher officials to give such assistance as might be required in the government of the district, by collecting taxes, arresting criminals, or supplying evidence with regard to the state of their local affairs. It is possible that the exegetai were introduced into the government of the towns when they were granted the privilege of electing senates; but in Alexandria, at any rate, the office of exegetes was not dependent on the existence of a senate.

19. The revenues of the country, in addition to the general authority exercised over them by the prefect, received the special supervision of the idiologos, who was appointed by the emperor, and who, in view of the position of Egypt in the imperial economy as the private property of the emperor, was virtually the steward of the country; he was nominally subordinate to the prefect, but, being independently appointed, would be likely to serve as a check on any attempt to vary the imperial orders with regard to the taxation of Egypt.[87] The directions as to the amount of revenue to be raised, its assessment, and the money when collected, passed along the usual channel of officials and subordinates, from prefect to strategos; but the actual collection was done by a special body of officers, the praktores, who were divided into classes according to the taxes with which they dealt—poll

tax,⁽⁸⁸⁾ corn tax,⁽⁸⁹⁾ bath tax,⁽⁹⁰⁾ stephanikon,⁹¹ and so forth; and for this purpose a number of the inhabitants of each village of sufficient income—which in one case was 1000 drachmæ—were chosen by the strategos from nominations by the village scribe.⁽⁹²⁾ That the liturgy of collecting taxes was a burdensome one, in respect of the time and expense involved, is shown by a deed in which a man who had been named as praktor appointed a deputy, and paid him 252 drachmæ yearly to do the work.⁽⁹³⁾ The praktores were assisted by another body, the epiteretai;⁽⁹⁴⁾ and, in the case of the wheat and barley taxes, by the paralemptai.⁽⁹⁵⁾ The money taxes were usually paid into the public or other bank of the village,⁽⁹⁶⁾ while the taxes in kind went to the village granary, which was in charge of the sitologoi,⁽⁹⁷⁾ who had to make monthly returns as to the amount of corn stored therein.

20. In addition to the strategos of the nome, there was a second check upon the collection of corn in the dekaprotoi, who were appointed to hold office in the toparchies, into which the nomes were divided, and to supervise the storage of grain in the granaries.⁽⁹⁸⁾

21. The collection of customs-duties at the stations on the Nile and on the roads leading across the desert, was in the hands of companies of farmers;⁽⁹⁹⁾ and other indirect taxes, such as the fees on sales and on the registration of contracts, were likewise farmed.⁽¹⁰⁰⁾ That the position of farmer of taxes was not a very profitable one, and, in fact, was probably little better than a liturgy, especially after Nero had reformed the system of collection by publishing tariffs, may be gathered from the reluctance to continue their work which is sometimes stated to have been shown by the farmers, and from the special orders which had to be issued by the prefects against compelling them to undertake the duties.⁽¹⁰¹⁾ The collection of some taxes, such as the poll tax, appears at some places to have been done indifferently by the farmers of the customs and the praktores:⁽¹⁰²⁾ it may be surmised that the latter, in places where a body of farmers existed, made

some arrangement with them to take over the work of revenue collection.

22. The domain lands, consisting of the large properties which had belonged to the Ptolemies, together with the possessions of state debtors, and those for which no heirs or claimants appeared, were administered, under the idiologos, by a dioiketes [103] —who was probably, like the idiologos, always a Roman—and a body of epitropoi or procurators.[104]

23. The administration of the large towns naturally stood on a somewhat different footing to that of the villages. Alexandria had been deprived of its senate by Augustus; [105] but it still enjoyed a separate body of officers, who were specially nominated by the prefect himself.[106] The exegetes answered to the strategoi of the nomes, having the general charge of the government of the city, and was privileged to wear the purple. The hypomnematographos was the counterpart of the royal scribes, and acted as the clerk of the city. The local courts were presided over by the archidikastes, who had also, however, as has been seen above, extraneous functions. There was, naturally, a body of police, whose commander was dignified with the title of strategos; and in addition to the agoranomoi and gymnasiarchs, whose place was similar to that which they held in the country towns, there was at least one imperial procurator—of Neapolis and the Mausoleum of Alexander—specially attached to Alexandria.[107] The Alexandrian citizenship in itself carried certain more or less substantial privileges, the chief of which was the exemption from poll tax and liturgies; the citizens also shared in the distributions of corn, and were entitled to be scourged with rods instead of whips; and it was only through the Alexandrian citizenship that an Egyptian could attain to the Roman, until Caracalla gave the latter privilege broadcast to all the provincials.[108] Severus had, a few years previously, restored their senate to the Alexandrians; [109] but there is no evidence to show how far it superseded the previous form of government.

24. At Ptolemais-Hermiou, the administration of the city on the Hellenic pattern, with archons and a senate, established on its foundation by the Ptolemies, was seemingly left to subsist as it stood by Augustus,[110] and Naukratis also probably preserved its separate magistrates.[111] Antinoopolis was built and organised by Hadrian as a Greek state, with a senate, prytany, and tribes.[112] And at the end of the century the chief towns of the nomes were granted the privilege of self-government. Arsinoe,[113] Herakleopolis,[114] Hermopolis,[115] and Oxyrhynchos[116] are known instances, but doubtless every other metropolis of a nome had its senate. At Thebes[117] also there were archons in the time of Hadrian; in this case, however, the office was probably a religious one, as it was hereditary, and the political importance of Thebes in the second century was extremely small.

25. So far as can be ascertained from the scanty evidence, the reorganisation of Egypt, which took place at the end of the third century, under Diocletian, effected more change in the titles than in the actual duties of the officials concerned in the government. The prefect of Egypt, to whose province Upper and Lower Libya—that is, Cyrene and Parætonium—were added, received the title of Augustalis. Middle and Lower Egypt, with Libya, were under his special supervision; and in place of the epistrategoi of the Thebaid, Heptanomis and Delta are found in the time of Theodosius II., the præsides of Arcadia, Augustamnica Secunda, Thebais, and Aegyptiaca, and of the two divisions of Libya, and the corrector of Augustamnica Prima. The military forces were placed under a dux, whose authority extended over the whole country, till about 380 A.D., when the province was split up into three military divisions—the limes Aegypti, including Lower and Middle Egypt, under a comes; the Thebaid, under a dux; and the two divisions of Libya, likewise under a dux.[118]

26. The prefect of Egypt was not only deprived of his control of the troops by the appointment of the

comes under the Diocletianic reorganisation; he was also superseded in his financial duties by a new official, the catholicus, who apparently took the place of the idiologos, but was not, as he had been, subordinate to the prefect. The dioiketes, who had special charge of the imperial domain land, continued to exist with the changed title of epitropos of the royal property.[119]

27. Among the subordinate officials the strategoi almost disappear in the Byzantine period, and their place appears to have been taken in the Arsinoite nome by the pagarchs, who were not, however, like them, appointed to the charge of a nome, but merely to that of a pagus or division of a nome.[120] In the Hermopolite nome the præpositus pagi held an identical position.[121] At Oxyrhynchos there is found another official, the logistes, who more nearly resembled the strategos in the extent of his jurisdiction over the whole nome, and who fulfilled similar duties:[122] he is once associated with the strategos.[123]

28. The local government of the towns continued in the hands of the senates; while in the villages the elders likewise remained as the chief authorities of their districts.[124] A few other minor officials appear— the ephor and the quadrarius, associated with the komarch, and subordinate to the præpositus pagi, and the exactores, who had taken the duties of tax collection which formerly belonged to the praktores: these were appointed by nomination for one year, a second year of office only being allowed if such were the custom of the district, or if no other suitable persons could be found.[125]

29. The military authorities still took a considerable part in the administration of justice, especially with regard to criminal offences. The correspondence of Flavius Abinnæus, prefect of the camp at Dionysias in the reign of Constantius II., shows that complaints were frequently laid before him with petitions for redress against injuries; and the superior officer whose aid he was requested to invoke was the dux, another military official.[126] That his judicial functions were

perhaps somewhat irregular, may be gathered from the fact that on one occasion a serious dispute as to jurisdiction arose between him and the civil officials.[127] However, though as a military officer he may not have possessed any statutory powers in such legal matters, his authority was unquestionably recognised; and he had the great advantage over the local officials, that his decisions could be promptly enforced by the soldiers under his command. It was probably this consideration more than any other which caused the frequent reference of criminal cases in Egypt to military officers.

30. In the sixth century fresh officials occur in subordinate posts: the epimeletes of the public treasury;[128] the ethnikos and embolator or arkarikarios, who were both collectors of taxes;[129] the pronoetes, who was also a financial official.[130] But it is interesting to observe how almost the whole government of a village, apart from the mere duties of tax-collection, seems to have passed into the hands of the wealthy landed proprietor in some cases in the Oxyrhynchite nome, where the leading house was that of Flavius Apion; so that on one occasion a village actually describes that house as its pagarch. This custom had been attacked by the laws against patronage; but the orders of the government were of little avail against the needs of the Egyptians.[131]

[See Note IX., p. 216, for a comparison of the ancient and modern local government of Egypt.]

CHAPTER II

THE FIRST CENTURY OF ROMAN RULE IN EGYPT, 30 B.C.–68 A.D.

AUGUSTUS.

30 B.C.–14 A.D.

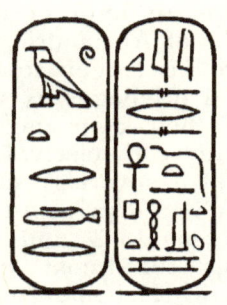

Buildings.—Alexandria: Nikopolis. Soknopaiou Nesos: peribolos of temple of Soknopaios. Tentyra: hypostyle, outside back wall, east and west walls of great temple; temple of Isis; Typhonium. Koptos: small chapel. Philæ: east wall, temple K; east and north walls, temple J. *Debot*: west wall of temple. Talmis: temple. *Dendur*: front wall of temple. Pselkis: pronaos completed.
[In almost all the cases where the name of Augustus appears on buildings, it merely shows that a work previously begun was being carried on. The small chapel at Koptos is perhaps an exception, and may have been entirely built in his reign. The propylon of the temple of Isis at Tentyra was dedicated for him. The inscription from Soknopaiou Nesos in the Ghizeh Museum refers to a building which has probably been destroyed. The building of Nikopolis is mentioned by Dio Cassius (li. 18).]

Inscriptions.—Hieroglyphic: L.D. iv. 69, 70, 71, 72, 73. Demotic: L.D. vi. 32. Greek: C.I.G. 4715, 4723, 4909, 5080; M.A. 61, 65; App. iii. 1; Rec. Trav. 1890, p. 62; Lumbroso, Documenti Greci del Mus. Egiz. di Torino, App. II. Trilingual: Sitzungsb. d. Kaiserl. Akad. zu Berlin, 1896, p. 469.

Papyri.—B.G.U. 174, 189, 543, 580; G.G.P. i. 45, 46, ii. 40; C.P.R. 224; Petrie, Hawara, p. 36, No. 244; Pap. B.M. 256 ᴿd, e, 262, 354.

Ostraka.—B.M. 12,612, 12,618 (R.E. iv. p. 183).

1. THE deaths of Antony and Cleopatra secured the immediate recognition of Augustus as their successor

by the population of Lower Egypt; and he was thus able to return to Rome, leaving to the prefect the greater part of the work connected with the settlement of the country. Before his departure, however, he took three steps to impress upon the Greeks of Alexandria that they were no longer to look for special privileges as from rulers of their own race, or to arrogate to themselves the position of a sovereign class. In addition to depriving them of their senate,[132] and thus destroying the most characteristically Hellenic part of the local government, he granted to the Jews of the city a renewal of all the rights and privileges which they had enjoyed under the Ptolemies, thus placing them on a position of equality with the Greeks, or even of superiority; for, on the one hand, they were allowed to choose an ethnarch or a council of elders to regulate their own affairs,[133] while the Greeks lost their right to elect a senate; though, on the other, they were liable to pay the poll tax, from which the Greeks were free. These concessions were granted to the Jews by Augustus, to whom that nation had been of considerable service, in the teeth of a request from the Greeks for their refusal. The third blow aimed at the Greek population, which if it had succeeded in its object would have been the heaviest of all, was the foundation of a new city, named Nikopolis, four miles east of Alexandria.[134] To this Augustus seemingly designed to remove the seat of government and the official

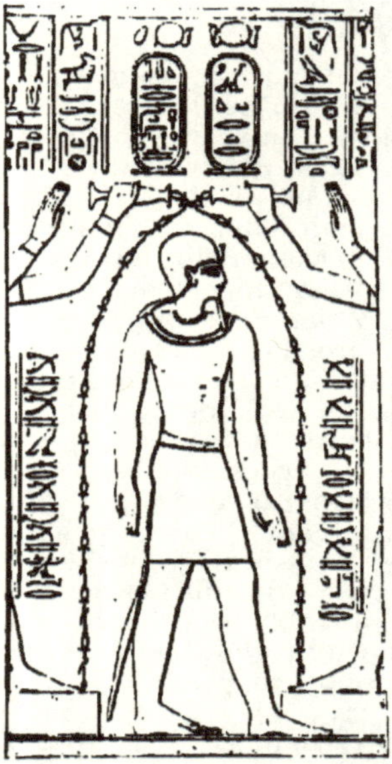

FIG. 1.—Augustus: Temple K, Philae.

SUBJUGATION OF UPPER EGYPT

celebrations of religion. But the new settlement never flourished, and only continued to exist as the camp of the Roman garrison.

2. The submission of Lower Egypt to the Roman government did not carry with it that of the southern districts, which for many years had been subject in little more than name to the kings of Egypt. So the first duties which fell to the new prefect, Cornelius Gallus, consisted in suppressing disturbances up the country. Heroopolis was the first city to rise against [29 B.C.]

FIG. 2.—Augustus adoring Isis: Tentyra.

FIG. 3.—Philæ: Temple of Hathor.

the Romans, and to be retaken.(135) A more widely

spread revolt was caused in the Thebaid by the arrival of the Roman tax-collectors; but the Egyptians were no match for the legions which followed. In fifteen days the rebels were crushed in two pitched battles, and the country was secured by the reduction of the towns of Boresis, Koptos, Keramike, Diospolis, and Ophieum. The prefect marched on to Syene, and on the island of Philæ met ambassadors of the king of the Æthiopians. The region beyond the First

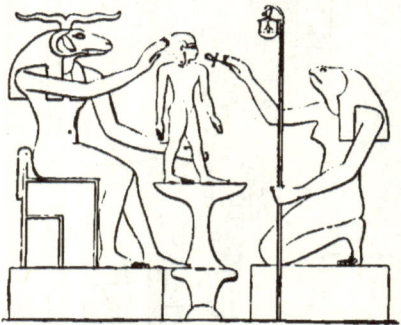

FIG. 4.—Khnum forming Augustus, and Hekt giving him life : Tentyra.

FIG. 5.—Talmis: Front of Temple.

Cataract had been for over a century entirely independent of Egypt; and Gallus, not caring to venture into

THE EARLIEST PREFECTS

unknown country, came to terms with the ambassadors, by which the border territory known as the Triakontaschoinoi was constituted a Roman protectorate, but left in the hands of the Æthiopians.[136]

3. This easy conquest of the country was celebrated by Gallus with such extravagant praise of himself, that he aroused the displeasure of his master. He caused statues to be set up in his honour, and inscriptions to be carved on public buildings; and Augustus, lest the Egyptians should hold the viceroy above the emperor, recalled him from his province; whereupon he committed suicide.[137]

4. His successor, Gaius Petronius, was called upon to suppress a rising of the Alexandrians — probably one

FIG. 6.—Tentyra: Temple from the south.

of the general riots in which the turbulent mob of the chief city of Egypt indulged from time to time.[138] It was, at any rate, easily quelled; and the soldiers were turned to the more useful task of clearing the irrigation canals, which had silted up during the reigns of the later Ptolemies to such an extent as seriously to diminish the amount of land available for cultivation.[139] The work was successfully accomplished, so that a rise of twelve cubits at Memphis, when the Nile was in flood, conferred as much benefit on the country as one of fourteen had done in previous years.

5. Ælius Gallus, the third prefect, was specially commissioned to subdue the districts of Æthiopia, Trogodytica, and Arabia. Through these the trade-routes from Central Africa and India ran; and the

[25 B.C.]

Romans, imagining that the valuable goods which they received along these channels were produced by their immediate neighbours, designed to get into their possession districts of such wealth. Gallus accordingly built a fleet at Cleopatris, and sailed to attack Arabia with a force of 10,000 Roman troops, 1000 Nabataeans, and 500 Jews, the two latter contingents being supplied by the client-kings Obodas and Herod. The expedition landed at Leuke Kome on the Arabian coast, where it wintered, and moved forward in the spring into the territory of the Sabaeans. But by the time that the Romans had reached the Sabaean capital, Mariaba, although they had nowhere met the Arabian forces in a regular battle, they had suffered so much from disease and want of water, that Gallus determined on retreat, without making any serious attempt on the town; and withdrew his troops to Nera Kome, whence he returned by way of Myos Hormos and Koptos.[110]

6. The expedition had failed largely through the

FIG. 7.—Augustus: Talmis.

FIG. 8.—Augustus: Debôt.

ignorance or incapacity of the prefect, who had wasted his time and forces by an unnecessarily long voyage and march. If he had obtained proper information about the country he intended to invade, as he might easily have done from merchants, he could have learnt that the route to be followed was the more southerly one from Berenike to the island Katakekaumene. It was possibly on account of this failure that, in the follow-

FIG. 9.—Talmis: Temple from behind.

ing year, the government of Egypt is found in the hands of Gaius Petronius once more.[141] During the absence of Ælius Gallus in Arabia, the Æthiopians had taken the opportunity to break off the friendly relations which Cornelius Gallus had established with them; and their muster of 30,000 ill-armed men had seized Syene, Elephantine, and Philæ, defeating the three Roman cohorts which were stationed in that district. Petronius, however, brought up a force of 10,000 infantry and 800 cavalry, and drove them back [24 B.C.

to Pselkis. There three days were spent in fruitless negotiations, at the close of which the Romans defeated them, and successively stormed Pselkis, Premis, and the Æthiopian capital Nabata. Leaving a garrison,

FIG. 10.—Dendur: Temple.

FIG. 11.—Pselkis: Temple and Pylon.

Petronius returned to Alexandria, only to be recalled next year by the news that his garrison was besieged. It was, however, speedily relieved; and Kandake, the queen of the Æthiopians, sent ambassadors to Rome to sue for peace, which was granted, and their territory evacuated.(142) A part of the Roman protectorate of the Triakontaschoinoi—the district between Syene, the former frontier town, and Hiera Sykaminos, known as the Dodekaschoinoi — was, however, now definitely

FIG. 12.—Hiera Sykaminos: Temple.

occupied by Roman troops as a military frontier, seemingly not subject to the civil authorities, and not organised, like the rest of Egypt, as a nome.(143) From this time the relations of Egypt and Æthiopia remained on the whole peaceful. A few years later a mission [13 B.C. from Kandake into Roman territory left a record on its return at Pselkis;(144) but with this exception nothing is heard of the Æthiopians for many years after the expedition of Petronius.

TIBERIUS.

14-37.

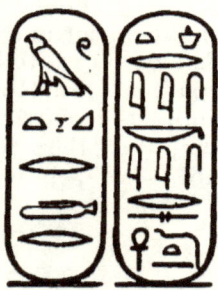

Buildings.—Philæ: temple J, west wall; east wall and wall of hypostyle, temple K; door M; colonnade F; colonnade D. Ombos: temple. Apollinopolis Parva: temple of Isis—peribolos. Koptos: temple of Ptolemy XIII. Tentyra: pronaos. Athribis: pronaos of temple of Thriphis.
[The buildings executed under Tiberius at Philæ were all continuations of earlier undertakings; as was the work on the temples at Koptos and Ombos. At Apollinopolis Parva, Tentyra, and Athribis, additions were made or completed to old temples.]
Inscriptions.—Hieroglyphic: L.D. iv. 74, 75, 76; Petrie, Koptos, xxvi. 6, 7, 8. Demotic: L.D. vi. 26, 27, 33. Greek: C.I.G. iii. 4711, 4716, 4716 b, 4963, 5074; M.A. 64; App. iii. 2, 3; Rec. Trav. 1890, p. 62. Latin: C.I.L. iii. 6589.
Ostraka.—P.S.B.A. vii. pp. 11 ff., Nos. 12, 13, 19, 21, pp. 195 ff., No. 1; ix. p. 198, No. 4.
Papyri.—B.G.U. 197, 636; Petrie, Hawara, p. 36, Nos. 41, 60, 166, 208, 212-4, 238; Pap. B.M. 195, 256 Ka, 276, 277, 357, 445.
Miscellaneous.—A stele of Tiberius adoring Horus and Isis (M.G.) from Apollinopolis Parva; a similar stele from Koptos (Petrie, Koptos, p. 22).

7. During the remainder of the reign of Augustus, and the whole of that of Tiberius, Egypt remained in a state of comparative tranquillity; so that by the tenth year of the latter emperor the three Roman legions which had formed the original garrison of the country had been already reduced to two.[115] The strict watch which Tiberius kept upon his ministers tended to preserve this tranquillity, by checking any exaction or oppression on the part of the officials which might

[23 A.D.]

have given occasion for disturbances among the people.

FIG. 13.—Tiberius: Philae.

Thus he rebuked the prefect Æmilius Rectus, who sent

FIG. 14.—Philae: West side of Great Court.

to Rome a larger amount of tribute than that which

had been fixed, for flaying his sheep instead of shearing them.(146)

8. The same strictness appears in his censure of Germanicus Cæsar, who, when sent out as governor of the East, took the opportunity of visiting Egypt on an

FIG. 15.—Tentyra: Portico of Temple. (Photo. by W. M. F. Petrie.)

antiquarian tour, ascending the Nile as far as Syene. He had, however, omitted to obtain permission from the emperor, and had thus broken the law laid down by Augustus, which forbade any Roman citizen of senatorial rank, without such permission, to enter Alexandria: he had also taken upon himself to open the public granaries in a time of scarcity, and allow the stores of wheat hoarded there to be sold, thus lowering the price of grain; and had gone about among the people in a Greek dress, without guards.(147) All these acts were capable of treasonable interpretation, especi-

FIG. 16.—Tiberius: Philæ.

FIG. 17.—Stele of Tiberius adoring Isis and Horus, in Ghizeh Museum. (Photo. by J. G. M.)

ally when done in Egypt, the province which gave to

its possessor the command of Rome, and which was always ready to embark on a new course of sedition

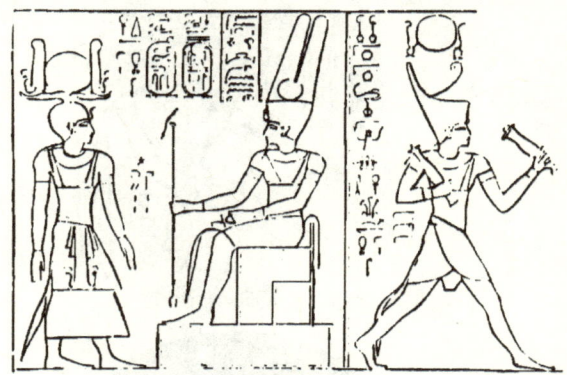

Fig. 18.—Tiberius : Philae.

with any leader who might call to it; and they were visited with severe reproof by Tiberius.

CALIGULA.

37-41.

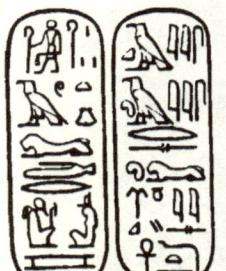

Buildings.—Tentyra: hypostyle of great temple. Koptos: passage dedicated to Khem-ra.
[The buildings of this reign were apparently only continuations of the older works.]
Inscriptions.—Hieroglyphic: L.D. iv. 76. Greek: C.I.G. iii. 5101; Sitzungsb. der Kgl. Preuss. Akad. 1887, p. 419, No. 125. Latin: P.S.B.A. xviii. p. 107.
Ostraka.—P.S.B.A. v. pp. 84 ff., B.M. 5790 c; vii. pp. 11 ff., No. 20.
Papyri.—C.P.R. 242; Pap. B.M. 177.

9. The last of the prefects appointed by Tiberius, Avillius Flaccus, succeeded for some years in keeping the various factions in Egypt quiet, if not satisfied, by administering even-handed justice to all ranks and classes alike, and by holding firmly under control both

the Alexandrian mob and the Roman soldiery. But on the death of Tiberius the reins of empire passed into the weaker hands of Caligula; and the old-standing enmity of Greeks and Jews soon found an occasion for open conflict in the eccentricities of the new emperor. The signal for the outbreak was given by the arrival of Agrippa at Alexandria on his way to the kingdom which his friendship with Caligula had secured him. The Jewish account of what followed, given by Philo and Josephus, naturally throws the whole blame on the Greeks; but it may be remarked that the visits of Agrippa and of his son to Alexandria were always coincident with riots. The newly-made king was well known to the Alexandrian money-lenders; and in his sudden elevation from bankruptcy to a throne the mob saw an opportunity for the coarse humour in which they delighted: they dressed up an idiot with a paper crown, and led him about the streets in mockery of the *parvenu* king. The disturbance once begun, as the Greeks might feel certain that Agrippa would lay the Jewish case before his friend the emperor, they proceeded to find a justification for their actions in the plea that the Jews had disregarded the order of Caligula for the erection of statues of himself in all temples, and to enter the Jewish synagogues for the purpose of placing therein such statues. By this stroke of policy they got the prefect on their side, and induced him to withdraw from the Jews the rights of citizenship, to have thirty-eight of the Jewish elders scourged by the public executioner, and to order all the houses in the Jewish quarter to be searched for concealed arms. Meanwhile the Greeks plundered and slew the Jews at their will.

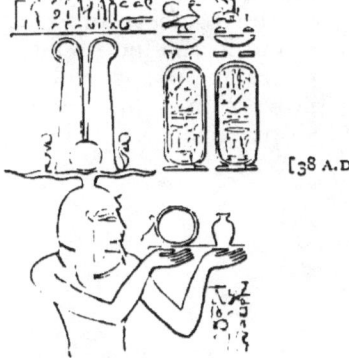

[38 A.D

FIG. 19.—Caligula: Tentyra.

10. The attempts of the Jewish community to lay

a complaint before the emperor were suppressed by Flaccus, until Agrippa took up their cause. His influence was sufficient to secure the disgrace and recall of the prefect, for which a colourable pretext might be found in the facts that he had not been able to keep the peace in his province, and had certainly exceeded his powers in depriving the Jews of the rights of citizenship: although neither of these arguments would be

FIG. 20.—Alexandria: Ruins of the Gymnasium. (Ainslie, Views in Egypt.)

likely to have any great weight with Caligula in the actual decision of the case, as the riots had arisen over the question of his own deification, and the Jews had been punished for opposing his wishes.

11. The precautions taken in effecting the deportation of Flaccus serve to show the strong position held by a prefect of Egypt. A centurion was specially despatched from Rome with a cohort of soldiers, and, on approaching Alexandria, waited till night fell before

he entered the harbour. He then hurried to suprise the prefect before any news of the arrival of the Roman vessel could reach him, arrested him at a supper party, and took him back on board without delay.

12. Agrippa had effected the disgrace of Flaccus; but he was unable to procure a favourable hearing at Rome for an embassy which the Jews sent to lay their case before Caligula. This embassy, which was headed by Philo, was confronted by another representing the Greeks, whose spokesman was Apion; and the two parties exhausted themselves in running about the palace after the emperor, and endeavouring to get a few arguments or explanations interposed in the discussion of domestic trivialities which occupied most of the attention of the court. Finally, as the only question of importance appeared to be the worship of the emperor, the Jews were glad to be dismissed by him with an affectation of contemptuous pity for a people who could not recognise that he was a god.(148)

CLAUDIUS.

41-54.

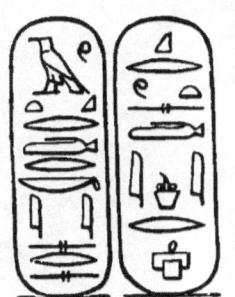

Buildings.—Tentyra: columns of great temple. Latopolis: corner pillars of pronaos and columns. Philae: west colonnade.
[Under Claudius the records of building refer only to the continuations of work previously begun.]
Inscriptions.—Hieroglyphic: L.D. iv. 77, 78.   Greek: C.I.G. iii. 4956, 4697 b; M.A. 47; App. iii. 4, 5. Latin: C.I.L. iii. 6624.
Ostrakon.—P.S.B.A. vii. pp. 11 ff., No. 14.
Papyri.—B.G.U. 37, 177, 297, 584, 611, 713; G.G.P. ii. 41; C.P.R. 4; G.O.P. i. 37, 38, 39; Pap. B.M. 139 a, 139 b, 165.

13. Agrippa reappeared in the tumults which broke out at Alexandria after the death of Caligula; and on this occasion the Jews were unquestionably the aggressors. They hoped to be able, under an emperor

[41 A.D.]

who was more favourably disposed towards their nation than the late one had been, to take vengeance on the Greeks; and Agrippa, whose influence was still strong at Rome, procured the countenance of Claudius for their claims and the restoration of the rights of citizenship and self-government which had been conferred upon them by Augustus. He went so far as to appear in public at Alexandria, and read aloud the imperial edict for the protection of the Jews.[149]

FIG. 21.—Claudius : Philæ.

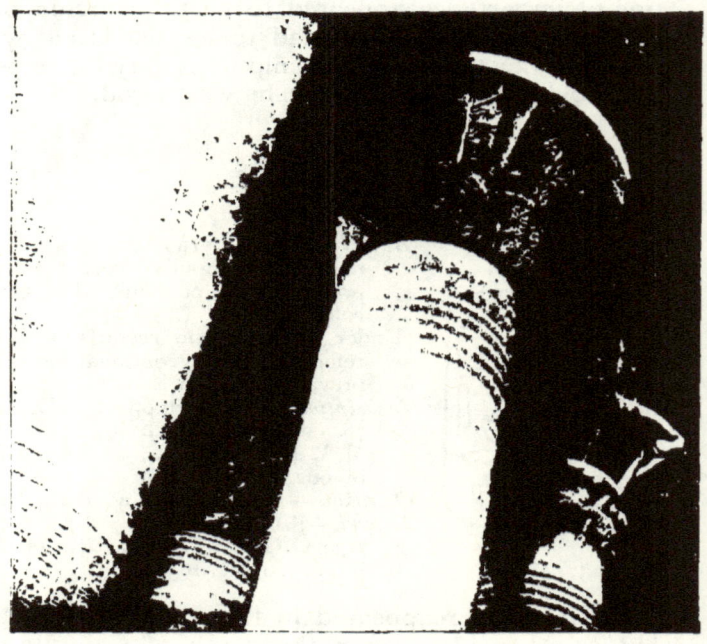

FIG. 22.—Latopolis: Capitals of columns. (Photo. by W. M. F. Petrie.)

TRADE WITH THE EAST

14. The hatred of Jews and Greeks, however, was not likely to be stilled by such measures, and when the younger Agrippa, who had been made king of Chalkis (53 A.D.) by Claudius, came to play the same part at Alexandria as his father, the Greeks, resenting his interference in their affairs, despite his friendship with the emperor, sent an embassy under Isidoros the gymnasiarch to Rome to make formal complaint of his behaviour.(150)

15. Since the time of the expedition of Ælius Gallus

FIG. 23.—Hermopolis Magna: Temple. (Description de l'Egypte.)

into Arabia, the Romans had learnt that the goods brought into the Red Sea ports by Arab vessels came, not from Arabia, but from India; and they rapidly took the trade into their own hands. The discovery was partly made by accident, when, in this reign, a Roman tax-collector was driven by a storm from the coast of Arabia to Ceylon;(151) but the government took systematic measures to secure the monopoly for ships from Egyptian ports. In addition to steps for the suppression of piracy in the Red Sea, a Roman fleet was sent about this time against Adane, the chief trading-centre of the Arabian coast, and destroyed it,(152) apparently for purely commercial reasons; and a special customs tariff was adopted, favouring the direct Indian trade by the imposition of a heavy import duty of twenty-five per cent. on goods from Arabian ports.

16. The development of trade, together with the advantages secured to the Egyptians by a settled and careful government, chief amongst which was the improvement of the irrigation system, brought a renewal of prosperity to the country, which was marked by the reopening of the Alexandrian mints under Claudius. Very little fresh coinage was put into circulation in the reign of Augustus, and by the time of Caligula the issue of local money had entirely stopped. It now, however, recommenced, and considerable issues of the debased silver tetradrachms, which served as the Alexandrian stater, were made. Still larger quantities were struck under Nero; indeed, so numerous were the coins then put into circulation, that in the hoards of the succeeding century they habitually form one-half of the total sum.(153

NERO.
54-68.

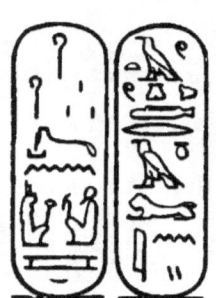

Buildings.—Karanis: propylon of temple of Pnepheros. Tentyra: east wall, colonnades, and columns of great temple. Koptos: temple of Ptolemy XIII. Ombos: west colonnade.

[The only building of Nero which appears to have been more than a continuation of previous work is the propylon at Karanis, which may have been erected wholly in this reign.]

Inscriptions.—Hieroglyphic: L.D. iv. 79, 80; Petrie, Koptos, xxvi. 9. Demotic: L.D. vi. 144. Greek: C.I.G. iii. 4699; M.A. 99, c; R.E.G. vii. p. 284, No. 10; Petrie, Illahun, p. 32; E.E.F. Report, 1895–96, p. 16, No. 2. Latin: C.I.L. iii. 30.

Ostraka.—P.S.B.A. v. pp. 84 ff., B.M. 5790 k, B.M. [no number]; vii. pp. 11 ff., Nos. 16, 22.

JEWISH RISING

Papyri.—B.G.U. 112, 181, 379, 591, 612, 650, 748; G.O.P. i. 99; Pap. B.M. 154, 181, 280, 281.
Miscellaneous.—Stele of Nero adoring Min, from Koptos, Petrie, Koptos, p. 22.

17. A fresh and unusually serious riot of the Greek and Jewish factions broke out soon after the accession of Nero. It was provoked by the expedition of a large body of Egyptian Jews to Palestine, with the object of setting Jerusalem free from Roman rule. The expedition itself was fruitless, but the religious fervour which had inspired it and sent it out, found further vent in a quarrel at Alexandria, where the Jews attacked the amphitheatre in which the Greeks were assembled, alleging the ill-treatment of certain of their fellows in justification; and, but for the

[55 A.D.

FIG. 24.—Nero: Tentyra.

FIG. 25.—Karanis: Interior of Temple of Pnepherôs and Petesouchos. (Photo. by J. G. M.)

active interposition of the prefect with a number of the Jewish elders, would have set fire to it. The Greeks naturally indulged in reprisals, until the Roman garrison had to be called out to protect the Jews, and secure them in their own quarter.(154)

18. Apart from Alexandria, however, Egypt was peaceful. Even on the southern frontier the tribes of the desert had ceased from troubling ; in great measure, no doubt, because of the waste which had been made of the debat

FIG. 26.—Nero : Ombos.

able ground above the First Cataract, and which secured peace because there was no plunder. A tribune, sent with a scouting party from Syene to Meroe, found nothing along the banks of the Nile but desert.(155)

19. This mission was connected with a great scheme of conquest in the Eastern provinces to which Nero was devoting his attention. One of the objects was the invasion of Æthiopia ; and for this purpose, just before his fall he despatched to Alexandria some of the German legions.(156) A year previously he had seem-

ingly been expected at Alexandria, as coins were struck bearing the type of the galley which was to convey him;[157] and when he heard of the proclama-

FIG. 27.—Karanis : Gateway of Nero in Temple of Pnepherôs and Petesouchos. (Photo. by J. G. M.)

tion of Galba as emperor by the troops, and of his approach, he thought of retiring to Egypt, or even of asking for the position of prefect of that country.[158]

20. On the whole, the internal condition of Egypt

had steadily improved during the first century of its government by the Romans. The immediate results of the conquest by Augustus, it is true, had not been favourable to its prosperity; the trade and agriculture had been rapidly deteriorating under the later Ptolemies, and the sudden removal of all the portable property of the court, representing a large amount of capital, from the country, did not tend to improve matters. There was no remission of taxation; a large quantity of corn was withdrawn yearly as tribute; the rate of interest was high—eighteen per cent.,[159] at any rate in one early instance; though shortly afterwards the rate, subsequently normal, of twelve per cent. is found;[160]—and all signs point to a general scarcity of money. The consequence of these difficulties may partly be traced in the several outbreaks under Augustus. But gradually, under the care of a succession of able prefects, the state of the country was improved. The frontiers were secured against invasion by the defeat of the Æthiopians by Petronius; the external trade of the country was enlarged by the development of the Red Sea traffic with India and the East; measures were taken, notably by Claudius, for the extension of manufactures and mineral workings; and the government encouraged agriculture by restoring the means of irrigation in the cleansing of the canals, first done by Petronius in the reign of Augustus, and subsequently by Balbillus in that of Nero. The increase in general prosperity is marked by the large issues of fresh coinage under Claudius and Nero. The decree of the inhabitants of Busiris and the Letopolite nome in honour of Nero and his prefect Balbillus,[161] which styles Nero the Agathos Daimon of the world, is probably more than a mere empty formula, and shows the actual feeling of the people towards the government which had done so much to improve the condition of the country.

FIG. 28.—Galley of Nero. (Bodleian.)

CHAPTER III

A Century of Prosperity, 68–182 A.D.

GALBA.

68–69.

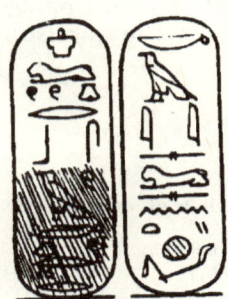

Buildings.—Thebes: small temple of Medinet Habu.
[At Thebes, the work done in previous reigns was still continued under Galba.]
Inscriptions.—Hieroglyphic: L.D. iv. 80. Greek: C.I.G. iii. 4957; Petrie, Koptos, c. vi. No. ii.

1. THE legions sent to Egypt by Nero went no farther

FIG. 29.—Galba: Thebes.

than Alexandria, and were recalled immediately on the accession of Galba; [162] since the idea of an invasion of Æthiopia was not one that was likely to attract the new emperor, and if that project was dropped, there was no need whatever for increasing the garrison of two legions in Egypt.

OTHO.

69.

Buildings.—Thebes: door of small temple of Medinet Habu.
[The building at Thebes was a continuation of earlier work.]
Inscription.—Hieroglyphic: L.D. iv. 80.

2. These two legions at first showed no desire to

FIG. 30.—Otho: Thebes.

rival the Roman armies of the West in the work of making emperors. They took the oath of allegiance to Galba, and on his murder they accepted Otho with equal readiness.[163] The three months' reign of Otho, however, did not seemingly give time for the news of his accession to spread over Egypt generally beyond Alexandria; coins were struck there for him at the imperial mint, but in the official and other documents of the upper country no emperor is usually recognised between Galba and Vespasian,[164] and Otho's name appears only in a single inscription on one of the temples whose erection was continued through all the changes of rulers.

VITELLIUS

69.

3. The news of the proclamation of Vitellius by the troops in Germany, however, induced the Egyptian army to take action, and they joined with the other legions of the East in finding a candidate of their own. In less than three months after the death of Otho and the accession of Vitellius, Vespasian, who had already been hailed as emperor by the troops under his command in Syria, was formally proclaimed at Alexandria [69, July 1st by the prefect Tiberius Julius Alexander.[165] With the support of all the legions of Syria and Egypt, he was secure in the possession of the East, and might have starved out Rome by simply cutting off the Egyptian corn supplies, as indeed he was advised to do by Mucianus.[166] But he preferred to take more speedy measures, and sent Mucianus with his own son Domitian to crush the forces of Vitellius in Italy.

VESPASIANUS.

69-79.

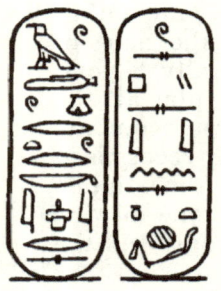

Buildings.—Karanis: temple of Pnepheros. Latopolis: architrave. Oasis of *Dakhêl*: temple of Ammon Ra.
[The gateway of the temple of Pnepheros at Karanis was dedicated for Vespasian. Apart from this, his name only appears on minor parts of buildings in progress.
Inscriptions.—Hieroglyphic: L.D. iv. 81. Greek: C.I.G. iii. 4719; E.E.F. Report, 1895-96, p. 16, No. 3; P.S.B.A. xi. p. 228. Latin: C.I.L. iii. 31, 32, 33, 34, 6603.
Ostraka. –P.S.B.A. v. pp. 84 ff., B.M. 5791 d, 5790 d, 5791 j, Leyden; vii. pp. 11 ff., No. 17; C.I.G. iii. 4863 b; Louvre, N. et E., Nos. 1, 2. *Papyri.*—B.G.U. 184, 251, 594, 595, 597, 644; Pap. B.M. 131, 140, 260, 261, 282; Petrie, Hawara, p. 36, No. 381.

4. Vespasian himself proceeded to Alexandria, that he might be ready to adopt the plan of starvation, if his army were defeated.[167] Very shortly after his arrival, however, he received the news of the defeat and murder of Vitellius, and of his own recognition at Rome.[168] He was naturally received in great state by the Alexandrians, who had not been favoured with the sight of a Roman emperor since the departure of Augustus after his conquest, and must have felt how greatly the position of their city was changed from that which it held in the days when it was the home of the kings of Egypt. So Vespasian found himself treated as a god. A blind man, and one with a withered hand, came to him to be healed, in accordance with advice which they said they had received from Sarapis; and the report went abroad that he succeeded in restoring them, the one by spitting upon his eyelids, the other by trampling upon him. He was also vouchsafed a vision in the temple of Sarapis, where he saw Basilides, one of the best known men in Alexandria, who was actually at that moment lying seriously ill many miles away.[169]

5. But the Alexandrians soon found out that their

god was essentially a man of business, who was so careful of mundane affairs as to increase the taxes and to claim payment of even the smallest debt from his friends; and they revenged themselves for their disenchantment by returning to the habits of scurrility

FIG. 31.—Karanis: Gateway of Vespasian in Temple of Pnepherôs and Petesouchos. (Photo. by J. G. M.)

with which they amused themselves at the expense of their rulers. A tax upon salt fish won for Vespasian the name of Kybiosaktes, and his anxiety about a loan of six obols, that of "the six-oboller." He replied to these witticisms characteristically enough, by ordering a poll tax of six obols to be laid on the Alexandrians, who had hitherto been exempt from the direct taxation to which all other inhabitants of Egypt were liable; but his son Titus intervened, and secured a pardon for the city.(170)

6. The two legions, the III Cyrenaica and XXII Deiotariana, which formed the chief part of the Roman garrison of Egypt, were summoned from Alexandria to

[71 A.D.]

FIG. 32.—Alexandria: "Cleopatra's Needle" and Roman tower. (Description de l'Egypte.)

reinforce the army which was besieging Jerusalem.(171) They remained there until the fall of the city, when they were apparently accompanied back to Egypt by Titus, who had taken his father's place as commander against the Jews. During his visit to Egypt he showed the same regard for the feelings of the people which had formerly led him to intercede with his father on behalf of the Alexandrians: he attended the consecration of a new Apis bull at Memphis, and lent to it the honour of an imperial presence, by appearing in

Fig. 33.—Roman Stele: in Ghizeh Museum.
(Photo. by J. G. M.)

state, crowned with a diadem. This action, however, while calculated to increase the popularity of the Roman government in Egypt by the countenance given to the national religion, was viewed with disfavour at Rome, as if it betokened a desire to seize the crown prematurely.[172]

TITUS.

79-81.

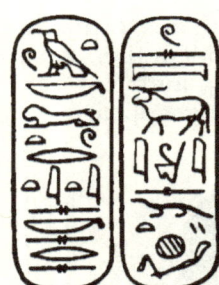

Buildings. - Latopolis: south and east walls of temple. Oasis of *Dakhel*: portal and sanctuary of temple of Ammon Ra.

[Under Titus, the only buildings recorded are continuations.]

Inscriptions.—Hieroglyphic: L.D. iv. 81. Greek: App. iii. 6.

Papyri.—Petrie, Hawara, p. 36, No. 321; G.O.P. i. 165.

7. Titus, however, who was the first Roman emperor, with the possible exception of Nero, to show any tendency towards a truly imperial policy in his dealings with the nations of the Greek East, and to forsake the old traditions of treating them as mere slaves of Rome, did not live long enough to exercise much influence on the destinies of the Empire.

FIG. 34.—Titus: Latopolis.

DOMITIANUS.

81-96.

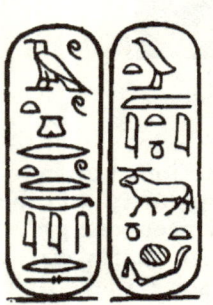

Buildings. — Koptos: bridge. Latopolis: east wall and columns of temple. *Kumer-Resras*: temple of Isis. Kysis: back wall of temple.

[The bridge over the canal at Koptos was wholly rebuilt under Domitian. The work done on temples was in continuation.]

Inscriptions.—Hieroglyphic: L.D. iv. 81. Greek: C.I.G. iii. 5042, 5043, 5044; Petrie, Koptos, c. vi., No. 4; (mentioned) E.E.F. Report, 1893-94, p. 10. Latin: C.I.L. iii. 35, 36, 37; Priv. Vet. 15, 18; Petrie, Koptos, c. vi., No. 3.

Ostraka.—P.S.B.A. v. pp. 84 ff., B.M. 5790 o, 5790 æ, 5789 f, 5788 e, 5790 h, 5791 i; vii. pp. 11 ff., Nos. 23, 24, pp. 89 ff., Nos. 1, 2.

Papyri.—B.G.U. 183, 190, 260, 526, 536, 596; G.G.P. ii. 42, 43; C.P.R. 1, 12; G.O.P. i. 45, 48, 72, 72 a, 73, 94, 104, 174, 175; Pap. B.M. 141, 142, 163, 216, 257, 258, 259, 285, 286, 287, 289, 290.

LOCAL DIVINITIES

8. The recognition of local deities, which had been semi-officially begun by Titus, was carried further under Domitian, by the issue of coins at Alexandria with the names of, and types specially belonging to, the several nomes.[173] The vigour of the various centres of worship, and the amount of hatred engendered thereby between the inhabitants of the nomes to which they belonged, is illustrated by an anecdote recorded by Juvenal, who during this reign was sent to hold a subordinate command in the camp at Syene.

FIG. 35.—Domitian: Latopolis.

He tells how the men of the neighbouring towns of Tentyra and Ombos in the Thebaid, the first of which persecuted the crocodile, while the second worshipped it, took the opportunity of a festival to have a fight; and one of the Ombites, who was caught while his fellows were running away, was killed and eaten by the Tentyrites.[174] A more serious instance is preserved by Plutarch, with reference to the towns of Oxyrhynchos and Kynopolis, in the Heptanomis, where the Roman troops had to be called in to put a stop to a war which had arisen in consequence of insults offered by the inhabitants of either district to the god of their neighbours.[175]

9. At Alexandria, however, the worship of Isis and Sarapis had long overshadowed that of all the other Egyptian gods; and from Alexandria the influence of these cults had spread into Italy, where they had gradually become fashionable in spite of the endeavours of the government to suppress them; until Domitian himself erected temples to Isis and Sarapis in Rome.[176]

NERVA.
96–98.

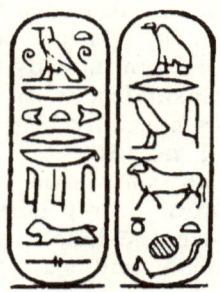

Building.—Latopolis: columns of temple.
[The only building recorded under Nerva was that of the temple of Latopolis, which was proceeding continuously.]
Inscriptions.—Hieroglyphic: L.D. iv. 82. Latin: P.S.B.A. xviii. p. 107.
Ostrakon.—P.S.B.A. v. pp. 124 ff., B.M. 5790 w.
Papyrus.—Pap. B.M. 143.

TRAJANUS.
98–117.

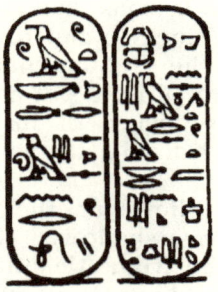

Buildings.—Panopolis: propylon of temple of Khem. Tentyra: propylon; Typhonium. Latopolis: columns. Philæ: temple O. Elephantine: Mammisi temple. Talmis: west wall of second court and forecourt of temple. Kysis: pylon of temple of Sarapis and Isis.
[The buildings completed in the reign of Trajan were the temple of Philæ, the propylon of the great temple at Tentyra, the pylon dedicated at Kysis, and the propylon at Panopolis. The other works mentioned were still in progress at his death.]

Inscriptions.—Hieroglyphic: L.D. iv. 82, 83, 84, 85; Cat. des Mons. p. 113. Greek: C.I.G. iii. 4713 c, 4714, 4716 c, 4823, 4824, 4843, 4984; M.A. 15, 70, 100; App. iii. 7, 8; R.A. 1889, p. 70; P.S.B.A. xviii. p. 107. Latin: C.I.L. iii. 24, 25, 38, 79.
Ostraka.—C.I.G. iii. 4864, 4865, 4866; P.S.B.A. v. pp. 124 ff., B.M. 5790 w, 5819 c, 5791 t, 5791 v, 5791 u, 5790 k, 5790 m, 5790 y, 5788 f, 5790 f, 5790 g, 5790 t, 5790 n, 5790 o, 5791 s, 5790 l, 5790 a, 5790 s, 5788 c, 5788 b, 5791 f, 5790 b, 5790 i, 5791 c, coll. Aquila Dodgson; vii. pp. 11 ff., Nos. 25, 25 a, pp. 195 ff., Nos. 2, 3, 4, 5; ix. p. 198, No. 1; R.E. iv. p. 183, L. 7648; Louvre, N. et E., No. 3; Lumbroso, Documenti Gr. del Mus. Egiz. di Torino, vii. 1.
Papyri.—B.G.U. 22, 44, 50, 68, 101, 140, 163, 196, 213, 226, 232, 252, 281, 350, 360, 415, 418, 446, 538, 715, 718; G.G.P. ii. 44; C.P.R. 11, 13, 28, 170, 171; Petrie, Hawara, p. 36, Nos. 132, 223, 298, 303; G.O.P. i. 46, 49, 50, 74, 97, 176; Pap. B.M. 171 a, 172, 173, 191, 202, 293, 476 a; Louvre, N. et E. 68.

10. Except at times of festivals, the Egyptians generally were quiet enough; so that at some date during the

Fig. 36.—Nerva: Latopolis.   Fig. 37.—Trajan: Latopolis.

reign of Trajan the Roman garrison was reduced by the withdrawal of one of the two legions which had been up till then maintained in Egypt.(177) Even a famine,—usually the signal for disturbances,—which was caused by the failure of the Nile to rise to a sufficient height in flood, passed quietly; partly through the prompt

FIG. 38.—Philæ: Temple of Trajan.

measures taken by the emperor, who sent back to Alexandria a fleet loaded with Egyptian corn from the stores accumulated in the public granaries.(178)

RISING OF THE JEWS

11. But at Alexandria there were always elements of

FIG. 39.—Trajan dancing: Tentyra.

FIG. 40.—Tentyra: Gateway of Trajan.

disturbance ready in the mutual hatred of the Greeks and Jews. The crushing policy adopted towards the whole Jewish nation after the destruction of Jerusalem had kept them quiet for a while. A local rising in Alexandria was easily put down by the government; but in the following year, while the greater part of the Eastern legions were away with the emperor, engaged in the Parthian war, there was a general revolt of the Jews in Egypt, Cyprus, and Cyrene, and to some extent also in Palestine and Mesopotamia. They massacred all

[115 A.D.]
[116 A.D.]

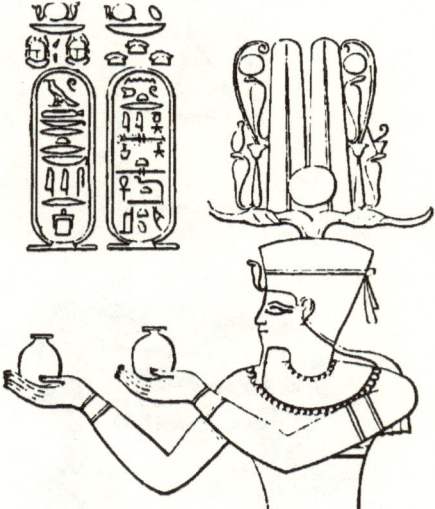

FIG. 41.—Trajan: Philae.

the Greeks who fell into their power, and succeeded in driving the rest into Alexandria, while they dominated the open country. The Greeks, besieged in Alexandria, retaliated by putting to death any Jews who had remained in the city; but they were unable to raise the siege until Marcius Turbo arrived with an army and fleet specially sent to suppress the rising in Egypt and Cyrene. Even then it needed a number of battles to break the spirit of the Jews, and the struggle went on for some months; but gradually all those of them who survived were driven into the desert, there to take up the profession of robbers. In Alexandria, the Jewish population was practically annihilated. In

FIG. 42.—Roman fortress of Babylon. (Description de l'Egypte.)

consequence of these disturbances, Turbo rebuilt the fortress of Babylon, which served also to guard the head of the canal which Trajan cut from the Nile to the Red Sea.[170]

HADRIANUS

117–138.

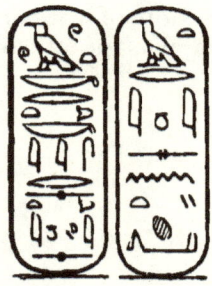

Buildings.—Antinoopolis. Tentyra: Typhonium. Latopolis: hypostyle. Philæ: temple G. Mons Claudianus: temple of Zeus Helios Sarapis.

[The temple at Mons Claudianus was probably a work of the reign of Trajan and Hadrian. The Typhonium at Tentyra does not appear to have had any further work done on it after this time. No inscriptions of Hadrian have been found among the ruins of Antinoopolis; but the town was certainly planned, and its building commenced, by him.]

Inscriptions.—Hieroglyphic: L.D. iv. 85, 86, 87. Greek: C.I.G. iii. 4713 f, 4721, 4722, 4723, 4724, 4725, 4726, 4728, 4732, 5081; M.A. (unnumbered); R.A. 1870, p. 314. Latin: C.I.L. iii. 39, 41, 42, 43, 44, 45, 77.

Ostraka.— C.I.G. iii. 4867, 4868, 4869, 4870, 4871; P.S.B.A. v. pp. 158 ff., B.M. 5790 e, i, l, p, s, u, 5791 a, g, h, k, l, n, 5788 c, 12,642, coll. C. Appleton; vi. pp. 207 ff., Nos. 1, 2; ix. p. 198, Nos. 2, 3; Louvre, N. et E. 4; Lumbroso, Documenti Gr. del Mus. Egiz. di Torino, vii. 3, 5.

Papyri.—B.G.U. 19, 53, 69, 70, 73, 109, 114, 136, 176, 182, 193, 231, 234, 250, 339, 352, 394, 420, 457, 459, 464, 465, 581, 647, 706, 742, 755; G.G.P. ii. 45, 45 a, 46; C.P.R. 17, 18, 24, 25, 26, 173, 178, 223, 240; Petrie, Hawara, p. 36, Nos. 83, 116, 166, 418; G.O.P. i. 34 v, 68, 75, 95, 100, 105, 106, 107, 188; Pap. B.M. 201 a, 208 a, 254, 255, 295, 297 b, 298, 299, 300.

12. These disturbances, which had not yet been quelled when Hadrian succeeded to the throne, had wrought great damage to the buildings of Alexandria; and when, in the course of his travels over the empire, he reached Egypt, he found ample opportunity for gratifying his passion for architecture in restoring and

renewing the temples and other public edifices of the capital.[180]

Fig. 43.—Hadrian : Philæ.

13. His patronage was also extended to philosophy, in the persons of the professors of the Museum; with whom he held discussions.[181] The advantage, however, which might possibly have been gained from such imperial condescension, was more than counterbalanced by the presentation to sinecure professorships at Alexandria of wandering sophists, who were apparently not required even to reside, much less to lecture, but only gave the glory of their names to the Museum in return

for their salaries. Such were Polemon of Laodicea and Dionysios of Miletos.[182]

14. The visit of Hadrian to Egypt unquestionably resulted in an artistic revival under Greek influence, which had been waning since the second century before Christ until this date. This revival is shown most markedly in the coinage, the types and style of which had been under Trajan strongly Egyptian in character,

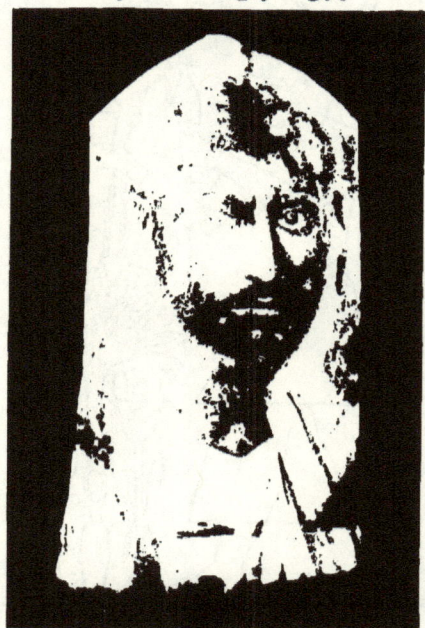

Fig. 44.—Mummy portrait: from Hawara.

but suddenly revert to Hellenism after the fifth year of Hadrian.[183] Another instance may be found in the series of mummy cases from several Roman cemeteries in the Fayum, notably those of Hawara and Rubaiyyat; on which the formal face modelled in wood or plaster is replaced, about this time, by a portrait of the deceased person whose body was inside the mummy case; and these portraits, executed

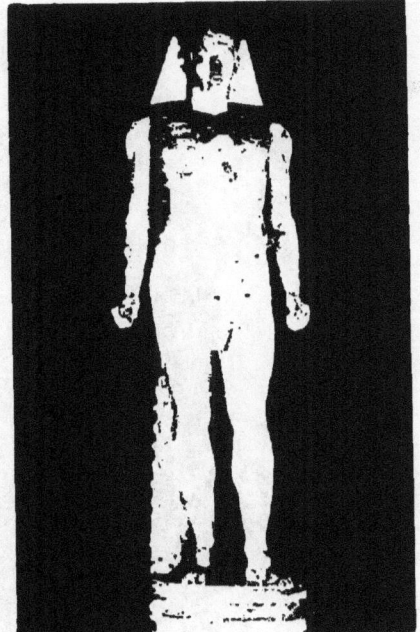

Fig. 45.—Statue of Antinous? (Vatican.)

Fig. 46.—Antinoöpolis: Arch of triumph. (Description de l'Égypte.)

Fig. 47.—Antinoöpolis. (Description de l'Égypte.)

in wax, show distinctly the traditions of Hellenistic art.[181]

15. Hadrian was, however, a student of, and believer in Oriental, as well as Greek ideas; and his curiously eclectic disposition is well illustrated by the fate of Antinous. This youth, a favourite of the emperor, was accompanying him on his voyage up the Nile. According to the commonly received account, Hadrian had consulted the Egyptian astrologers, who promised him some prolongation of life or fortune if he would sacrifice his most cherished possession; and thereon Antinous drowned himself, or was drowned, to secure the fulfilment of the promise.[185] Whatever the exact circumstances of his death were, he was honoured by Hadrian with a memorial in the shape of a city, named after him Antinoopolis, built in Greek fashion and granted a constitution on the Greek model; while he was made the hero-god of the district, which was constituted into an Antinoite nome. The emperor, to secure the prosperity of his new city, constructed a road from it across the desert to the Red Sea, ending at Berenike; but it does not appear that any important part of the Indian trade was diverted along this line from the old-established route through Koptos.[186]

16. A second visit was paid to Egypt nine years [131 A.D.

FIG. 48.—Cartouche of Sabina.

later by the emperor with his wife Sabina. But little is recorded of this visit beyond the names of Hadrian and his followers scratched on the northern colossus at Thebes, which they visited, according to the usual

FIG. 49.—Hadrian approaching Alexandria. (British Museum.)

FIG. 50.—Hadrian greeted by Alexandria. (British Museum.)

custom of Roman tourists in Egypt, to hear the musical sounds which proceeded from it at sunrise.[187]

ANTONINUS PIUS.

138-161.

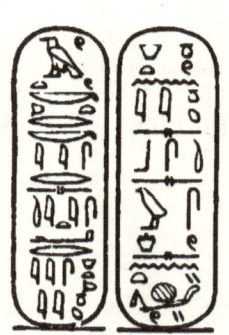

Buildings.—Alexandria : gates to east and west. Tentyra : east door. Apollinopolis Parva : peribolos of temple of Harpokrates. Thebes : antehall of small temple of Medinet Habu. Latopolis : sculptures. Syene : basilica. Tehonemyris : sekos and pronaos of temple of Amenebis.

[The inscription of Antoninus is the latest that is found on the temple of Medinet Habu. The work done at Tehonemyris and Apollinopolis Parva was rebuilding. The gates of Alexandria are mentioned by Malala (xi. 280) and John of Nikiou (c. 74).]

Inscriptions.—Hieroglyphic : L.D. iv. 87. Demotic : L.D. vi. 30. Greek : C.I.G. iii. 4683 b, 4713 b, 4766, 4831, 4832, 4955, 5050 ; App. iii. 9, 10, 11 ; Rec. Trav. xvi. p. 44. Latin : C.I.L. iii. 6625.

Ostraka.—C.I.G. iii. 4873, 4874, 4875, 4876, 4877, 4878, 4879, 4880, 4881, 4882, 4883, 4884, 4884 b ; P.S.B.A. v. pp. 158 ff., B.M. 5790 f, t, 5851 a, 12,070, 12,460 ; vi. pp. 207 ff., Nos. 3, 4 ; Louvre, N. et E., Nos. 5, 6, 7, 8, 9, 10, 11 ; Lumbroso, Documenti Greci del Mus. Egiz. di Torino, vii. 4.

DISTURBANCES AT ALEXANDRIA

Papyri. B.G.U. 5, 6, 16, 17, 20, 31, 51, 52, 55, 78, 85, 86, 87, 88, 90, 95, 99, 100, 102, 104, 105, 107, 110, 111, 113, 133, 134, 135, 137, 142, 143, 152, 153, 155, 160, 166, 167, 169–172, 188, 191, 201–212, 214, 227, 239, 254, 256, 257, 262, 263, 265, 272, 273, 278–280, 284, 285, 288–290, 293, 294, 299–301, 328–331, 340, 348, 353–355, 357, 358, 372, 391, 416, 422, 427, 438–443, 453, 462, 463, 468, 469, 472, 488, 489, 492, 512, 516, 517, 524, 544, 545, 587, 593, 610, 613, 619, 626, 635, 638, 645, 661, 696, 697, 702, 704, 710, 717, 720, 723, 729, 741, 747; Pap. Gen. 5, 6, 8, 8 bis; G.G.P. i. 47, ii. 46 a, 47, 48, 49, 50 a, 50 b, 50 c, 51, 52, 53 a, 54; C.P.R. 15, 22, 23, 31, 193, 194, 206, 230; Louvre, N. et E. 17, 19, 19 bis; Petrie, Hawara, p. 36, No. 116; G.O.P. i. 89, 98, 101, 171; Pap. B.M. 178, 196, 296, 301, 303–310, 312–321, 323, 358, 376, 438, 466, 469 a; Rivista Egiziana, 1894, p. 529.

17. The reign of Antoninus passed peaceably in Egypt, with the exception of an outbreak among the Alex-

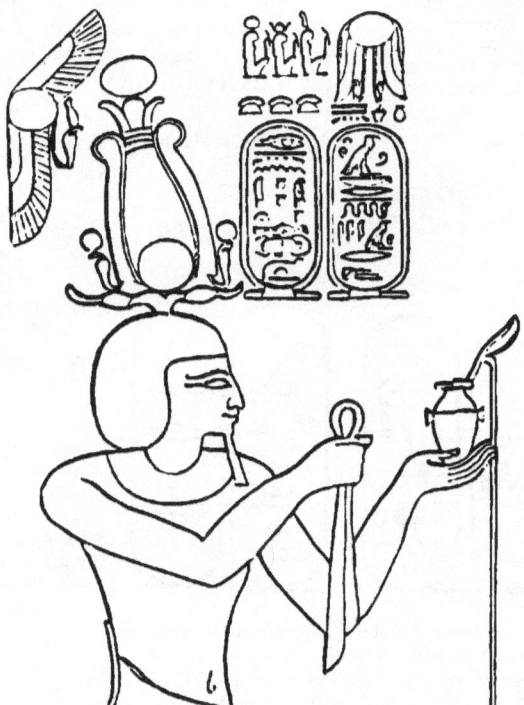

FIG. 51.—Antoninus Pius: Tentyra.

andrians, in which the prefect — probably M. Sempronius Liberalis — was killed. This disturbance is said to have brought upon the city the severe displeasure of the emperor; but he is also reported to have subsequently visited Alexandria, and to have built a hippodrome and the gates known as those of the Sun and of the Moon, which were at the east and west ends of the main street which intersected the city.(188)

18. In the first year of Antoninus was celebrated the completion of a Sothiac period of 1460 years, when the new year's day of the movable calendar had come round to the day on which the dog-star Sirius rose heliacally. The particular year was probably decided for political considerations, as the astronomers were not agreed upon the results of their observations.(189)

138 A.D.

FIG. 52.—Phœnix: Coin of Antoninus Pius. (Bodleian.)

MARCUS AURELIUS.

161–180.

L. VERUS.

161–169.

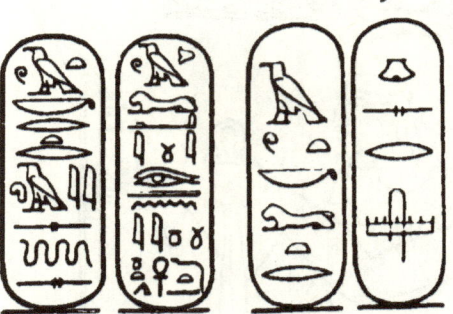

Buildings.—Busiris: temple repaired. Antæopolis: temple rebuilt. Latopolis: outer west wall of temple. Philæ: temple G.

[The building at Latopolis still continued. At Busiris and Antæopolis old work was repaired. The erection of temple G at Philæ was perhaps completed in this reign, as the inscription of Aurelius is the latest found there.]

Inscriptions.—Hieroglyphic: L.D. iv. 87, 88. Greek: C.I.G. iii. 4701, 4704, 4712, 4767. Latin: C.I.L. iii. 13, 49, 67; P.S.B.A. xviii. p. 107.

Ostraka.— C.I.G. iii. 4888; P.S.B.A. vii. pp. 195 ff., No. 7; Louvre, N. et E., No. 13.
Papyri.— B.G.U. 18, 26, 49, 55–59, 66, 74, 77, 79, 80, 91, 119, 123, 127, 154, 194, 195, 198, 219, 224, 225, 233, 238, 240, 241, 282, 283, 298, 302, 324, 327, 347, 359, 387, 393, 410, 414, 421, 431, 434, 461, 513, 514, 520, 521, 525, 537, 541, 542, 598, 603, 604, 607, 629, 631, 654, 666, 708, 722; Pap. Gen. 3; G.G.P. ii. 50 d, 50 e, 50 f, 53 b, 53 c, 53 d, 53 e, 53 f, 55, 56, 57, 58, 108; C.P.R. 5, 14, 16, 246; Petrie, Hawara, p. 36, No. 401; G.O.P. i. 51, 62 K, 76, 88, 90, 173; Pap. B.M. 168, 170, 182 b, 198, 206 c, 324, 325, 327–340, 368, 470, 471.

19. The unusual event of a revolt among the native Egyptians, as distinct from the Alexandrians, occurred under Marcus Aurelius. The disturbance began among the Bucolic troops, who were recruited from among the inhabitants of the country, and employed for home service. It soon assumed a national and religious character. The leader of the rebels was a priest, Isidoros, and he administered to his followers, when they took the oath of fidelity, the flesh of a Roman officer whom they had captured and slain,— an act of ceremonial cannibalism which was typically Egyptian. The Roman troops were defeated, and Alexandria almost fell into the hands of the insurgents; even when Avidius Cassius came from Syria with reinforcements, he was unable to meet them in battle, but devoted himself to sowing dissensions in their ranks; and by these means he was able to break up their league, and crush the separate bands in detail.(190)

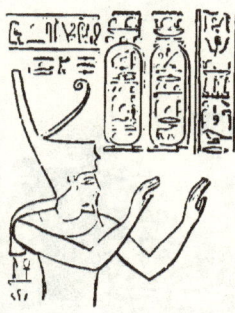

FIG. 53.—Aurelius: Latopolis.

[172 A.D.]

20. Very shortly after the suppression of this rebellion, came a military revolt, at the head of which the victorious general Avidius Cassius found himself. He was said to have been intriguing with the empress Faustina, in the hope of seizing the imperial power after the death of Aurelius; but a false report that

[175 A.D.]

this event had occurred, led him to allow his troops to proclaim him emperor. Leaving his son Mæcianus in Alexandria to take charge of Egypt, he went to Syria to win over the army there, and was promptly acknowledged by them. But the revolt collapsed as rapidly as it arose: while Aurelius was preparing for war, Cassius was killed by a centurion, and Mæcianus likewise put to death by the troops in Alexandria.[191]

Fig. 54.—Antæopolis: Temple. (Description de l'Egypte.)

21. The emperor, notwithstanding this collapse, visited the East; but the rebels escaped without severe punishment. Most were rewarded for their timely submission by a free pardon; and even those most deeply implicated, such as the children of Cassius and Gaius Calvisius Statianus, the prefect of Egypt, escaped with fines and banishment.[192]

GROWTH OF TRADE

COMMODUS.
180-192.

Buildings.—Karanis: temple of Pnepheros. Latopolis: west wall and colonnades of temple.
[The work done at the temple of Karanis consisted in restoration of the propylon.]
Inscriptions. Hieroglyphic: L.D. iv. 88, 89. Greek: C.I.G. iii. 4683; E.E.F. Report, 1895-96, p. 16, No. 4. Latin: C.I.L. iii. 49.
Ostraka.—P.S.B.A. vi. pp. 207 ff., No. 5; vii. pp. 195 ff., No. 6.
Papyri. B.G.U. 12, 28, 39, 60, 71, 72, 81, 82, 92, 115-118, 120, 124, 126, 128, 129, 138, 188, 200, 242, 243, 264, 270, 342, 361, 432, 433, 506, 515, 578, 590, 622, 649, 651, 658, 662, 731; Pap. Gen. 18; G.G.P. i. 48; ii. 50 g, 50 h. 50 i, 53 g, 59; C.P.R. 27, 29, 174; G.O.P. 69, 79, 91, 96, 166, 185; Pap. B.M. 166 b, 341-343, 439, 460, 472.

22. The clemency of Aurelius did not long avail the family of Cassius, as one of the first acts of Commodus, on his accession, was to put them to death.[193]

FIG. 55.—Commodus: Latopolis.

23. During the greater part of the period now under review, the prosperity of Egypt appears to have been well maintained at the level which it reached under Nero. The broader views of imperialism which he first put into practice encouraged the development of the provinces; and a similarly enlightened policy was pursued by his successors. The trade with the East continued to extend; in the reign of Antoninus or Aurelius, Roman merchants had got as far as China;[194] and the voyage to India had been shortened by the discovery of the monsoon and the consequent abandonment of the coast for the direct route across the open sea from the Arabian Gulf to India. The

amount of the Eastern trade is shown by Pliny, who estimated the annual value of the imports from Arabia and India at one hundred millions of sesterces ;[195] and alternative routes for the land journey, in addition to the recognised ones from Myoshormos and Berenike to Koptos, were provided by Trajan, who renewed the canal connecting the Nile with the Red Sea, and by Hadrian, in his road from Berenike to his new foundation of Antinoopolis. This trade was now chiefly in Egyptian hands, and its profits went to enrich the country. Agreeably with the development of trade, the rate of interest dropped to ten or twelve per cent. ;[196] and the issue of coinage continued to be steadily plentiful, while the standard was kept up alike in fineness and in weight. But in the latter part of the reign of Antoninus, complaints began to be made about the pressure of taxation. The first instance preserved of a decree of the prefect, ordering those who had left their villages in order to escape the burden of liturgies to return home, and promising a remission of outstanding debts to those who obeyed, is dated in the seventeenth year of Antoninus ;[197] but shortly afterwards, similar decrees seem to have become frequent.[198] The Bucolic war dealt a serious blow to the agriculture of Egypt ; spread as it was over several years and over the greater part of the country, while the rebellious troops were drawn from the native cultivators of the ground, its effects were far more serious than those of the only similar war which had occurred in Egypt since the Roman rule had been firmly established—the Jewish revolt under Trajan, which did not concern the Egyptians so much as the Romans and Greeks of the ruling classes. And the results are shown by the fact that the corn supply from Egypt to Rome had, under Commodus, to be supplemented by the institution of an African corn fleet.[199] There was also a distinct drop in the standard of the coinage. The mournful reference, in a letter of about this period, to the hardness of the times, probably gives accurately enough the general feeling of the Egyptian farmers.[200]

CHAPTER IV

THE DECAY OF THE PROVINCIAL SYSTEM

PERTINAX.

193.

Papyri.—B.G.U. 646; Pap. B.M. 473. [B.G.U. 46, dated in his reign, was written after his death.]

1. THE short reign of Pertinax was recognised by the Egyptians; and incidentally the documents dated by it give evidence of the length of time which it took for news to travel from Rome to Egypt. He was proclaimed emperor at Rome on 1st January; and on 6th March the prefect of Egypt issued orders for a fifteen days' festival in celebration of his accession; a decree, the issue of which would naturally have been the first act of the authorities on hearing of the event it commemorated.[201] He was murdered on 28th March; but on 19th May this fact was still unknown in the Fayum, as an official document was then dated with his name.[202]

DIDIUS JULIANUS.

193.

[PESCENNIUS NIGER.]

[193-194.]

[*Ostrakon.*—P.S.B.A. vii. pp. 195 ff., No. 33.
Papyri.—B.G.U. 454; G.G.P. ii. 60.]

2. The successor of Pertinax at Rome, Didius Julianus, was not, however, accepted in Egypt. No

coins were struck for him by the Alexandrian mint, nor has his name been found in any papyrus. The Egyptians had their own candidate for the throne in Pescennius Niger, the Roman general in Syria, who

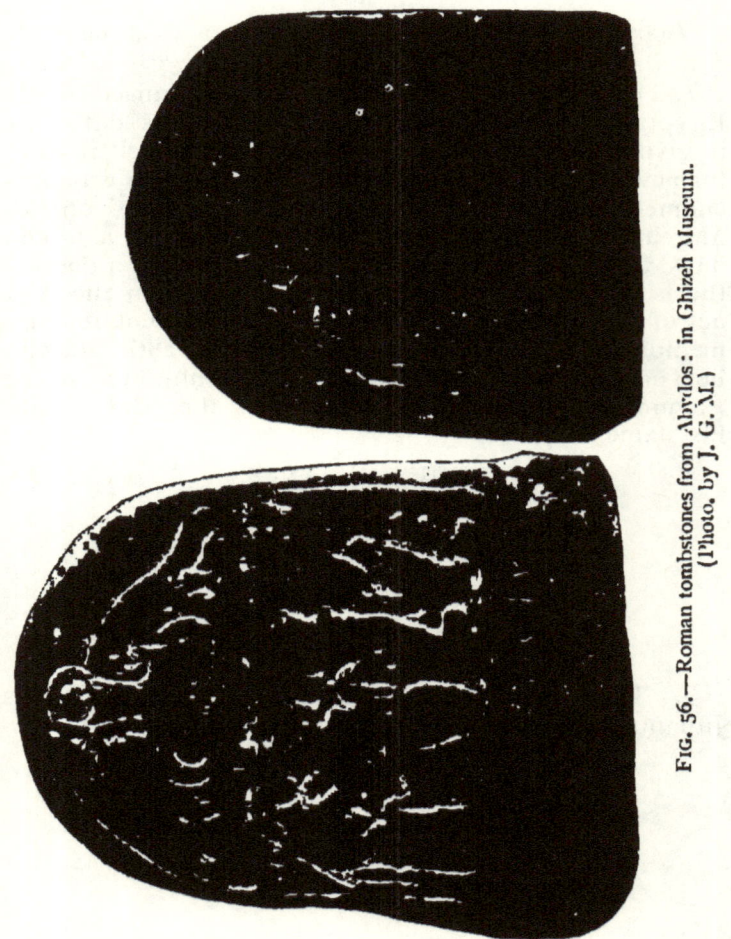

Fig. 56.—Roman tombstones from Abydos: in Ghizeh Museum. (Photo. by J. G. M.)

had won popularity amongst them while he commanded the troops at Syene, who guarded the frontier against the wandering tribes of the desert; the reason for this popularity being the firm hand with which he kept his men in order, and prevented them from plundering, according to the usual custom, those whom they were set to protect. He was declared emperor by the Syrian legions, and the Egyptian army and people joined his side.[263]

SEVERUS.

193–211.

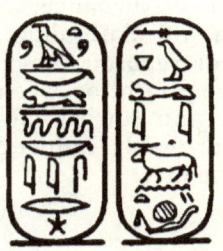

Buildings.—Latopolis: north and south walls.
Inscriptions.—Hieroglyphic: L.D. iv. 89. Greek: C.I.G. iii. 4680, 4863, 4980, 4981, 4982, 4983, 4984; Petrie, Koptos, ch. vi., No. 5; M.A. 72. Latin: C.I.L. iii. 14, 15, 50, 51, 52, 6580.
Ostraka.—C.I.G. iii. 5109^1, 5109^2; P.S.B.A. vii. pp. 195 ff., No. 32.
Papyri.—B.G.U. 2, 10, 15, 25, 41, 42, 45, 61, 62, 63, 67, 97, 98, 106, 108, 121, 139, 156, 199, 215, 216, 218, 220, 221, 266, 291, 326, 345, 346, 382, 392, 430, 473, 484, 527, 577, 639, 652, 653, 663, 705, 756; Pap. Gen. 16, 17; G.G.P. ii. 61, 62; C.P.R. 48, 49, 50, 51, 52, 53, 54, 55, 228; G.O.P. i. 54, 56; Pap. B.M. 156, 345–348, 451, 474.

3. In the struggle which followed, the decreasing importance of the Egyptian granaries became evident. Severus, the rival of Niger, as soon as he was master of Rome, hastened to secure, not Egypt, but Africa, in order to protect the corn-supply of the capital; showing that it was no longer possible for the master of Egypt to starve Rome into submission, as Vespasian had proposed to do.[204] Ultimately, the troops of Niger [194 A.D.] were defeated by Severus at

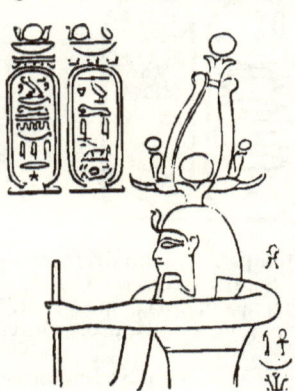

FIG. 57.—Severus: Latopolis.

Cyzicus; and the latter thus secured undisputed possession of the empire.(205)

[196 A.D.] 4. Some time afterwards, he visited Egypt, and restored to the Alexandrians the privileges of local self-government by a senate, which had been taken away from them by Augustus.(206) The general tranquillity which had prevailed for many years in Alexandria —only one disturbance, in the reign of Antoninus, having been recorded since the last great fight between the Greek and Jewish factions, eighty years before this date—probably induced the emperor to confer this favour on the city.

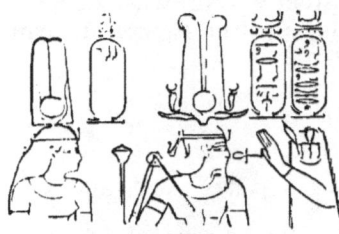

FIG. 58.— Severus and Julia: Latopolis.

CARACALLA.
211-217.

GETA.
211-212.

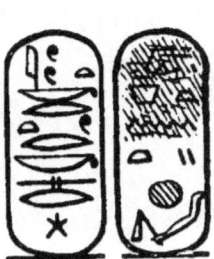

Buildings.—Latopolis: outer walls of temple. Alexandria: camp.
Inscriptions.—Hieroglyphic: L.D. iv. 89, 90. Greek: C.I.G. iii. 4986, 4987, 4988, 4989, 4990, 4991, 4992, 4993, 4994; M.A. 69, 103, 104, 105, 108; App. iii. 12; Petrie, Koptos, ch. vi., No. 6.
Ostraka.—C.I.G. iii. 5109³, 5109⁴; P.S.B.A. ix. p. 198; Lumbroso, Documenti Greci del Mus. Egiz. di Torino, vii. 2.
Papyri.—B.G.U. 64, 145, 159, 186, 222, 223, 266, 275, 321, 322, 336,

356, 362, 529, 534, 614, 617, 618, 637, 655, 711; Pap. Gen. 1; C.P.R. 33, 35, 45, 56 62, 239; G.O.P. i. 108; Pap. B.M. 217, 322, 349, 350, 352.

Miscellaneous.—Statue from Mendes. Colossal head from Koptos.

5. Caracalla, his son, also visited Alexandria; but

FIG. 59.—Caracalla and Geta: Latopolis.

FIG. 60.—Geta: Latopolis.

with less pleasant results for the inhabitants. They had exercised their talent for satire at his expense, scoffing at him for his mimicry of heroes like Alexander and Achilles, and for his murder of his brother Geta. On his approach to the city, the Alexandrian populace went out to receive him with honour, which he appeared to reciprocate. After a few days, he announced that he wished to enroll as soldiers those of the youths of the city best fitted to bear arms; and, having thus collected a large body of men upon a plain outside the city walls, he surrounded and charged them with his troops. The

FIG. 61.—Colossal head of Caracalla: from Koptos. (Photo. by W. M. F. Petrie.)

FIG. 62.—Caracalla: Latopolis.

FIG. 63.—Statue, face recut to likeness of Caracalla: in Ghizeh Museum. (Photo. by J. G. M.)

massacre which ensued was continued by the Roman soldiers on their return into the city, where they entered the houses and slew the inhabitants. Caracalla also abolished the games, put down the syssitia, and ordered Alexandria to be divided into two parts by a wall; at the same time directing the legionaries who had hitherto been stationed outside the walls at Nikopolis, to take up their quarters inside the city.[207]

6. It was probably shortly before the visit of Caracalla to Egypt that the procurator Titianus was assassinated by the orders of Aurelius Theocritus, a freedman of the emperor's, who held a commanding position in Egyptian affairs.[208] This was not the first time that a freedman had been the virtual ruler of Egypt. Basileides, a freedman of Claudius, had exercised the chief influence in Alexandria up to the time of the accession of Vespasian; and, still earlier, Julius Severus had been actually made prefect by Tiberius.

MACRINUS.

217-218.

Papyrus. Pap. B.M. 351.

7. A more novel step was taken by Macrinus, who, immediately on his accession to the throne, recalled Julianus the prefect of Egypt, and sent with Basilianus, the new prefect, a senator, Marius Secundus, as second in command. The rule of Augustus, which forbade the appointment of senators to administrative rank in Egypt, was thus for the first time broken.[209]

ELAGABALUS.

218-222.

Inscriptions.—Greek: C.I.G. iii. 4996; App. iii. 13; R.E.G. 1891, p. 46.
Papyri.—B.G.U. 296, 413, 452, 458, 518, 633, 667; G.G.P. i. 49; C.P.R. 8, 32; G.O.P. i. 61; Pap. B.M. 166 a, 352, 353, 477.

8. Basilianus and Marius, however, were not left for long in peaceful enjoyment of their offices. As soon as Elagabalus had been proclaimed emperor by the Syrian troops, the Roman garrison in Alexandria declared themselves on his side, thus following the precedents set in the cases of Vespasian and Pescennius Niger, both of whom were nominated in Syria and subsequently accepted in Egypt. But the citizens, as the new claimant to the throne professed himself to be the son of their old enemy Caracalla, were naturally for opposing him, and supported Basilianus, who had put to death the couriers who brought the news from Syria. A general battle in Alexandria was the result, in which the military got the better, Marius being killed; and Basilianus fled to Rome.[210]

ALEXANDER SEVERUS.

222-238.

Inscriptions.—Demotic: L.D. vi. 10. Greek: C.I.G. iii. 4705, 4997, 4999, 5000, 5001, 5002, 5068.
Papyri.—B.G.U. 35, 659, 716; C.P.R. 7, 21, 36, 63-69, 75, 81-83, 225, 243; Louvre, N. et E., No. 69; G.O.P. i. 35^v, 77; Pap. B.M. 176, 180.

9. A justification for the action of Macrinus in disregarding the rule of Augustus may be found in the greatly diminished importance of Egypt, which was, as has already been pointed out, no longer the sole, or

FIG. 64.—Wady Khardassy: Greek tablets.

even the chief, granary of Rome, and was reduced to poverty alike in wealth and spirit. Thus it was no longer to be apprehended that a man of influence would find it easier to gather the materials for a rebellion in Egypt than elsewhere. A still more striking example of this decline in importance is preserved in the reign of Alexander Severus, who, when one Epagathus had led a mutiny of the prætorian guards at Rome, despatched him to Egypt as prefect, as though this was a place where he would

FIG. 65.—Roman lamp in form of a boat. (Petrie Collection.)

be removed from any chance of making mischief. It later transpired that the seeming honour was merely a step to removing Epagathus from the company and the memory of the praetorian guards, whom the emperor feared to offend, and then quietly having him executed.(11)

MAXIMINUS.
235-238.
Inscriptions.—Greek : C.I.G. iii. 5003.
Papyri.—B.G.U. 735; G.G.P. ii. 67; C.P.R. 6, 84; Pap. B.M. 212b.

GORDIANUS I.

GORDIANUS II.
238.

BALBINUS.

PUPIENUS.
238.

GORDIANUS III.
238-244.
Inscriptions.—Greek : C.I.G. iii. 5004-5008.
Papyri.—B.G.U. 84, 141 ; R.E.G. vii. p. 299, No. 3 ; G.O.P. i. 80.

PHILIPPUS.
244-249.
Inscriptions.—Greek : C.I.G. iii. 5009, 5010, 5069.
Papyri.—B.G.U. 7, 8, 253 ; G.G.P. ii. 68, 71 ; C.P.R. 85 ; R.E.G. vii. p. 299, No. 5 ; G.O.P. i. 81.

10. A province which had reached such a low degree of importance as that shown by the foregoing events, counted for little in the making and unmaking of emperors which followed the death of Alexander Severus. The Egyptians seem to have acquiesced in the decisions of fate and the western provinces ; and the officials at Alexandria also recognised without question any claimant who was set up. Such were the two Gordiani in Africa, for whom coins were struck in Egypt simultaneously with those of Maximinus, whom they sought,

but failed, to overthrow.(212) In one way only did Egypt share with the rest of the East a power in the empire —by its poverty. The inability of the government to collect the revenue in the Eastern provinces compelled Philip to make peace with the Goths on the Danube.(213)

DECIUS.

249-251.

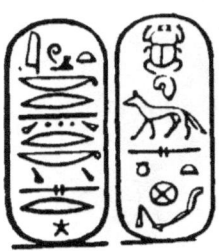

Building.—Latopolis: west wall of temple. [The name of Decius is the last of those which occur on the walls of the temple of Latopolis.]
Inscription.—Hieroglyphic: L.D. iv. 90.
Papyri. B.G.U. 287; C.P.R. 20, 37; R.E.G. vii. p. 299, No. 1.

11. A new disturbing element was beginning to make its presence felt in Egyptian politics; the growing strength of Christianity obliged the rulers of the country to recognise it. There had, indeed, been occasional attempts, of a more or less local character, made during the second century with a view of putting down the new religion; but the first general attack upon it was made in the reign of Decius, when a systematic test was ordained of compelling every person to do sacrifice, on pain of denunciation and death if they refused; while those who fulfilled the test received a certificate from a magistrate, witnessing to the due performance.(214)

250 A.D.]

FIG. 66.—Decius: Latopolis.

GALLUS.

251-254.

Papyrus.—Pap. Gen. 9.

ÆMILIANUS.
252-254.

VALERIANUS.
253-260.

Inscription.—Greek: App. iii. 14.
Papyri.—B.G.U. 14, 746; C.P.R. 176; Pap. B.M. 211.

GALLIENUS.
260-268.

Inscription.—Greek: C.I.G. iii. 4839.
Papyri.—B.G.U. 244, 552-557, 579, 743, 744, 745; G.G.P. ii. 69; C.P.R. 38, 39.

[MACRIANUS I.]
[MACRIANUS II.]
[QUIETUS.]
[261-262.]

[*Inscription.*—Greek: Petrie, Koptos, c. vi., No. 7.
Papyrus.—G.G.P. i. 50.]

12. In the general state of revolution which pervaded the Roman Empire during the time of Gallienus, Egypt shared to the full. At first the Egyptians followed, as they had so often previously done, the lead of Syria, and recognised as emperors Macrianus with his sons Macrianus and Quietus.[215] But when these had fallen, the first two in Illyricum, the third at Emesa, the Alexandrian mob ventured to experiment in the making of an emperor on its own account, and compelled Marcus Julius Æmilianus, the prefect, to ac-

[262 A.D.]

FIG. 67.—Inscription of Quietus: from Koptos. (Petrie Collection.)

cept their nomination. For a few months the Egyptian emperor ruled with vigour; he drove back the Blemmyes, who were harassing the Thebaid, and was preparing an expedition, probably destined against Æthiopia, when Theodotus arrived to support the cause of Gallienus in Alexandria. During the contest which followed, the city was laid waste by the opposing parties, who established themselves in different quarters, and made the intervening space a desert; the wall which Caracalla had built across the city probably serving to mark the boundaries of the two factions. Finally, Theodotus got the victory, captured Æmilianus, and sent him as a prisoner to Rome, while Alexandria was left in ruins, and infected with disease. So great was the mortality caused by these various troubles, that it is reported that the numbers of the inhabitants between the ages of fourteen and eighty were only equal to those of between forty and seventy in former times; that is to say, that the population had been reduced to barely a third of its former numbers.[216]

FIG. 68.—Coin of M. Iulius Æmilianus. (British Museum.)

CLAUDIUS II.

268-270.

Papyrus.- G.G.P. ii. 70.

13. During the last few years the power of the vassal state of Palmyra had been steadily growing under its prince Odænathus; and when, after his death, his widow Zenobia aspired to independence from Rome, one of her first movements was to occupy Egypt. Odænathus, it is true, had been made by Gallienus commander of the Eastern provinces, in which Egypt would be included; but he had never been recognised

there. An Egyptian named Timagenes, in the first year of Claudius, invited the Palmyrenes to enter the country; and, in response to his invitation, Zenobia sent an army of seventy thousand men, under Zabdas. The Romans, however, though inferior in numbers, made a dogged resistance: they were at first defeated; but when the main Palmyrene army withdrew, leaving a small garrison of some five thousand men, these were expelled by Probus, a Roman general. Zabdas and Timagenes thereon returned, and were defeated by Probus; but when he attempted to cut off their retreat near Babylon, the superior local knowledge of Timagenes secured the victory for the Palmyrenes, and Probus committed suicide.[217] [268 A.D.]

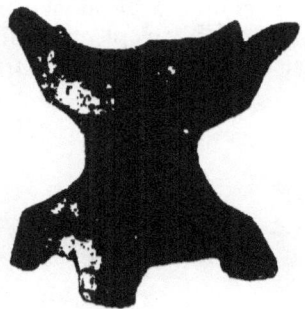

FIG. 69.— Miniature altar. (Petrie Collection.)

14. During the whole of the reign of Claudius the authority of the Roman government in Egypt was practically confined to Alexandria. The Palmyrenes had allied themselves with the Blemmyes, who were of kindred Arab race, and from their homes above the First Cataract of the Nile had recently been threatening the Roman frontier, which had remained undisturbed since the days of Augustus. They

FIG. 70.— Altar of M. Aurelius Belakabos: from Koptos. (Photo. by W. M. F. Petrie.)

possibly found support also at Koptos, where a corps of Palmyrene archers had been stationed by the Roman government. The two Arab tribes now ruled the whole of Upper Egypt, and finally possessed themselves, in part at least, of Alexandria.[218]

QUINTILLUS.

270.

AURELIANUS.

270-275.

Papyri.—C.P.R. 9; Pap. B.M. 214.

15. The Palmyrene government, in spite of the fact that its armies were fighting against the Roman troops, had not definitely renounced its allegiance to the Roman emperor; and when its partisans obtained a footing in Alexandria, they struck coins which bear the head of Aurelian on the obverse, while that of Vaballathos the son of Zenobia appears on the reverse.[219] But [270 A.D.] Aurelian soon broke relations with Zenobia, and went to Egypt to recover that country. He succeeded in driving the Palmyrene forces and their adherents into the suburb known as the Brucheion, and there besieged them. They were forced by hunger to capitulate; and Aurelian destroyed the greater part of the quarter which they had held, together with the walls of Alexandria.[220]

16. There was still a considerable element of disturbance left in Egypt after the expulsion of the Palmyrenes from Alexandria. The most dangerous enemy of the Romans was Firmus, the leader of the native Egyptian party, who was acting in concert with the Blemmyes and the remnants of the Palmyrene army. He actually held Upper Egypt, and even threatened Alexandria; but Aurelian returned to Egypt and defeated him.[221]

TACITUS.

275-276.

PACIFICATION OF EGYPT

PROBUS.
276–282.
Papyrus.—B.G.U. 419.

17. The Blemmyes from the southern frontier of Egypt now dominated the whole of the Thebaid, and necessitated the attention of the Roman government; and it was only by degrees that Probus, who had been left in command of Egypt by Aurelian, drove them back to their homes. He had also to deal with attacks on the western frontier made by some of the wandering tribes of the Libyan desert; and it was not until six or seven years had passed that he finally recovered from them Ptolemais and Koptos, the two chief military stations of Upper Egypt. He had, in the meantime,

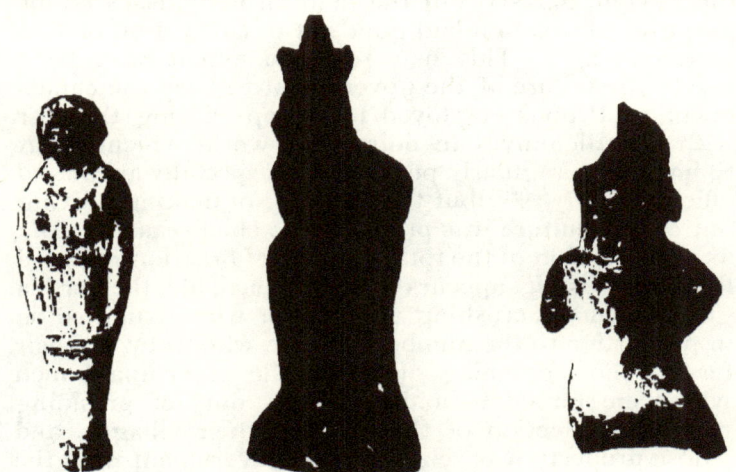

Fig. 71.—Roman terra-cotta figures. (Petrie Collection.)

after the death of Aurelian and the short reign of Tacitus, been named as emperor by the Egyptian legions in opposition to Florianus, the brother of Tacitus; and the Syrian army, reversing the order hitherto prevalent, accepted the choice, which was approved by the remainder of the empire.(222)

CARUS.
282–283.

Papyri.—G.O.P. i. 55, 55 a, 55 b.

CARINUS.
283–285.

18. The economic history of Egypt from the time of Severus to that of Diocletian shows nothing but a decline from bad to worse. The oppression of the taxes was such that large numbers of the cultivators of the land were driven to leave their homes and live the life of brigands; and a record shows that, in one part of the Fayum, one-sixth of the land formerly assessed for purposes of taxation had gone out of cultivation or was unoccupied.[223] This may to some extent have been due to the failure of the government to keep the canals open, as Probus employed his troops during the war with the Blemmyes in doing this work, which ought to have been regularly performed by specially appointed officials yearly;[224] but the difficulty of making a living out of agriculture was probably the chief reason. And as no remission of the total amount of taxation required from each district appears to have been made, the burden grew the more crushing upon those who struggled on in proportion to the number of those who threw up their farms; most crushing of all on the unfortunate men who were forced to undertake the duty of presiding over the collection of the taxes in their villages, and whose property was seized by the government until the full amount of the taxes had been paid into the official bank.[225] The difficulty found by Philip in raising the imperial revenues from the East has already been mentioned; and the rapid deterioration in the size of the coinage—it could not deteriorate much in fineness—shows, further, the embarrassments of the government. The latter fact explains away to some extent the rise in prices—as, for example, that of corn, from eight

drachmæ to sixteen or nineteen drachmæ an artaba—in the course of the century ;[226] and the farmers were the less able to benefit by this rise, as the greater part of their produce was paid directly in kind to the State by measure and not by value ; while the rise in prices had brought with it a rise in the wages which had to be paid to the labourers, who at the beginning of the century were receiving from one and two-thirds to three drachmæ a day ; and, forty years later, obtained from four to six drachmæ.[227] The position of the Egyptian farmers, especially those who held large amounts of land, must have been desperate before Diocletian took in hand the reform of the empire.

CHAPTER V

THE STRUGGLE BETWEEN THE STATE AND THE CHURCH, 284-379 A.D.

DIOCLETIANUS.

284-305.

Building.—Philæ : arch.
[The arch at Philæ was probably part of a scheme of fortification for the island, executed under Diocletian.]
Inscriptions.—Greek : C.I.G. iii. 4681, 4892.   Latin : C.I.L. iii. 22 ; M.A., E.
Papyri.—B.G.U. 13, 94, 286, 373, 624 ; G.G.P. ii. 72, 74, 75, 76, 78, 110 ; C.P.R. 40, 41 ; R.E.G. vii. p. 299, No. 2 ; G.O.P. i. 43, 58, 59, 71.

1. THE defeat of the Blemmyes by Probus had only checked their inroads for the moment. From year to year they renewed their attacks on Upper Egypt, finding no resistance, and probably some help, among the inhabitants, who could scarcely suffer more from their plundering than they did from that of the Roman government. The garrison at Syene was quite incapable of keeping them in check ; and Diocletian devised a new plan for the protection of the Thebaid. The military frontier of the Dodekaschoinoi had long been Roman only in name ; and the diminished Roman army in Egypt was unable to spare the troops required for its occupation, while little revenue was to be obtained from the narrow strips of land here available for cultivation ; indeed, there is no evidence that the Dodekaschoinoi was ever regarded as a source of revenue by the Romans ; it was certainly never organ-

ised in the same manner as the rest of the country for financial purposes. So Diocletian withdrew the Roman

FIG. 72.—Philæ: Arch of Diocletian.

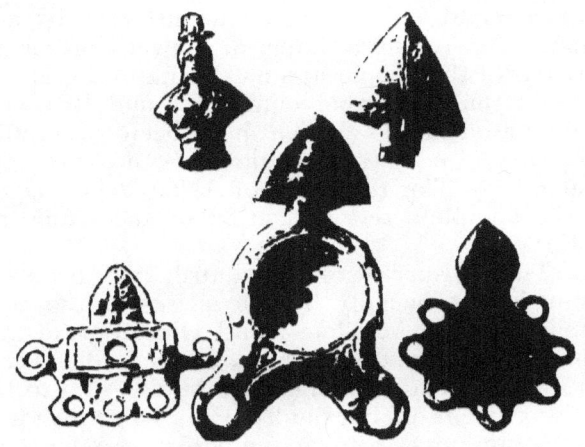

FIG. 73.—Roman lamps and handles. (Petrie Collection.)

frontier from Hierasykaminos to Syene, and invited the Nobatae, one of the wandering tribes of the western desert, to settle in the Nile valley, and to protect Upper Egypt against the Blemmyes, promising them an annual subsidy in return for this service. The Blemmyes were at the same time subsidised by the Roman government, in order to buy off their ravages; and the fortifications of the new frontier were strengthened.(228)

[295 A.D.] 2. Upper Egypt had scarcely been reorganised, when disturbances broke out in Alexandria. Lucius Domitius Domitianus, a Roman officer known to the Egyptians by the nickname of Achilleus, revolted, and was accepted by the Egyptians as emperor. Diocletian was obliged to come in person to Egypt in order to put down the revolt. He besieged Alexandria for eight months, and finally took it by storm; and a great part of the city was destroyed in the sack which followed.(229)

FIG. 74.—Coin of Domitius Domitianus. (British Museum.)

[297 A.D.]

[296 A.D.] 3. The revolt of Achilleus was in progress when Diocletian introduced his monetary and economical reforms; and its nature, as an attempt by a Roman commander to seize imperial power, rather than an uprising of the people against Roman rule, is shown by the fact that the rebel emperor found it advisable to adopt the changes which had been ordered by his adversary, and struck coins of the new monetary system.(230) The reduction of Alexandria was followed by the complete reorganisation of the whole province of Egypt.

4. The prosperity of Alexandria had been seriously diminished, especially by the sieges in the revolts of [302 A.D.] Æmilianus and Achilleus; and Diocletian decreed that a portion of the corn tribute, which had hitherto been sent by Egypt to Rome, should be diverted to the relief of the citizens of Alexandria.(231) In gratitude for this act of kindness from an emperor who had certainly

PERSECUTION OF CHRISTIANS

no reason to love them, the Alexandrians set up the column, still standing, known as Pompey's pillar.[232]

5. The latter part of the reign of Diocletian was a time of considerable disturbance in Egypt, owing to the persecution of the Christians, who now numbered amongst them a large proportion of the population, especially in Lower Egypt. The new system of government desired to secure, amongst other things, a more distinctly religious position for the emperor, in the hope that one to whom sacrifices were offered, and who was almost a god upon earth, might be more secure against assassination than the military emperors of the last century had been.[233] This desire was met by the resistance of the Christians; and the struggle provoked thereby was nowhere more keen than in Egypt, where the traditions of the country might have led the government to expect that all and more than they asked would have been granted at once, and that Diocletian would have been deified as readily as Caligula had been. But Egyptian fanaticism did not die out in those converted to Christianity; and the endeavours of the Roman officials to secure the worship of the emperor were met by an obstinacy which frequently degenerated into foolishness and wanton provocation. It would be difficult to decide with any approach to accuracy the number of those who were executed on religious grounds in Egypt; but they were certainly many, and of all classes of society.[234]

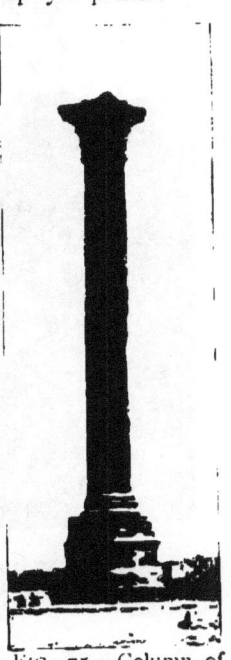

FIG. 75.—Column of Diocletian at Alexandria.

GALERIUS.   MAXIMINUS.
            AND
305-311.   305-313.

Inscription. Latin: M.A. 78.
Papyri. B.G.U. 408, 606; G.O.P. i. 102.

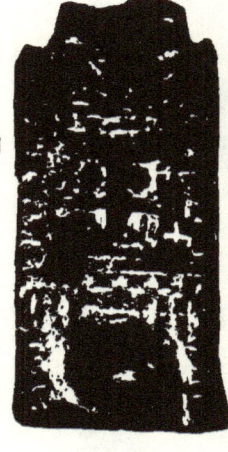

[313 A.D]

FIG. 76.—Roman lamp in form of a gateway. (Petrie Collection.)

6. The persecution was carried on steadily by Galerius and Maximinus, the latter of whom earned the special hatred of the Christians.(235) After his defeat by his rival Licinius, he designed to retreat on Egypt, and raise a fresh army there; though it may be doubted whether that country alone could have supplied any force capable of withstanding the troops of his rival.(236) To the support of Licinius, when in his turn he had to defend his possession of the East, Egypt only contributed eighty triremes out of a total of three hundred and fifty.(237)

CONSTANTINUS.   LICINIUS.
            AND
313-337.   313-323.

Inscriptions.—Greek: App. iii. 8; Rec. Trav. xvi. p. 44.
Papyri.—B.G.U. 349, 409, 411; Pap. Gen. 13; C.P.R. 233; G.O.P. i. 42, 53, 60, 84, 103.

Inscriptions.—Greek: C.I.G. iii. 4770. Latin: C.I.L. iii. 17, 18; M.A. 13; Bull. de la Soc. des Antiq. de France, 1888, p. 273.
Papyri. Pap. Gen. 10; C.P.R. 10, 19; G.O.P. i. 52, 83, 83a, 92.

7. As soon as Constantine obtained sole power, Christianity became the recognised religion of the State. But the Egyptian Christians had no sooner been relieved from persecution by the government, than they found fresh occasion for trouble in sectarian quarrels. The dispute which arose between Athanasius

[323 A.D.]

and Arius on the relationship of the Father and the Son, besides its theological importance, had political consequences which profoundly affected the history of Egypt.(238) The emperor was called upon to decide the point at issue in its earliest stage; Alexander, the bishop of Alexandria, appealed to him, as also did Arius; and as his letter, declining to pronounce an opinion, and endeavouring to pacify the opponents, produced no effect, he summoned a council of bishops [325 A.D at Nicæa to formulate a creed.(239) Their decision led to the excommunication and banishment of Arius; but when he offered a written explanation, the emperor revoked the order of banishment, and directed Athanasius, who was now bishop of Alexandria, to receive Arius into the Church again; and, upon the refusal of Athanasius to obey this order, he was summoned before a fresh council of bishops at Tyre, deposed, and [335 A.D. banished.(240)

8. Thus Constantine had been placed in a peculiar position with relation to the Christian Churches of Egypt. He was looked upon, to a certain extent, as arbiter of theological quarrels, with the civil power at his hand to enforce his decisions; but these decisions were only accepted by the parties in whose favour they were given, and consequently the civil power became an instrument of constant use for the settlement of ecclesiastical matters. The natural consequence of this confusion of the functions of Church and State was, that the bishops began to arrogate to themselves the rights of civil officials; and the charge of attempting to levy a tax, in the shape of a linen garment, for the support of the Church, was laid against Athanasius, who would thereby be infringing what had always been regarded in Egypt as the sole prerogative of the emperor. It is true that taxes had previously been assigned by the rulers of Egypt, alike native, Greek, and Roman, for the expenses of the worship of the national gods; and Athanasius may have held that he was entitled to claim assistance for his religion in a similar manner; but his unauthorised action was taken

to be one of the signs of a design to overthrow the government of Constantine.

9. Relations were constantly strained between this emperor and the people of Alexandria. They had supported his rivals Maximinus and Licinius; and this fact, taken together with the notorious unquietness of the Alexandrians, probably contributed to the decision of Constantine, to set aside the city which had been the chief one of the Greek East in favour of Byzantium, when he wished to found a new capital for the empire. This slight upon Alexandria did not tend to improve the feeling of the inhabitants towards the emperor; and one Philumenus attempted to raise a rebellion in Egypt, with the assistance, as it was said, of Athanasius; but his plans were discovered and crushed before any serious rising could occur.

CONSTANTIUS II.

337–361.

Papyri.—B.G.U. 21, 316, 405, 456; Pap. Gen. 11; C.P.R. 247; G.O.P. i. 66, 67, 67 a, 85, 86, 87, 189; Pap. B.M. 231–237, 239–248, 251, 403–418.

10. The confusion of civil and religious functions led to yet more serious consequences, when the death of Constantine placed Egypt in the hands of his weaker son Constantius. Athanasius now returned to Alexandria; and at first the support of the two other partners in the empire, Constantine II. and Constans, protected him against any interference by Constantius, who alone of the three belonged to the opposing Arian creed.[241] But as soon as the death of Constantine II. left a freer hand to Constantius, he deposed Athanasius, and had Gregory elected as patriarch of Alexandria by a council of bishops held at Antioch. It was not, however, until an armed escort was sent with him that Gregory ventured to enter Alexandria; and the metropolitan church was held against him by the supporters of Athanasius, till Syrianus, the general in command of the escort, threatened to storm it.[242]

Athanasius thereupon withdrew, and sought refuge at Rome, where he secured the support of Constans and of Julius the bishop of Rome; and their joint threats and arguments, after a conference at Constantinople between Constantius and Athanasius, secured the conclusion of an agreement, whereby the emperor and the bishop promised each to restore his theological opponents to the places from which they had been ejected. Athanasius accordingly once more resumed his office in Alexandria, where his supporters had kept up a continual disturbance in his absence; they had even succeeded in expelling the Arians from many monasteries, and in burning the metropolitan church, of which they had been dispossessed.(243)

11. That the fear of civil war with Constans was the chief reason which had prompted Constantius to make peace, was shown by the fact that, immediately after the death of his brother, he directed Athanasius to leave Egypt. This direction was disregarded, and it was over a year before Constantius ventured to take further steps. At length Syrianus the general threatened Athanasius with expulsion by force of arms, and carried his threats into effect by attacking him in church. The bishop, however, escaping from the general slaughter, took refuge with his friends; and they successfully concealed him from the emperor's emissaries, who were ordered to produce him dead or alive. Meanwhile the Arian party chose for their patriarch George of Cappadocia, who at once began a course of vigorous measures against his opponents, relying upon the assistance of the government to crush all those who disagreed with him.(214)

JULIANUS.

361-363.

Papyrus. G.O.P. i. 93.

12. The accession of Julian put a new aspect on the religious conflicts of Alexandria. During the disputes between the Athanasians and Arians of the last two

reigns, both parties had had, at any rate, one common ground, in the destruction or conversion to Christian uses of all temples and other monuments of polytheism, and they could exercise themselves in this work without any fear of drawing down upon their heads the displeasure of the government. But now the followers of the older religions had the emperor on their side, and they proceeded to take their revenge. They preferred formal complaints against Artemius, the military commander in Egypt, and George, the bishop; and, though Julian refused to see a deputation which came to Constantinople to bear these complaints, he summoned Artemius before him, and condemned him to death, seemingly for misuse of his authority. As soon as the news of his execution reached Alexandria, the mob rose and attacked George, against whom they had been cherishing a grudge, as well for a proposal made by him to the late emperor that a special house tax should be laid on Alexandria, as for destroying their temples; they murdered him in the street, and with him Dracontius the imperial treasurer, and Diodorus, a count.[245]

13. These acts of violence were tacitly approved by the government, though the emperor wrote to say that if there should be similar outrages again perpetrated, he would punish the offenders. But it is probable that they were as much the work of the Athanasian faction as of the pagans, or at any rate of the mob, who held no particular opinions, and were ready to support the party who were most violent at the moment. At any rate, Athanasius forthwith reappeared in triumph; and though Julian first published an edict expelling him from Alexandria, as one who had been banished and had returned without permission, and subsequently wrote threatening to fine the prefect if Athanasius were found in Egypt, he does not appear to have left the capital, but to have enjoyed sufficient security in the homes of his followers.[246]

JOVIANUS.

363-364.

14. The Athanasian party at length had an emperor of their own sect in Jovian; and their leader was able to come out of concealment, and to resume once more the functions of patriarch of Alexandria.[247]

VALENS.

364-378.

Buildings.—Athribis: tetrapylon. Alexandria: gates of Brucheion. [The building at Athribis is only known from the inscription preserved in the Ghizeh Museum. The erection of the gates of the suburb of Brucheion at Alexandria is mentioned by John of Nikiou (c. 82).]
Inscription.—Greek: App. iii. 15.
Papyrus.—G.G.P. i. 54.

15. This state of peace between the Egyptians and the government, however, was of short duration. The partition of the empire between Valentinian and Valens gave Egypt into the charge of the latter, and as he was an Arian, he came at once into conflict with the majority of the Egyptian Christians. The popularity of Athanasius, indeed, enabled him to procure the revocation of an edict of banishment which the prefect had issued against him on the ground that the original order of Constantius banishing him had never been revoked, and he held his bishopric thenceforth in peace till his death. But his successor Peter was imprisoned [373 A.D.] by direction of the emperor, and the Arian patriarch Lucius, who had been originally elected by his party in the time of Julian, was supported by the imperial troops in what is described by the orthodox historians as a course of violent persecution.[248] His worst offence, however, in their eyes seems to have been that he assisted in the enforcement of a new law, which abolished the privilege which the monks claimed of exemption from military service.[249] If any troops were to be recruited in Egypt, where whole towns such as Oxyrhynchos, or even whole districts like the Fayum,

were under monastic vows, it was out of the question to recognise such a claim to exemption; but the monks stoutly resisted the attempt to force them into the army, and many of them preferred to risk death fighting against, rather than with, the imperial troops.

377 A.D.] 16. The need of increased armaments was brought home to the government by an incursion of the Saracens, who advanced by the head of the Red Sea across the eastern frontier under the command of their queen Mavia, although they were nominally vassals of the Roman Empire. The imperial forces were apparently unequal to the task of meeting them, and they had to be bought off by a treaty, of which the only recorded but probably least substantial conditions were the marriage of a daughter of Mavia to the Roman general Victor, and the provision of an Egyptian bishop for the Saracens.[250]

17. The reforms of Diocletian apparently produced a temporary improvement in the economic condition of Egypt, or at any rate effected a check in the downward course of its finances. There is negative evidence for this in the absence of the complaints which had been so frequent during the previous century with regard to the burden of taxation; although this may be due to the comparative rarity of documents belonging to this period. There was certainly a revival of trade with the East, when, in the reign of Constantine, Frumentius negotiated treaties of commerce with the Axumitæ of Abyssinia; and Theophilus did likewise a few years later with the Homeritæ of Arabia.[251] These two nations now controlled the Æthiopian and Indian trade as they had done up to the time of Augustus; the Roman merchants having allowed the monopoly which the government then secured for them to slip out of their hands. Before long, however, tokens of an increase in the poverty of the empire begin to be again noticeable in the edicts of Constantius and Valens. The former forbade the custom of patronage, by which

communities in Egypt put themselves under the protection of some wealthy or influential individual, preferably an official, who could assist them in any difficulties with the government;[252] while Valens issued special orders that the curiales, who were responsible for the payment of taxes, should be prevented from moving from the towns into the country, and that they should, if they fled to the desert with the object of becoming monks, be seized and brought back.[253] Perhaps the most striking evidence, however, is to be found in the law of Valens, which decreed that tribute should not be paid in money;[254] and, agreeably with this, it is noticeable that comparatively few coins of the period between Constantius and Justinian are found in Egypt, while the evidence of the papyri shows that small accounts were commonly paid in kind.

CHAPTER VI

Establishment of the Supremacy of the Christian Church, 379–527 A.D.

THEODOSIUS I.

378–395.

Inscriptions.—Greek: App. iii. 16. Latin: C.I.L. iii. 19.
Papyri.—Pap. Gen. 12; Pap. Leyden Z.

1. The troops which had been raised by the violent methods adopted by the officers of Valens were scarcely likely to be ready to serve the government which had pressed them, if any chance of escape were offered. Consequently, in the reign of Theodosius, the Egyptian legions were partly drafted into Macedonia, where there would be less facility for desertion; and the garrison of Egypt was completed by the transfer to it of a number of Goths who had been recruited for the imperial army.[255] This was the first recorded departure from the rule which had been observed by previous emperors, that the Egyptian levies should be reserved for service in their own country.[256]

2. Immediately on his accession, Theodosius decreed that the whole of the Roman Empire should become Christian;[257] and this decree was vigorously enforced in Alexandria and Lower Egypt, though in the upper country the authority of the government was scarcely strong enough to secure its observance, even if the officials had cared to do this. For the most part, however, they were either too prudent administrators or too lukewarm Christians—if indeed they were not

actually pagans, as the more fanatical bishops and monks frequently asserted to try to force religion upon an unwilling people : the more so as the manners and habits of the leaders of the Christians were not such as to excite admiration in men possessed of any culture.

3. In Alexandria itself, the prætorian prefect Cynegius, [385 A.D.] with the imperial troops, assisted the patriarch in the work of conversion. The temple of Sarapis was the chief point round which the struggle raged. The followers of the older religion gathered to defend it, till the streets became the scene of furious battles ; at length they were driven into the temple, which they fortified, and were only expelled by the military after much bloodshed. This and most of the other temples captured by the Christians were turned into churches, and the leaders of the philosophical schools were forced to withdraw from Alexandria.(258)

ARCADIUS.
395-408.
Papyri.—G.G.P. ii. 80, 81, 81 a, 82.

4. From this time the history of Egypt was chiefly determined by the patriarchs of Alexandria, and during the next fifty years, in particular, little is recorded except with regard to the quarrels of the bishops and their followers, which gave the authorities almost as much occupation as did the forced conversion of the pagans. The position of authority in the government, arrogated to himself by the bishop of Alexandria, as well as the spirit in which theological controversy was carried on, is well illustrated by the history of the dispute which arose with regard to the anthropomorphist conception of God held by the greater part of the Egyptian Church. Theophilus, the patriarch, as though those who did not agree with him were rebels against his authority, and therefore against that of the emperor, took a body of soldiers and destroyed a number of the monasteries of Nitriotis which were inhabited by his theological opponents.(259) In the civil

SUPREMACY OF CHRISTIAN CHURCH [379-527 A.D.]

power thus arrogated by the patriarchs there may be found an anticipation of the Papacy of the Middle Ages.

FIG. 77.—The Red Monastery: Interior looking west.
(Photo. by J. G. M.)

THEODOSIUS II.
408–450.
Papyrus.—B.G.U. 609.

5. If the patriarch interfered with the authority of the imperial government by using the soldiers for his own purposes, the imperial officials also took their part in religious questions. Thus when Theophilus died, and a quarrel arose over the election of his successor, Abundantius, the general in charge of the Roman troops in Egypt, joined in the fray, though his support did not bring victory to the party which he joined.[260]

[415 A.D.] 6. The new patriarch, Cyril, fell foul of the Jews, who had, during the three centuries which had elapsed since their virtual extermination under Trajan, grown numerous and influential once more in Alexandria.

The origin of the quarrel is obscure : probably it was nothing more than the hatred of the Jews and Christians for one another, coupled with a desire on the part of the mob to plunder the Jews, who were far the richest part of the community. In any case, plunder of the Jews was what actually resulted ; their quarter of the city was sacked, and they were all driven from their homes.[261]

7. This expulsion and robbery of the chief merchants of Alexandria, the people on whom the prosperity of the city depended, by a mob of monks and vagabonds, was an act which the government could not well overlook. So Orestes, the prefect, tried to interfere ; but his troops were insufficient to quell the disturbance, and he only drew the hatred of the monks upon himself. He was attacked in the street, and wounded by a stone ; and the victory remained with Cyril.[262]

8. It was probably the friendship of Orestes, and the consequent enmity of Cyril, which led to the murder of the philosopher Hypatia. The monks, elated at their success, sought to sweep out all the pagans, amongst whom they counted the prefect, from Alexandria ; and they attacked Hypatia, and murdered her in the Church of the Cæsareum.[263]

9. Since the treaty of Diocletian had interposed the Nobatæ as a buffer State between the Roman frontier at Syene and the land of the Blemmyes, there had been comparatively little trouble experienced in Upper Egypt from the wandering tribes of the desert. The kings of the Nobatæ had fulfilled the task to which they had agreed, of making war on the Blemmyes, and had established their authority over the whole of the old Roman military frontier. But, in the latter part of the reign of Theodosius II., the Blemmyes once more appeared in Egyptian territory, and ravaged the Great Oasis, defeating the Roman garrison, and carrying away the inhabitants as captives ; though they subsequently restored the latter to the governor of the Thebaid, seemingly in order to be free from the encumbrance of guarding prisoners, when their line of retreat was threatened by the neighbouring tribe of the Mazices.[264]

MARCIANUS.

450-457.

10. This renewal of inroads by the Blemmyes was a sign that the Nobatæ had failed to keep the terms of the agreement on which they had been settled in the 453 A.D.] Nile Valley; and the general Maximinus undertook an expedition to punish both of the tribes. He inflicted a severe defeat upon them, and compelled them to make a peace for one hundred years, to release all Roman captives, to pay compensation for damage done, and to surrender hostages; the last stipulation being one to which neither the Blemmyes nor the Nobatæ had ever before submitted. On their side, they obtained leave to visit the temple of Isis at Philæ, and at stated times to borrow her statue, and take it into their own country in order to consult it; a strange condition for a Christian Roman to include in the terms, which shows that the old religion could still be recognised for motives of policy.

11. Very shortly after the conclusion of this treaty, Maximinus died; whereupon the Blemmyes and Nobatæ at once disregarded their agreement, and invaded the Thebaid, in which they found and recovered the hostages whom they had recently given. But Florus, the prefect of Alexandria, returned to the attack, and compelled them to agree to peace again.[265]

12. The relations between the government and the Church in Alexandria were growing still more strained. The former represented the ideas of Constantinople, the latter those of Egypt; and when the emperor, to deprive the Alexandrian mob of their usual leader in their risings against his representative, obtained at a general council at Chalkedon the excommunication of Dioscorus, the patriarch of Alexandria, and sent to replace him an orthodox bishop in the person of Proterius, the populace of Alexandria rose against the imperial nominee, and the imperial troops who escorted him defeated them, and drove the leaders into the temple of Sarapis, which they burnt with those in it. It needed a reinforcement of

THE RIVAL PATRIARCHS

two thousand men and a regular sack of Alexandria to secure the new bishop on his throne; and their guilt was brought home to the citizens by a stoppage of the public games, closure of the baths, and withdrawal of the corn supply.[266]

LEO I.
457-474.

13. The bishopric of Proterius, however, was of short

FIG. 78.—The White Monastery: North door. (Photo. by J. G. M.)

duration. Since it was only by the help of the army he had been put in office, so soon as the commander of that army was called away to Upper Egypt, the Alexandrians rose in rebellion, and chose a monk named Timotheus Ælurus as their patriarch. Before the prefect could return to Alexandria, they had murdered Proterius. But, in spite of this unmistakable evidence as to the feelings of the people, the emperor was persuaded by the advice of the bishops to refuse to recognise a heterodox priest; and he proceeded to set aside the choice of the Egyptian Church in favour of a nominee of his own, Timotheus Salophaciolus.(267)

LEO II.
474.

ZENO.
474-491.

14. At length the troubles which arose after the accession of Zeno at Constantinople brought for a time to the throne a ruler whose religious opinions were those of the Egyptian Church, in the person of Basilicus, [475 A.D.] who succeeded in expelling Zeno from his capital. He forthwith restored Timotheus Ælurus to Alexandria; and that priest held the office of patriarch until his death, which occurred just in time to save him from fresh deposition by Zeno, who had recovered his throne.(268) The Alexandrians then chose Peter Mongus, who was, as usual, deposed by the emperor's orders in favour of his old nominee, Timotheus Salophaciolus. He, however, also soon died; and thereon a fresh dilemma was created by the choice of the people falling upon John. The new patriarch had formerly been sent as representative of the Egyptian Church to Constantinople, to ask that they might in future choose their own bishops; and he had been required by the emperor, before the desired favour was granted, to swear that he would not take the bishopric if it were offered to him. In view of this oath, Zeno apparently thought

it the lesser of two evils to disregard John and recall Peter Mongus, who had been chosen by the Church on a previous occasion. He agreed to the publication by [482 A.D. the emperor of an edict, styled the Henotikon, which was intended to restore the ecclesiastical position of things which had existed before the Council of Chalkedon had proclaimed war on the opinions of the Egyptians; and, accordingly, provided that the decrees of that council should be left in oblivion. Peter, however, almost immediately disregarded the agreement, and banished from the Egyptian monasteries all monks who held to the Chalkedonian decrees; to which measure the emperor replied by sending a reinforcement to the garrison of Egypt, and deporting the ringleaders of the Alexandrians to Constantinople.[269]

ANASTASIUS.

491-518.

Papyri.—Pap. B.M. 113[5a]; G.G.P. i. 55; G.O.P. i. 141.

15. Peace was secured at length by the death of Peter, and the election of Athanasius to the bishopric; and for the rest of the reign of Zeno and the whole of that of Anastasius, the religious troubles of the Egyptians were lulled to rest.[270] It was well for the maintenance of Roman rule in Egypt that they were so ended, as the Persians, who had for some time been threatening the Eastern frontier, invaded the Delta. The imperial forces were unable to defend the open country; but they held Alexandria until the invaders retired, in spite of difficulties caused by the insufficiency of supplies in the city.[271]

16. With the view of distracting the attention of the Persians from Egypt, Anastasius sent an embassy to the Homeritæ of Arabia, to arrange for an attack by them upon the neighbouring territories of Persia from the south.[272]

JUSTINUS I.

518-527.

17. A second embassy was sent to the same Homeritæ by Justinus; and the results achieved were satisfactory, as far as promises went. The king of the Homeritæ undertook to invade the Persian territory, and to keep open the trade route between Egypt and India. The promises, however, do not appear to have been kept.(273)

18. In addition to grasping at the chief power in the government of Egypt, the Christian Church seems during this period to have concentrated in its hands most of the wealth of the country. The monastic corporations certainly held large quantities of land, which were cultivated by the monks; and the account in the life of Schnoudi, how his monastery fed the prisoners recovered from the Blemmyes for three months, at a cost of 265,000 drachmæ, with 85,000 artabai of wheat and 200 artaba of olives, is not improbably correct.(274) The manner in which whole districts

FIG. 79.—The White Monastery: South wall. (Photo. by J. G. M.)

were under monastic vows has already been noticed; and this would mean that the produce of all the work of the inhabitants would pass through the hands of the superiors of the monasteries. These corporations were strong enough, both in their influence and in their buildings, to resist any undue exactions on the part of the government, and thus to secure their general prosperity and the comfort of each individual member. Those who were not monks, however, suffered severely both at the hands of the government tax-collectors and at those of the wandering desert tribes, whether Saracens on the east, Blemmyes on the south, or Mazices on the west frontier.[275] Most of all, perhaps, did Alexandria suffer. The expulsion of the Jews by Cyril dealt a most serious blow to the trade of the city, as the plunderers who seized their houses had neither the ability nor the desire to continue their business. Thus a few years later an additional supply of corn [436 A.D. for the relief of the citizens, in spite of a considerable decrease in population, was necessary.[276]

CHAPTER VII

Union of Temporal and Religious Power, 527-668 A.D.

JUSTINIANUS I.
527-565.

Papyri.—B.G.U. 305, 364, 370, 673, 736; Pap. B.M. 113[5b]; G.G.P. i. 56, 57, 58, ii. 85; G.O.P. i. 125, 133, 140, 142, 143, 145, 146, 147, 148, 197, 205, 206.

1. THE first work in Egypt to which the attention of Justinian was called was the quarrel of the rival

FIG. 80.—Byzantine sculptures: from Ahnas. (E.E.F. Report.)

patriarchs; and he tried to settle the matter by sending a nominee of his own. But the patriarchs from Constantinople, in spite of the assistance given them by the imperial troops, were never able to hold their position long; and when the second of Justinian's nominees was expelled by his flock, he was perforce accompanied by all other Egyptian bishops who dissented from the national Monophysite beliefs.(277)

2. Justinian met force with force, and gave the new patriarch, Apollinarius, the office also of prefect, so that the ruler of the Church would have more readily at his hand the soldiers who were required to enforce his decisions upon, and collect his revenues from, the people under his care. The new patriarch signalised his arrival by a general massacre of the Alexandrian mob, who refused to receive or listen to him, and even stoned him in the church where he endeavoured to address them; and thus succeeded in removing the most turbulent among the elements in the country opposed to his rule.(278)

3. This action on the part of Justinian with regard to the patriarchate virtually amounted to little more than a transference of all the temporalities of the Egyptian Church to the prefect of Alexandria; as henceforward that official, though nominal patriarch, exercised no religious influence, and probably performed a minimum of religious functions. The people of Egypt looked up to the Monophysite or Jacobite patriarch, who was elected by the Churches, and in whose hands the spiritual government of the country accordingly lay.

4. In addition to uniting the offices of prefect and patriarch, Justinian began to make regular use of the monks and their establishments for military purposes. The strong monasteries of Upper Egypt had for long served as refuges to the surrounding population during the plundering inroads of the desert tribes; and now, to protect the passes under Mount Sinai on the road to Egypt from Syria, which had fallen into the hands of the Persians, a group of buildings was erected to

serve the purposes both of monastery and fort, and was garrisoned with monks.(279)

FIG. 81.—Byzantine capital: from Ahnas. (E.E.F. Report.)

5. Any advantage which might have accrued to the Roman Empire in its struggle with the Persians from the treaties concluded by Anastasius and Justinus with the Homeritæ of Arabia, was soon nullified by the quarrels of that people with the kingdom of Axum, on the opposite coast of the Red Sea. These quarrels arose out of the Indian trade, in which both nations had considerable interest. The Axumitæ accused their neighbours of killing Roman merchants, and undertook the duty of punishing them; and Hadad the king of Axum made a successful expedition into Arabia; after which he sent an embassy to Alexandria to renew friendly relations with the Roman government, which were to be strengthened by the despatch of an Egyptian bishop to Axum.(80)

6. For a few years the Indian trade flowed smoothly through this channel, to the satisfaction of Justinian, who thus succeeded in diverting to his own dominions what had latterly been a source of profit to his enemies

the Persians; since, when the Red Sea route was blocked by the Homeritæ, the only alternative line for the silk and spices of the East to reach Europe was through Persian territory. It was, however, necessary for Roman ambassadors to visit both Arabia and Abyssinia from time to time; and at length a fresh quarrel led to a determined attempt on the part of

FIG. 82.—Coptic tombstones: in Ghizeh Museum.
(Photo. by W. M. F. Petrie.)

Elesbaan, the king of Axum, to reduce the Homeritæ to dependence. His expedition was immediately successful, and he set up a follower of his own as king; but the new ruler was shortly deposed in favour of Abraham, who, when an Axumite army was sent to reduce the country, won it over to his side, and defeated a second. The Axumitæ were thereon obliged to make peace; and the hopes of the Romans—that they might succeed in harassing the Persians from this quarter—came to nothing.(281)

7. On the Southern frontier, the treaty made with the Blemmyes and Nobatæ after their defeat by Maximinus and Florus had been observed fairly well, to judge by the absence of any record of raids from this quarter during the century that had elapsed since that time. But Justinian, whether in consequence of renewed raids by these tribes on the termination of the hundred years for which the treaty had been made, or with a view of putting a stop to the continuance of pagan rites in the temples of Philæ, which had been secured by the provision in the treaty empowering the barbarians to visit the sacred island yearly for purposes of worship, sent Narses the Persarmenian up the Nile, with orders to destroy the temple of Isis at Philæ; which he did, imprisoning the priests, and bringing the statues to Constantinople.(282)

8. A policy similar to that which has been suggested by the action of Justinian with regard to the temples of Philæ was shown earlier in his reign in his treatment of the philosophical school of Alexandria, which had been one of the chief strongholds of the older religions, till he strictly enforced a law against their teaching, and drove the leading professors to take refuge with the Persians.

JUSTINUS II.
565-578.

Inscription.—Greek: C.I.G. iv. 8646.
Papyri.— B.G.U. 306; G.O.P. i. 126, 134, 149, 195, 199.

9. The policy of Justinian with regard to the Blemmyes soon proved an unwise one. The Roman government was not strong enough to keep its neighbours quiet by force of arms, and the destruction of the temple of Isis at Philæ had removed the one object in Roman territory for which they felt respect; so they resumed their plundering raids, and obliged the commander of the Thebaid, Theodorus, to renew the fortifications of Philæ.(283)

TIBERIUS II.

578-582.

Papyri.—B.G.U. 317; G.G.P. i. 60; G.O.P. i. 135, 144, 193, 198, 202.

10. Further measures were necessary, however, as these fortifications were insufficient in themselves to stop the attacks of the desert tribes; and Aristomachus, the general of the Egyptian troops under Tiberius, was obliged to undertake a campaign against the Nubians and Mauretanians, whom he defeated.[281]

11. Egypt seems to have been rapidly drifting into a

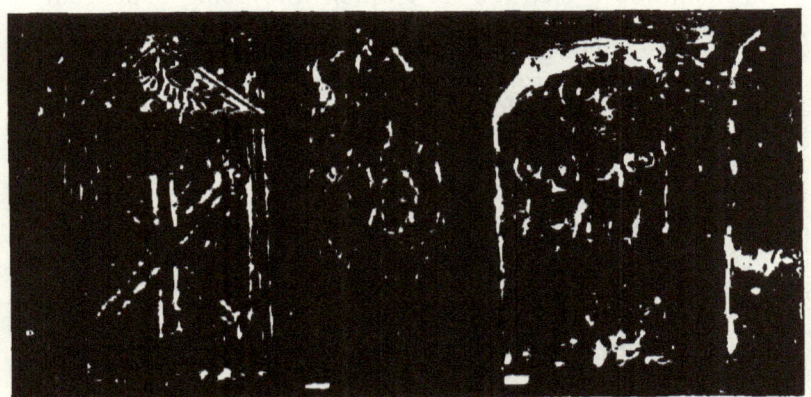

FIG. 83.—Coptic tombstones: in Ghizeh Museum.
(Photo. by W. M. F. Petrie.)

state of anarchy, while officials and subjects alike did what was right in their own eyes, and the government at Constantinople seemed capable of nothing but vacillation. Aristomachus was accused of having behaved too presumptuously in his command, and was arrested and brought to Constantinople; but was promptly pardoned, and justified his pardon by his victory above mentioned.

MAURICIUS.
582-602.

Papyri.— B.G.U. 255, 295, 303, 390, 395, 397, 399, 400, 402 ; Pap. B.M. 113⁴, 113ᵃᵛ ; G.G.P. ii. 86, 87, 88 ; Louvre, N. et E. 20, 21 bis, 21 ter ; Rev. Egypt. iv. pp. 58 ff., No. 17 ; G.O.P. i. 136, 137, 150, 201, 207.

12. Further evidence of the chaotic state of affairs is given by some events of the next reign. Certain men plundered the two villages of Kynopolis and Busiris, in the Delta, "without authorisation from the prefect of the nome"; and when the officials at Alexandria threatened them with punishment, they collected a body of men, and seized the corn which was being sent from the country to Alexandria,—thus a famine was caused in the city. The government acted with its usual vacillation: John, the prefect of Alexandria, was deposed, but as soon as he had offered an explanation, was reinstated. This measure, naturally, did not check the riots in the country, and an army was required to crush the revolt. Another outbreak of brigandage, under one Azarias, occurred at Panopolis, but proved less serious.[285]

PHOCAS.
602-610.

Papyri.—B.G.U. 3, 365 ; Rec. Tr. vi. p. 63, No. 5.

13. When Heraclius raised the standard of revolt against Phocas, Egypt became for a time the main seat of the war. Bonakis was sent thither to secure the country for the Heraclian party ; and, after he had defeated the imperial general of Alexandria outside the walls, was received into the city with enthusiasm by the clergy and people. All Egypt thereon made common cause with the insurgents, two of the prefects alone standing to the side of Phocas ; but reinforcements from Constantinople, under Bonosus, soon arrived and made their headquarters at Athribis. In a battle which shortly afterwards took place, Bonakis was killed, and the remnants of his troops were driven into Alexandria.[286]

14. Bonakis was succeeded in his command by Niketas, who collected the Heraclian forces at Alexandria, and went out to attack Bonosus again. On this occasion the insurgents were successful; but Bonosus rallied his troops at Nikiou, and continued to threaten Alexandria till another defeat had been inflicted on him, when he fled to Constantinople, leaving Niketas master of the country.(287)

HERACLIUS I.
610–641.

Papyri.—B.G.U. 314, 319, 368, 370, 398, 401, 725; Pap. B.M. 113(b), 113(m), 483; Louvre, N. et E. 21; Rec. Tr. vi. p. 63; R.E. iv. pp. 58 ff., No. 18; G.O.P. i. 138, 139, 151, 152, 153; Journal of Philology, xxii. p. 268.

15. During the whole of the sixth century the pressure

FIG. 84.—Designs from fragments of Coptic pottery. (Petrie Collection.)

of the Persians on the eastern frontiers of the Roman Empire had steadily increased; and it was beginning to be seriously felt in Egypt when Heraclius was recognised as emperor. As the Persian armies advanced, numerous fugitives from Syria and Palestine took refuge in Egypt; and when the enemy invaded the Delta, the refugees were driven into Alexandria. This city was thus crowded with a great multitude of people wholly dependent for their support on charity; and when the difficulty of feeding them, which chiefly fell [616 A.D.] upon the patriarch John, became an impossibility, through a failure of the harvest, John fled to Cyprus with the imperial general Niketas, and left the province of Egypt to the Persians.(288)

16. The new governors of Egypt entered into their inheritance quietly, and almost naturally; as the Persian army was largely drawn from Syria and Arabia, whose tribes had been in contact and relationship with the native Egyptians from time immemorial. Thus they had no great difficulty in ruling Egypt; the wealthier classes had probably a large intermixture of Arabs amongst them, who welcomed the rule of their kinsmen, while the fellaheen at the worst only changed masters, and possibly preferred the government of an Oriental to that of a Greek monarch.

FIG. 85.—Coptic painted pottery. (Petrie Collection.)

17. The Persian rule in Egypt lasted for ten years, until the revolt of the Arabs, under the inspiration of the teaching of Mohammed, deprived the king of Persia of his most effective soldiers, and gave the Romans a chance of recovering some of their lost provinces in the East. Heraclius marched through Syria into Egypt, and drove out the Persians; with them went the patriarch Benjamin, who had received his appointment with their approval when John, the Roman prefect-patriarch, fled, and who would consequently be regarded by the Romans less as a bishop

chosen by the Egyptians than as a rebel who had taken office under the Persians.

18. The Romans, however, were not left for long in the peaceful possession of Egypt, though the inhabitants of the country raised no disturbance at the fresh change of rulers. The Arabs, whose revolt from Persia had enabled Heraclius to recover Egypt, soon began to push forward against the frontiers of the Roman Empire, and to threaten Egypt. For awhile they were bought off by subsidies ;(289) but, on the stoppage of payments, the Saracen general 'Amr-ibn-al-'Asi entered Egypt with [639, Dec. an army of three thousand men, and, after a month's siege, captured the frontier fortress of Pelusium. He then advanced against Babylon, where Theodorus the prefect was collecting the Roman troops, and intending to attack the Arabs after the inundation in order to protect the sowing of the crops; but 'Amr, who had received considerable reinforcements from Arabia, surrounded and defeated the Romans at Heliopolis. He [640, July. then blockaded the fortress of Babylon, and overran the Fayum and Middle Egypt, the garrisons of which retired down the river.(290)

19. The Roman army had not made much show of resistance against the invaders, largely on account of the dissensions among their leaders, and the lukewarmness or treachery of the Coptic population. A number of the leading Copts had actually gone over to the Arabs; the most noted among whom was George, a prefect, who began openly to help them after the battle of Heliopolis.(291)

20. In the course of the autumn, 'Amr advanced Northwards towards the Delta, and drove all the Roman troops before him into it. He was unable, however, to penetrate it, and was obliged to turn back and secure the Rif.(292)

CONSTANTINUS II.

641.

21. After the death of Heraclius, the government

officials at Constantinople decided to try a waiting policy in Egypt; they directed Theodorus to pay tribute to 'Amr, and so keep him quiet, and at the same time to be on the alert for any chance to attack him. Reinforcements for the Egyptian army were also promised, but never arrived. In the meantime, 'Amr took Babylon, and a few weeks later Nikiou, from both of which the garrisons retired to Alexandria.(293)

[641, April 9th.]

HERACLONAS.
641-642.

22. The city of Alexandria was now subjected to a regular siege; but it was in no condition to withstand one. Theodorus the prefect, had been summoned to Rhodes; and the two leading commanders left in the city, Domentianus and Menas, quarrelled till they came to open conflict. Added to this was the opposition of the clergy to the new emperor Heraclonas, on the ground that he was the offspring of an uncanonical marriage between Heraclius and his niece Martina. At length Theodorus returned, and settled the quarrel by expelling Domentianus; and at the same time Cyrus the patriarch arrived, with authority to conclude peace. Peace was what the Romans and Egyptians alike desired; so Cyrus went to Babylon, and came to terms with 'Amr. He agreed that tribute should be paid by the Alexandrians, and that the Roman forces should evacuate Alexandria in eleven months, on condition that in the meantime there should be a cessation of hostilities, and that the Jews and Christians should thereafter remain unmolested.(294)

[641, Oct. 17th.]

CONSTANS II.
642-668.

23. In accordance with the agreement, Theodorus and his troops withdrew from Alexandria at the end of the specified time, and the Roman Empire in Egypt was ended.(295)

[642, Sept. 17th.]

24. There is little detailed evidence for judging of the general condition of Egypt during the last century of its government by the Romans. But the impression produced by reading its history is one of hopeless poverty. The cultivators of the soil were merely regarded as so many machines for raising corn; and corn became almost the only industry and currency of Egypt.(296) What wealth there was, was concentrated in a few hands, and whole villages, as has been already seen, became dependent on some rich man.(297) The consequence of this poverty was shown in the indifference with which the Egyptians regarded any change in their government, and the entire absence of any attempt to take a part in deciding who should rule in the State or the Church. They had sunk so low, that even religious controversy could not rouse them. Only in Alexandria the factions in the circus could raise a fight from time to time, and distract the attention of the populace from the laborious task of opposing the Arabs to the more congenial one of breaking each other's heads.(298)

CHAPTER VIII

THE REVENUES AND TAXATION OF EGYPT

1. THE amount which was to be contributed by Egypt to the imperial treasury was a matter for the special consideration of the emperor year by year. He not only decided how much revenue was to be raised in the province, but issued special directions as to the manner in which it was to be collected.[299] His orders were addressed to the prefect, from whom they passed in turn to the epistrategoi, strategoi, and village authorities. Each of these officials determined, in regard to assessed taxes, how the amount required from his own district should be divided among the smaller districts which were comprised in it. Thus the prefect fixed the sum to be paid by each epistrategia, the epistrategos that by each nome in his province, the strategos that by each village in his nome, while the village authorities decided and collected the payments due from each individual.[300]

2. The most important of all the taxes levied in Egypt was the corn tax, which was collected in kind from the villages, and used to furnish the tribute of corn sent to feed Rome. For the purpose of this tax there was kept an elaborate register of lands under cultivation,[301] by the aid of which the village authorities assessed upon the farmers the amounts respectively payable. In determining these amounts, they were directed to have special regard to the rise of the Nile, so that lands which had been out of the reach of the flood in any particular year should be more lightly taxed

than those which had been fertilised by the inundation.(302) The exact manner in which the incidence of the tax was ultimately decided is not certain; but it appears probable that each village as a whole was liable to pay a certain amount, and that this liability was met, in the first instance, by any common property which the village possessed, while the surplus over and above what this produced was divided amongst the individual members of the community, at rates which were most likely calculated on the amount of land each held and the crops raised on each holding.(303) In one list, which apparently refers to this tax, the rates vary from two and a half to seven artabai per aroura, the commonest rate being four and twenty-seven fortieths artabai.(304) The actual work of collection of the tax was in the hands of the sitologoi and their assistants,(305) who also had charge of the public granaries, and were required to make monthly returns of the corn stored therein to the strategos.(306) The amount required from the village, known as embole or epibole, was drawn from these granaries and transported to the river by carriers, who were obliged to keep a certain number of camels or asses for the public service, and received in return a regular allowance.(307) It was then delivered to the shipmasters on the river, who conveyed it to the imperial granaries at Alexandria; all the expenses, up to and including delivery at Alexandria, being paid by the authorities of the village which sent the corn.(308) The lands of Alexandria and the Menelaite nome were specially exempt from this tax.(309)

3. Payments for the corn tax were made, in some instances, in money instead of in kind; and the tax was in these cases received by the praktor of corn taxes, in place of the sitologos.(310) Probably it was open to a farmer to pay in the value of the corn for which he was liable, in place of the corn itself.

4. Another tax, payable, like the embole, in corn, and collected by the sitologoi, was the annona. Details as to this tax are rare; but it appears probable that it was for the supply of the allowance of corn made to

Alexandria, as the embole was for that to Rome and Constantinople.[311]

5. In connection with the corn tax should be mentioned the custom by which each year the local authorities supplied to the farmers in their district seed-corn, at the rate of an artaba of corn for each aroura farmed.[312] This corn was repaid after harvest to the granaries, with an addition of two choinikes to the artaba, or one-twenty-fourth, as interest, and a varying sum for cost of collection.[313] The interest on the loan doubtless went into the common store of the village to assist in meeting the demands for Rome and elsewhere.

6. The sitologoi had to meet a further charge upon the village granaries in the form of certain payments for charitable purposes, which were made in corn;[314] but it does not appear whether the supply for these payments was raised by a special tax, or whether it came from the common property of the village.

7. In place of the corn which was exacted from the farmers whose land was sown for this crop, those holdings which were used for growing garden produce, or as vineyards, fig-plantations, palm-groves, or olive-yards, were liable to a tax payable in money, and collected by the praktores of money taxes. The rate, however, cannot be determined, and the manner of assessment even seems to have varied. In one case the tax was ten drachmæ per aroura,[315] in another list it was from twenty to forty,[316] while in a third the payments made bear no fixed proportion at all to the amount of land held.[317] An allowance was made in the collection of this tax, as in that of the corn tax, for unoccupied or waste lands.[318]

8. There were other taxes on land, payable in money, the nature and amount of which is at present obscure. A charge of "naubion" is several times mentioned;[319] but there is nothing to show what its precise object was, beyond the fact that it appears among other imposts levied on real property; nor what its rate was, except in one instance, where it seems to have been assessed at approximately one hundred drachmæ per

aroura.[320] Entries of receipts for "geometria" are also found on the same lists with most of the taxes already mentioned;[321] but the particulars relating to this charge cannot be determined: it was possibly the surveyor's fee for his work in connection with obtaining the necessary particulars of each estate for the government.

9. House property was subject to a tax, which was collected by the same praktores as the land taxes, which were payable in money. It may be a chance merely that the three receipts for this tax which have been preserved are for a hundred drachmæ or multiples of a hundred;[322] but in the absence of other evidence it is perhaps reasonable to suppose that the rate was a hundred drachmæ for each house. Another tax, apparently levied only on house property, was that described as arithmetikon, which also was usually collected by the praktores. The sums entered as received from this source, however, are much smaller than those from the house tax;[323] but they do not give any guidance as to the manner of the assessment.

10. The cattle taxes were levied on the various kinds of flocks and herds separately; receipts for payments in respect of oxen,[324] sheep,[325] and camels[326] are found; and taxes were doubtless also laid on goats and asses, though no examples of these occur. Only in regard to the tax on camels is it possible to conjecture the rate of the impost; in this case the entries of receipts are almost invariably multiples of ten drachmæ, which suggests that that sum was the tax on each camel. One instance, however, is preserved of a tax receipt for twenty drachmæ paid on ten camels;[327] but this may have been an instalment only.[328] For the purposes of these taxes a yearly census of all kinds of live stock liable to them was taken by the local authorities.[329] For the collection of this branch of the revenue the praktores were responsible.

11. All inhabitants of Egypt between the ages of fourteen and sixty, with the exception of certain privileged classes, were liable to pay a poll-tax.[330]

Numerous receipts for payments of this tax exist on ostraka, dating from the first and second centuries; these show it to have risen from sixteen drachmæ for each person under Nero to seventeen about the first year of Trajan, and further to twenty soon after the accession of Antoninus Pius.(331) This rise may possibly be connected with the depreciation of the coinage, which proceeded in about the same proportion. A census was taken from house to house every fourteen years specially with a view to this tax; the returns were sent in to the strategos and royal scribe of the nome, the laographoi of the village, and the village scribe, and gave full particulars as to the inhabitants of each house; (332) and interim returns had to be furnished to state any changes which took place in families between the census years.(333) From the poll-tax Alexandrian citizens were exempt,(334) and doubtless also Romans domiciled in Egypt; so, too, were the Katoikoi, who were the descendants of the Greek soldiers originally settled in Egypt by the Ptolemies, and held their lands, nominally at any rate, on condition of liability to military service.(335) It appears also that a certain number of priests at each temple were allowed to be exempt.(336)

12. Another direct tax was the stephanikon, which was levied, so far as is known, only about the beginning of the third century; (337) and may have been in theory a revival of the old custom of making a national present to the king on his accession, which was, however, extended into a sort of recurrent "benevolence." It was collected by special praktores, and consisted in payments of sums of four drachmæ.

13. A tax was also paid by traders of all descriptions, the sums payable being reckoned on the monthly receipts of the business in each case. This was therefore a kind of income-tax; but the percentage charged cannot be discovered, though both on ostraka and papyri there are numerous entries of payments on this account.(338)

14. The indirect taxation was chiefly levied in the

CUSTOMS AND DUES 123

form of customs and entrance dues, which were collected, not only from merchants and others entering the country, but also from those passing from one part

FIG. 86.—Tariff-Stele of Koptos: in Ghizeh Museum. (Photo. by J. G. M.)

of the province to another, as a sort of *octroi*. Thus, in addition to the custom-houses, of which records have been preserved, at Syene for the Nile trade,[339] at Koptos for the desert road from the Red

Sea,[340] and in the Fayum for goods from the Sahara,[341] there were stations at Schedia,[342] two hundred and forty stades above Alexandria, where toll was collected from boats passing to and from the city, and at Hermopolis[343] for the trade between Upper and Lower Egypt. A stele found at Koptos[344] gives the rates charged there on passengers and equipages, which were as follows: steersmen from the Red Sea, ten drachmæ; boatswains, ten drachmæ; seamen, five drachmæ; shipwrights, five drachmæ; artisans, eight drachmæ; prostitutes, one hundred and eight drachmæ; women entering the country, twenty drachmæ; wives of soldiers, twenty drachmæ; camel tickets, one obol; sealing of ticket, two obols; ticket for the husband in a departing caravan, one drachma; all his women at four drachmæ each; an ass, two obols; a waggon with a tilt, four drachmæ; a ship's mast, twenty drachmæ; a ship's yard, four drachmæ; a funeral to the desert and back, one drachmæ four obols. The charge for camel tickets is found also in the Prosopite and Letopolite nomes, at the head of the desert roads to Nitriotis and the Fayum.[345] The duty on goods, both imported and exported, collected at the stations of Soknopaiou Nesos,[346] Karanis,[347] Philadelphia,[348] and Bacchias[349] in the Fayum, was an *ad valorem* charge of three per cent.; and it may be assumed to have been the same at other custom-houses; except that at the Red Sea ports there was apparently a preferential duty against goods coming through Arabia.[350] In addition to the customs, there was a further charge made at the Fayum stations for the maintenance of a guard along the desert roads. The collection of these taxes was sold to farmers.

15. Other indirect taxes, which were farmed in the same way as the customs,[351] were the enkyklion, a fee of ten per cent. on sales; [352] a fine of five per cent. on inheritance,[353] and one at a similar rate on the manumission of slaves;[354] and a fee, apparently of one-sixth per cent., for the registration of legal documents.[355] Also, in case of failure to fulfil a contract,

it was customary for a fine to be inflicted for the benefit of the treasury.(356)

16. An extraordinary burden which was laid upon the inhabitants of Egypt consisted in the posting-rights claimed by officials ; and though these were expressly restricted by decree of the prefect to the right to demand lodgings, and this only by those who had the proper authorisation from headquarters, the numerous officials who were continually journeying about must still have been a source of very considerable expense to their hosts.(357) Attendance on the higher officials was probably a hereditary liturgy, as it is recorded to have been in the case of a man whose duty it was to row in the State-boat of the governor of the Thebaid ; (358) this practice was perhaps derived from the slave-labour of slave-families who had settled into other work. A similar liturgy appears in another instance at Oxyrhynchos, where each tribe in turn had to supply a sailor to serve on a public boat engaged in the transport of corn.(359) The most burdensome, however, of the liturgies which were laid upon the Egyptians were the local administrative posts, such as that of strategos or praktor ; (360) even in the earlier and better years of Roman rule it was stated in an official decree that many strategoi had been ruined by their term of office ; (361) while the labour of the work of collecting taxes which fell on the praktor may be judged from the fact that a man nominated to the post paid a deputy two hundred and fifty-two drachmæ yearly, which would represent about six months' wages.(362) Under these circumstances, it was not remarkable that many men fled from home to escape these burdens ; as they might feel that they were bound to lose all they had, and so might as well let their property be confiscated without having three years' worry in addition to the loss. From these liturgies Alexandrians were exempt,(363) and therefore also Romans ; priests, too, could claim a similar freedom,(364) which was also accorded to veterans for a period of five years after their discharge.(365)

17. The work of repairing the dykes and clearing the canals partook somewhat of the nature of a liturgy, inasmuch as it was compulsory, though really it was joint labour for a common purpose. Every cultivator of land had to give five days in the summer of each year to this work, for which he received a certificate;[366] or, if he preferred, he could apparently purchase exemption at the rate of five days' wages of a labourer, which amounted to six drachmae and four obols in the second century.[367]

18. During the later period of the Roman rule, the Egyptians were required to furnish supplies for the imperial troops;[368] the earliest instance of this is in the reign of Diocletian.[369] One case is found of a money payment made for this same object by the Church of Apollinopolis Magna on account of a troop of soldiers quartered in a monastery.[370] It was perhaps this tax which Valens fixed at the rate of a soldier's clothing for every thirty arourai of land.[371]

19. Temple property was not, as such, exempt from taxation. It paid the ordinary taxes;[372] and there were, in addition, special taxes levied under the names of altar-tax[373] and tax on offerings;[374] the former of which appears to have been calculated at the rate of four per cent. on the receipts of the temple.[375] It would seem, also, that the State exacted a due on each calf sacrificed.[376] These charges possibly represented the share claimed by the emperor in the offerings made to the gods. Another tax is mentioned in connection with the two first-named, under the title of lesoneia;[377] but it can only be supposed, from its association, to have been a tax on temples. The priests also paid a special tax, known as epistatikon,[378] but nothing definite is recorded about the rate or object of this payment. On the other hand, a subvention was given from the imperial treasury towards the expenses of maintenance of the temples of the gods; in which respect the Roman emperors followed the practice of their Greek predecessors.[379]

20. While the whole of Egypt was, in theory, the

private property of the Roman emperor, certain lands were in a special sense his domain. These consisted of the old royal inheritance of the Ptolemies, which was increased by confiscation of the estates of debtors to the treasury and criminals, and by the reversion of unclaimed land;[380] though, on the other hand, domain-land, at any rate of the two latter classes, was from time to time sold.[381] The land was let out to cultivators by the imperial procurators; and an example is preserved of a notice, stating what royal lands were wanting tenants.[382] Quarries and mines also belonged to the imperial domain, and were usually worked directly by the State, convict labour being employed under the direction of a military guard.[383]

CHAPTER IX

Religious Institutions

1. The religious ideas of Egypt had, by the time of the Roman conquest, been influenced and modified to a considerable extent by those of the Greeks, especially where there was most mixture of races. The process of modification had gone forward, however, unequally in different directions: some of the old Egyptian gods remained almost unaffected, even in districts where there was a strong Greek element; others were simply identified in name with the Greek divinities who most nearly resembled them; while the attributes and worship of others were entirely remodelled in accordance with Greek taste. To these varying developments of the Egyptian religious system there was to be added the purely Hellenic theology which was preserved by many of the more cultured Greeks; and a certain leaven of Roman ideas was introduced for reasons of State by the new government. Outside of all the rest —Egyptian, Greek, and Roman—stood the Jews, who had exercised little or no influence on the ideas of the Egyptians, and were unaffected in their turn by Egyptian theology; although the influence of the philosophy of Alexandria is strongly marked in some of the later Jewish writings.

2. The least modification of the ancient Egyptian system was naturally found in the country districts, where the cultivators of the soil, who had never been touched by Greek learning, and whom the Greek priests had no desire to proselytise, continued placidly to wor-

ship the gods of their ancestors in the manner of their ancestors. The Fayum papyri have preserved numerous records of the priesthood, possessions, and services of Soknopaios—a form of Sebek, the crocodile god of the Arsinoite nome—which enable a fairly complete idea of the general nature of local Egyptian worship to be formed.(384)

3. There was at Soknopaiou Nesos—the modern Dimeh—a temple of Soknopaios, in which he was associated with Isis Nepherses.(385) This temple was probably the centre of worship for the peasants of the whole district; an inscription in the Ghizeh Museum

FIG. 87.—Stele from Soknopaiou Nesos: in Ghizeh Museum. Photo, by J. G. M.

refers to the rebuilding of its precinct wall by the shepherds of Nilopolis,(386) while another inscription calls Soknopaios the god of the nome, and requires copies of a decree of the prefect, relating to the privileges of the priests, to be set up in proper places throughout the nome.(387) These priests were organised in five tribes,(388) membership of which appears to have been hereditary, and, in the case of a woman, not to have been changed by marriage ; (389) and the affairs of the priesthood were placed in the general charge of a college of five elders, representing the five tribes.(390)

In most respects the priests were scarcely to be distinguished from the ordinary peasant ; many of them were unlettered, (391) and they were not devoted exclusively to the service of the temple, but were free to pursue other occupations ; (392) like the modern dervishes, who belong to religious fraternities and join in festivals, but work like ordinary individuals for their living. They had certain restrictions laid upon them ; the wearing of woollen garments and long hair being forbidden ; (393) and they had to be solemnly circumcised by leave of the high priest in childhood.(394) On the other hand, they received a daily allowance of an artaba of corn throughout the year, and an extra amount of four artabai daily at feast times, which seem to have occupied nearly half the year, and during which they would be required to be in attendance at the temple ; (395) and a subvention was paid towards the expenses of the temples by the State. They claimed

FIG. 83.—Column with figures of priests: at Rome. (Photo. by W. M. F. Petrie.)

exemption from forced labour, and this privilege was more than once definitely affirmed by orders from the prefect, although in terms which suggest that it was not always respected by the local authorities.(396) They were not, however, free from taxes, which they would naturally have to pay in respect of the lands which they occupied and cultivated in the intervals of their priestly duties ; but a certain number of priests at each temple were allowed to escape the poll-tax.(397) The temples also had to pay taxes on their landed property ; though the temple buildings themselves were perhaps exempt.(398)

4. With Soknopaios at Soknopaiou Nesos were associated Sokonpieios (399) or Sokopiaiis,(400) which are probably variant names of another form of Sebek, and Enoupis,(401) who was probably Anubis. Other local deities of the Fayum were Pnepherôs and Petesouchos, whose temple has been found at Karanis ; (402) Sokanobkonneus, who appears to have been the god of Bacchias ; (403) Phemnoeris, who may have belonged to Hexapotamos ;(404) and Sukatoimos.(405) Of these, Petesouchos and Sokanobkonneus may be regarded as local forms of Sebek, the most generally accepted form of whose name, Souchos, is found at Arsinoe, Nilopolis, and Soknopaiou Nesos in the Fayum,(406) and also in an inscription from a site in the nome of Ombos.(407)

5. Other local deities, whose worship persisted until Roman times without any recorded identification of their personalities with Greek gods, are Thriphis, the pronaos of whose temple at Athribis was dedicated under Tiberius ; (408) Amenebis, whose temple at Tchonemyris in the Theban Oasis was rebuilt under Antoninus, and to whom an inscription of homage was found at Kysis in the same Oasis ; (409) Thoeris, whose worship at Oxyrhynchos continued to the beginning of the fourth century ; (410) Mandoulis, to whom many votive inscriptions were written by the soldiers stationed at Talmis ; (411) and Srouptichis, mentioned in inscriptions at Khardassy.(412) Bes is represented in the work at

Tentyra, dating from the time of Trajan, and Roman terra-cotta figures of him are found; and Phthah ap-

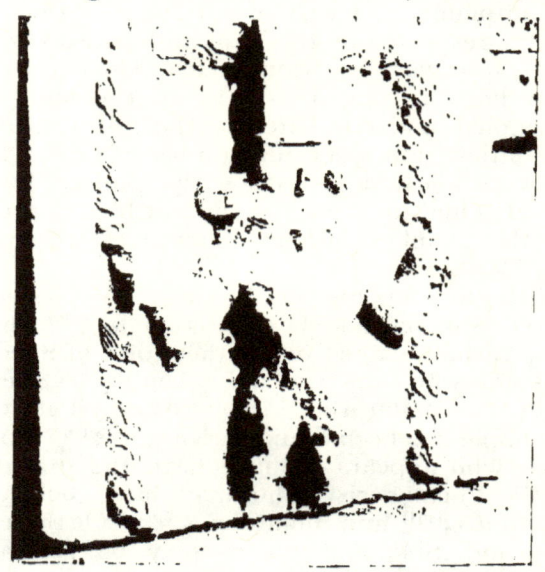

FIG. 89.— Figure of Bes: Tentyra. (Photo. by W. M. F. Petrie.)

pears on the coins of Hadrian; but neither is mentioned in inscriptions.

FIG. 90. Phthah: Coin of Hadrian. (British Museum.)

6. It was much more common, however, when the Greeks found that the attributes of an Egyptian god resembled those of a Greek, for them to identify the two and unite their worship. Such a tendency was nothing foreign either to Egyptian or Greek theology, both of which systems had pursued this process of identification from the earliest times. And there were obvious advantages in the economy thus effected, especially for the Greeks, who, in most Egyptian country towns, would not be sufficiently numerous or sufficiently wealthy to build or endow a temple for

their own gods, and could thus simply get the enjoyment of the existing establishments. It is not to be supposed, however, that the union of the deities went farther than their names; Pan Khem was still Pan to the Greek, and Khem to the Egyptian, neither race really assimilating the religious conceptions of the other. It was only in such rare cases as that of Sebek, for whom as the crocodile god the Greeks could not find an equivalent, that they accepted the Egyptian ideas.

7. The most patent instances of this assimilation may be found in the Greek names of the nomes and towns of Egypt. When the Greeks conquered the country, they renamed many of the old nome capitals by the simple process of taking the nearest Greek equivalent to the god who was worshipped in each town, and styling it as his city: thus Thebes, the city of Amen, became Diospolis; and Tes-Hor, the town of the raising of Horus, was called Apollinopolis.

8. Instances of the worship of gods under double names, however, are not very common in the Roman period. At Pselkis there was a temple of Hermes Pautnuphis, to whom inscriptions of homage were addressed either under his compound name or a single one.(413) Pan Khem was worshipped at Panopolis and in the neighbouring districts of the desert.(414) At Tentyra and at Philae temples were built to Aphrodite as identified with Hathor.(415) Zeus Ammon, one of the earliest of the joint gods, is commonly represented on coins (416); and a dedication to him with the addition of a third name, Chnubis, is found in a quarry near Philae.(417) In the last instance there appears to have been a conjunction of the two ram-headed gods Khnum and Amen.

Fig. 91.—Zeus Ammon: Coin of Hadrian. (British Museum.)

9. In Alexandria and Ptolemais Hermiou, where the Greek element was large enough to support temples without relying on the native endowments, the old

Egyptian deities had for the most part passed out of sight, and the gods were worshipped under purely Hellenic attributes. The arrival of the Roman officials and garrison would bring a considerable accession of strength to this party, who had hitherto consisted mainly of the direct descendants of the Ptolemaic settlers, with such of the Alexandrian philosophers as thought it worth their while to worship anything. The Roman official religious inscriptions, as distinct from private expressions of homage, are usually in the names of Greek gods, and the religious types on the coins struck at Alexandria are mainly Greek rather than Egyptian. Even on the nome coins, which, as representing a quasi-local issue, might have been expected to bear figures of the old nome gods, the usual type is one chosen from the Greek point of view by the authorities at Alexandria.[418]

10. Zeus was known mainly in his compound forms. His Graeco-Egyptian title as Zeus Ammon has already been noticed; and as Zeus Helios Sarapis he was worshipped at Canopus,[419] and two temples were

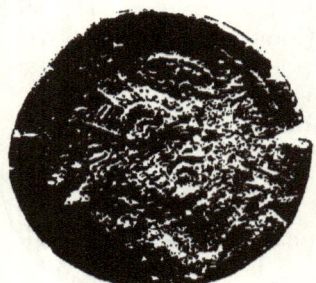

FIG. 92. — Pantheistic Zeus Sarapis: Coin of Hadrian. (British Museum.)

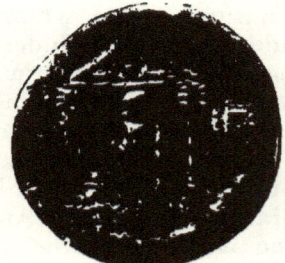

FIG. 93.—Temple of Zeus: Coin of Trajan. (British Museum.)

erected to him at Mons Claudianus in the reign of Hadrian;[420] to this title also a pantheistic type on the coins is attributable.[421] An altar dedicated to Zeus Helios Soter was found at Ptolemais Hermiou, and an inscription to Zeus Helios opposite Koptos.[422] On a coin of Trajan a temple of Zeus, presumably at Alexandria, is represented, within which is a statue of the Greek Zeus, naked and holding a thunderbolt.[423] The type of Zeus is a common one on Alexandrian coins; but, with the exception of the busts of Zeus Olympios and Zeus Nemeios on tetradrachms of Nero,[424] issued

FIG. 94.—Zeus: Coin of Trajan. (British Museum.)

FIG. 95. — Hera: Coin of Nero. (British Museum.)

probably in connection with local games at the time of his intention to visit Egypt, there are no special forms that can be identified.

11. Hera, on the other hand, scarcely appears at all in Egypt. As Juno she is associated with Jupiter Ammon Chnubis in the Latin inscription mentioned above;[425] and the bust of Hera Argeia is found in the same series of Neronian tetradrachms as the local types of Zeus.[426]

12. The only traces of the worship of Poseidon and

FIG. 96.—Poseidon: Coin of Claudius II. (British Museum.)

FIG. 97. — Kybele: Coin of Julia Domna. (British Museum.)

Kybele are in the coin types; and to Kronos there exists one dedication in the Ghizeh Museum, from Apollinopolis Parva.[427]

13. To Apollo, jointly with Sarapis and Isis, a temple at Senskis, near the emerald mines of the eastern desert, was dedicated;[428] an inscription of homage to him was found at Kysis in the Theban Oasis, and another, of unknown origin, is in the Ghizeh Museum.[429] A Sphinx from Ombos, with a dedicatory inscription to Apollo and other gods, has been discovered.[430] Among the Apollo types on the coins, which are not uncommon,

FIG. 98.—Apollo: Coin of Nero. (British Museum.)

FIG. 99.—Helios: Coin of Hadrian. (Bodleian.)

should be noticed the figures of the Apollo of Kanachos at Branchidae, on coins of Antoninus Pius,[431] and the busts of Apollo Pythios and Apollo Aktios in the "games" series of Nero.[432]

14. Helios, in the simple form, as distinguished from the pantheistic Zeus Helios Sarapis, is represented by purely Greek types on the coins,[433] even the nome coins of Heliopolis and Diospolis Magna.

15. Artemis likewise occurs only on coins, and in the Greek form of the huntress goddess:[434] and Selene also is always represented by a Greek type.[435]

FIG. 100.—Artemis: Coin of Antoninus Pius. (British Museum.)

FIG. 101.—Selene: Coin of Julia Paula. (British Museum.)

16. Athene is, next to Zeus, the most frequently represented of the Greek divinities on coins, but no

Fig. 102.—Athene: Coin of Gallienus. (British Museum.)

Fig. 103.—Temple of Athene: Coin of Antoninus Pius. (British Museum.)

inscriptions to her have been as yet discovered. Her temple at Alexandria is found on a coin of Antoninus Pius; (436) and she furnishes the type for the nome coins of Sais and Oxyrhynchos.(437) The Saite form is that of the goddess holding an owl, identified as Athene Archegetis, with reference to the idea that Athens was a colony of Sais, while at Oxyrhynchos she appears holding a double axe, usually of Egyptian form, with rounded edges. In both these localities she had taken the place, in the mind of the Alexandrians, of the Egyptian goddess Nit; (438) but it is noticeable that no reference to her occurs in the papyri from Oxyrhynchos.

17. Ares similarly appears on the nome coins, in the Upper Sebennyte nome, as the supplanter of a native god, Horus.(439) He is represented, both here and on the Alexandrian series, in a typically Greek form.

Fig. 104.—Ares: Coin of Hadrian. (Bodleian.)

18. Other Greek deities who occur very occasionally on the coins are Hermes,(440) Pan,(441) Dionysos, and Aphrodite.(442) The local identifications of the first two with Mandoulis and Khem have already been mentioned, and the compound deity Hermanubis will

be noticed later. Among the people, however, Aphrodite was very popular, to judge by the number of small

Fig. 105.—Dionysos: Coin of Trajan. (British Museum.)

Fig. 106.—Pan: Coin of Hadrian. (British Museum.)

Fig. 107.—Hermes: Coin of Claudius II. (British Museum.)

terra-cotta figures of her which are found in Egypt; and a figure of Aphrodite is entered in a list of articles pawned on a papyrus from Oxyrhynchos. A statue of Aphrodite set up in the reign of Antoninus has been discovered, and a small chapel south of the great temple at Ombos was apparently dedicated to her in the reign of Domitian.(443)

19. Demeter, as the goddess of corn, was a popular goddess at Alexandria; and a reference to priests of Demeter, apparently at Hexapotamos, is found in the

Fig. 108.—Demeter: Coin of Antoninus Pius. (British Museum.)

Fig. 109.—Rape of Persephone: Coin of Trajan. (British Museum.)

Fayum papyri.[444] The types of Demeter on coins are common;[445] and two empresses—Messalina[446] and Sabina[447]—are represented in the form of Demeter.

20. Persephone did not share in the popularity of Demeter; and the only representation of her is one, apparently copied from a picture, on a coin of Trajan.[448]

21. Triptolemos, on the other hand, occurs several times, and is shown scattering seed from a bag, standing in a car drawn by two serpents, Agathodæmones.[449]

Fig. 110.—Triptolemos: Coin of Hadrian. (British Museum.)

Fig. 111.—Dioskouroi: Coin of Trajan. (British Museum.)

22. The worship of the Dioskouroi was naturally familiar at Alexandria, where the Pharos was dedicated to them; and in this connection they are represented on a coin of Trajan, standing on either side of Isis Pharia.[450] They were known, however, outside Alexandria as well, a stele was dedicated to them at Soknopaiou Nesos,[451] and in the Fayum papyri there occurs an oath in their name.[452]

23. The identification of Herakles with Harpokrates, one of the specially Alexandrian deities, through the form of Haroeris, the elder Horus, prevented his appearing to any extent in the Greek theology of Egypt, as in this case the local god overshadowed the imported one. With one exception, in the time of

Fig. 112.—Herakles: Coin of Trajan. (Bodleian.)

Trajan, it was not until the reign of **Maximianus** that Herakles as a simple type was represented on the Alexandrian coins,(453) the groups of the labours of Herakles on the large bronze series of Antoninus (454) being pictorial rather than religious; and on the coins of Maximianus his appearance is, of course, due to the special fancy of the emperor.

24. Asklepios and Hygieia were deities of considerable importance in the Alexandrian system, and an interesting inscription, relating to the restoration of their temple at Ptolemais Hermiou in the reign of

FIG. 113.—Asklepios: Coin of Severus Alexander. (British Museum.)

FIG. 114.—Hygieia: Coin of Severus Alexander. (British Museum.)

Trajan, is preserved.(455) Their figures are frequently found on coins.(456)

25. The distinctively Alexandrian triad of **Sarapis, Isis,** and **Harpokrates** stands by itself in the development of Graeco-Egyptian religion, and presents the most complete instance of the fusion of the two theologies. It was in accordance with the Egyptian custom that the triad was appropriated to the Greek city as its foundation, and all three of the deities were originally Egyptian. But the leading member of the triad was practically unknown, a mere local form of Osiris-Apis, whose temple happened to stand on the site of Alexandria,(457) until he was brought under Greek influence.

FIG. 115.—Sarapis: Coin of Hadrian. (Bodleian.)

SARAPIS

Then there was built up, out of sources partly Greek and partly Egyptian, the conception of a god whose popularity quickly outstripped that of any other deity, local or foreign, in Egypt, and spread even to Rome. The new deity had none of the attributes of the bull Apis; but, in virtue of his connection with the lower world, as an Osirian, he was identified with the Greek Hades; and a statue of Hades by Bryaxis was imported under Ptolemy I. or II., and adopted as the type of Sarapis.(458) This statue was placed in the great temple of Sarapis at Alexandria, and is represented therein on the Alexandrian coins.(459) The Sarapeion of Alexandria, as the temple of the chief god of the capital city, became in a way the special government temple; and in this connection it was used

Fig. 116.—Head of Sarapis. (Plaque in Petrie Collection.)

Fig. 117.—Temple of Sarapis: Coin of M. Aurelius. (British Museum.)

Fig. 118.—Sarapeion and Hadrianon. (British Museum.)

to house the great public library of Alexandria. An adjunct to the temple known as the Hadrianon, was apparently built by Hadrian, on whose coins it is shown;(460) and this may perhaps be identified with the library of Hadrian, to which an edict of the prefect Flavius Titianus refers as newly erected for the reception of the State archives.[161] A temple of Sarapis is also mentioned in this period as existing at Oxyrhynchos;[162] a pylon was dedicated to Sarapis and Isis at Kysis in the Great Oasis under Trajan;[163] a temple was built to them at Senskis under Gallienus;[164] and numerous evidences of Sarapis-worship, in the form of prayers addressed to him and references to his neokoroi, are found in the Fayum papyri.[165] The extent to which, in the last-named district, the worship of Sarapis had supplanted that of the local gods Soknopaios and Sokonpieios—may perhaps be judged from the fact that, in the papyri, ten prayers addressed to Sarapis are found, as against two to the local gods.[166] And when Christianity became the ruling religion in Egypt, the temples of Sarapis at Alexandria and of Isis at Philæ were the last strongholds of the older faith.

FIG. 119.—Sarapis: Coin of Hadrian. (British Museum.)

FIG. 120.—Isis and Sarapis. (Vatican Museum.)

26. Isis, the consort of Sarapis, never underwent the same process of Hellenisation, but always remained one of the most purely Egyptian deities. There is a curious contrast between the development of Alexandrian concep-

tions of these two closely linked gods. Sarapis lost practically all his original Egyptian attributes, and was worshipped in Greek forms, by Greek ideas; while a tendency was shown to unite him with Zeus and Helios in a single personality, as Osiris had been united with Ra. Isis, on the other hand, is always represented by statues of Egyptian type, and her temple, as shown on Alexandrian coins, is Egyptian;[467] and, instead of becoming identified with other deities, she was more frequently localised with some distinctive epithet. Thus, at Alexandria, she was worshipped as Isis Pharia,[468] Isis Plousia,[469] Isis Sothis,[470] and Isis of Menuthis;[471] at Mons Porphyrites an altar was found, dedicated to Isis Myrionymos;[472] Isis Nanaia was one of the deities of Nabana in the Fayum,[473] and it was probably to

FIG. 121.—Temple of Isis: Coin of Trajan. (British Museum.)

FIG. 122.—Isis Pharia: Coin of Antoninus Pius. (British Museum.)

FIG. 123.—Isis Sothis: Coin of Faustina II. (British Museum.)

her that the Nanaion at Alexandria was dedicated;[474] Isis Nepherses and Isis Nephremmis were associated with Soknopaios at Soknopaiou Nesos[475], and were also worshipped at Nilopolis;[476] and at Hiera Sykaminos she is addressed as Rhodosternos.[477] In addition to these, she is associated with Sarapis in dedications at Kysis and Senskis, as already mentioned ;[178] a propylon at Tentyra was erected to her under Augustus ;[179] and stelæ dedicated to her

FIG. 124.—Isis: Coin of Nerva. (Bodleian.)

FIG. 125.—Isis suckling Horus: Coin of M. Aurelius. (Bodleian.)

have been found at Apollinopolis Parva, where there was a hereditary prostates of Isis, and at Pathyra.[480] There was also a temple of Isis at Oxyrhynchos.[481] The great centre of Isis-worship, however, was at Philæ, where inscriptions of homage continued to be

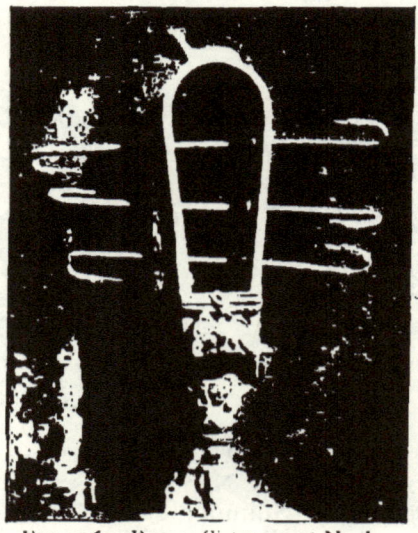

FIG. 126.—Bronze Sistrum: at Naples. (Photo. by W. M. F. Petrie.)

written down to the middle of the fifth century,[4.2] though the persistence of the old paganism here was probably due in part to political motives; as the Nobatæ, whose territory extended up to the Roman frontier, were worshippers of Isis, and resorted yearly to Philæ to borrow the temple statue for a brief space of time: and thus the temple of Isis might be able, by its sanctity, to protect Philæ, if not the whole Roman frontier, against the raids of the Nobatæ.[18.5]

27. The worship of Harpokrates, who, as Har-pa-khruti, or Horus the infant, was the remaining member of the Alexandrian triad, shows a development more nearly resembling that of Isis than that of Sarapis. Like Isis, he remained Egyptian, and was localised elsewhere than Alexandria; but this localisation was apparently accomplished by a certain variation of type, to judge

Fig. 127.—Horus as a child in military dress. (Terra-cotta in Petrie Collection.)

Fig. 128.—Harpokrates: Coin of Trajan. (British Museum.)

by the representations on the Alexandrian coins. At Alexandria itself, Harpokrates was worshipped as a child; at Herakleopolis Magna, he was identified, through the form of Haroeris (the elder Horus), with Heracles; at Mendes, he appears as a bearded man, with the local ram's horn; at Pelusium, his distinguishing attribute is a pomegranate; at Canopus, he is represented with the body of a crocodile from the waist downwards; at Taua and Buto, his type is the Egyptian one of a youth sitting on a lotus flower.(484) Apart from the coin types, official recognition of Harpokrates is rare: the base of a statue of him was found at Alexandria,(485) and he is mentioned in connection with the temples of Soknopaios at Soknopaiou Nesos,(486) and of Zeus Kapitolios at Arsinoe,(487) and associated with Isis in the stele from Apollinopolis Parva;(488) he also appears among the gods of Nabana in the Fayum.(489) But that the worship of Harpokrates or Horus was popular among the common people throughout Egypt, is shown by the multitudes of terra-cotta figures, usually of poor workmanship and evidently intended to suit the wants of the lower classes, which are found.(490) And he appears, with Sarapis and Isis, in the types of the Roman coinage under Julian, when the revived paganism sought its inspiration mainly from Egypt.

FIG. 129.—Osiris with stars: from Koptos. (Photo. by W. M. F. Petrie.)

OSIRIS AND HERMANUBIS

28. Osiris, in Alexandria at any rate, was completely overshadowed by Sarapis. In the Roman period there is no mention of him in papyri or inscriptions; nor does he appear on coins, except in the peculiar type of the Canopic vases with a human head, some of which represent him wearing the atef crown,[491] and others with a crown of rams' horns, uraei, disk, and plumes.[492] At Koptos, however, where he was worshipped as Min, dedications to him are found down to the time of Nero.[493]

29. Hermanubis was as distinctively Alexandrian a deity as Sarapis. His name, like that of Sarapis, was borrowed from the older Egyptian mythology, which had a compound of Horus and Anubis, or Har-m-Anup;

FIG. 130.—Hermanubis: Coin of Hadrian. (British Museum.)

FIG. 131.—Temple of Hermanubis: Coin of Antoninus Pius. (British Museum.)

and, as Sarapis for the Greek included the attributes of Hades, so did Hermanubis those of Hermes.[494] A temple of Hermanubis, presumably at Alexandria, is represented on coins of Antoninus Pius.[495]

30. There was also an interesting development of Nile-worship at Alexandria, where the river-god was to a certain extent assimilated with Sarapis.[496] His temple, with the statue inside it seated on rocks, appears on a coin of Hadrian;[497] and either his bust, or his figure reclining on a hippopotamus or a crocodile, with small figures up to the number of sixteen, representing the cubits of the flood-rise, is commonly found as a type.[498] As the consort of Nilus, Euthenia was

brought into the rank of the gods, and appears on the coins either alone [499] or with her husband.[500]

FIG. 132.—Temple of Nilus: Coin of Hadrian. (British Museum.)

FIG. 133.—Nilus: Coin of Nero. (Bodleian.)

FIG. 134.—Nilus: Coin of Trajan. (British Museum.)

FIG. 135.—Euthenia: Coin of Livia. (British Museum.)

31. The Roman conquerors of Egypt did not add many fresh religious ideas to those they found already existing in the country. Perhaps the only distinctively Roman worship known was that of Jupiter Capitolinus, to whom a temple was dedicated at Arsinoe. There is preserved a fairly long record of the procedure at this temple in the reign of Caracalla, which shows it to have been mainly a centre for the worship of the imperial family in general and the reigning emperor in particular.[501] The festivals recorded to have been celebrated there during a period of three months are: two in honour of the deified Severus, one to celebrate

the proclamation of Julia Domna as mother of the armies, and seven variously relating to Caracalla; together with a feast to commemorate the birthday of Rome. A Capitolium, which may have been a temple of Jupiter Capitolinus, also existed at Oxyrhynchos.[502]

32. The worship of the emperors was more Egyptian than Roman. From time immemorial the rulers of Egypt had occupied a semi-divine position in the minds of their subjects; and an emperor who was far away at Rome would be even more an object of mysterious awe than one who might be seen from time to time by his people. Consequently, though Augustus and Tiberius discouraged the desire to deify them in their lifetime, Caligula had no sooner expressed his designs on godhead than the Alexandrians wholeheartedly fell in with his wishes, and worshipped him. So, also, when Vespasian visited Alexandria, immediately after his proclamation, the people expected him to work miracles of healing.[503] Augustus himself is named Zeus Eleutherios on the propylon of the temple of Isis at Tentyra,[504] and on an inscription from Arsinoe;[505] and a decree of the inhabitants of Busiris and the Letopolite nome addresses Nero as the Agathos Daimon of the world.[506] An inscription of the reign of Caracalla shows that, in addition to priests of "the emperors," presumably Severus and Caracalla, there were at Alexandria priests of Trajan and Antoninus Pius, and of the Hadrianeion, which was probably devoted to the worship of Hadrian.[507] There was also a Hadrianeion at Memphis, and a Caesareum is mentioned in an Oxyrhynchan papyrus.[508]

33. The Roman government exercised a kind of general supervision over the religious affairs of Egypt through the "high priest of Alexandria and all Egypt," who was a Roman probably appointed directly by the emperor.[509] He had not only the supreme authority over the priests of the whole of the province,[510] but was also charged with the control of the treasures of the temples.[511]

34. There is no direct evidence how far the worship

of the Fortune of the city of Alexandria persisted in Roman times; though the Tycheion is represented on

Fig. 136.—Temple of Tyche: Coin of Antoninus Pius. (British Museum.)

Fig. 137. Tyche: Coin of Hadrian. (British Museum.)

Fig. 138.—Tyche of Alexandria: Coin of Antoninus Pius. (British Museum.)

Fig. 139.—Alexandria: Coin of Hadrian. (British Museum).

Fig. 140.—Roma: Coin of Antoninus Pius. (British Museum.)

Fig. 141.—Roma: Coin of Antoninus Pius. (Bodleian.)

coins, and Tyche is a favourite type; one interesting variety gives the Tyche of Alexandria. The types of Alexandria and Rome probably have no religious meaning.

35. As has already been remarked, the Jews, who formed an important section of the community, especially in Alexandria, stood wholly apart in religious matters from Egyptians, Romans, and Greeks. There was, however, one development of Jewish ideas which was peculiar to Egypt, in the sect of the Therapeutai, described by Philo.[512] This sect existed in a settlement near Lake Mareotis, where they lived a monastic life, devoted wholly to study and meditation. Both men and women were admitted to the community, and each member had a separate cell, where he remained alone for six days out of the week, only meeting his fellows in the synagogue on the seventh day and in a festival held every fiftieth day. This contemplative life was not unknown in Egypt among the followers of the old national religion, who had perhaps been first induced to it by Buddhist missionaries from India; but the fact that the Jews, who were most unlikely to have consciously borrowed any ideas from a foreign creed, were found adopting the same eremitic seclusion, suggests that the habit was at any rate encouraged by the physical character of the country. In Egypt, the desert is always close at hand for those who wish to retire from the world; and it exercises a peculiar fascination, easier to feel than to describe, over minds which have risen to a higher religion than mere fetichism, tempting those who enter it to stay and think their lives away. The same religious tendency was shortly afterwards displayed to a wider extent in the Christian Church, and, borrowed by it from Egypt, spread throughout Europe.

36. The introduction of Christianity into Egypt is reported to have taken place in the reign of Nero, when the Apostle Mark visited Alexandria.[513] No records of the earliest years of the Alexandrian Church are preserved, beyond the list of bishops, but it rapidly

assumed a place among the philosophical sects of the city, influencing them and in return receiving influence; and, as Alexandria was the home of more schools of thought than any other place in the Roman world, so Christianity there not unnaturally developed an unusually large number of peculiar ideas. The earliest Egyptian heresy was Gnostic, founded by Basilides of Alexandria in the time of Hadrian;[514] which mainly consisted in an attempt to blend Christianity and the old Egyptian magic; and the Christian Gnosticism was further extended by other Alexandrian philosophers.

37. The first appointments of Christian bishops in Egypt outside Alexandria were made in the reign of Aurelius, when Demetrius, patriarch of Alexandria, nominated three;[515] and shortly afterwards the catechetical school of Alexandria was founded by Pantænus for the training of Christian students.[516] The growing importance of the Christians was marked in the reign of Severus by the first organised persecution in Egypt.[517] This, however, did not check the spread of the religion; and about thirty years later it was found advisable to increase the number of Egyptian bishops from three to twenty.[518] Fresh persecutions were ordered by Decius and Valerian; but Gallienus, who had quite enough political difficulties to face in Egypt without complicating them by religious ones, stopped the persecution and granted liberty of religion to the Christians.[519]

38. This edict of toleration enabled the Christians to build themselves churches; and the small church of Al Mu'allakah at Old Cairo may be dated to very shortly after this period.[520] In a papyrus from Oxyrhynchos of about 300 A.D., reference is made to the north and south churches,[521] and doubtless most other large towns were similarly provided. But these churches were all ordered to be destroyed, and the Christians to be forced to change their belief, by Diocletian; and for some years the persecution continued.[522]

39. The "conversion" of Constantine, however,

brought Christianity into power; and for the next two centuries the Christians were constantly active, except during the brief reign of Julian, in trying to root out the pagans; and they pursued their work as relentlessly as the ministers of the old religion had tried to suppress Christianity. Perhaps the most notorious instance of the ruthlessness of the monks was the murder of Hypatia at Alexandria, at the instigation of the patriarch Cyril.(523) But every bishop, and every abbot, apparently thought himself at liberty to do as he liked with pagans and their property. Thus Macarius, bishop of Tkoou, and his companions made a raid on a village, and burnt not only a temple and three hundred and six idols, but also the high priest.(524) The life of Schnoudi represents him as similarly engaged in attacking villages near Panopolis, and even Panopolis itself, and burning houses and temples for the glory of God; (525) so that it is not to be wondered at that the people of Panopolis made complaint of him to the governor.(526)

40. It is difficult to say what position the government intended to take up with regard to paganism. Apparently it was left to the discretion of each local official whether he interfered in the religious disputes of his districts; and the average official would probably be satisfied if the peace was not too flagrantly broken. Here and there a zealous Christian governor might assist the local ecclesiastics in their holy war, as Cynegius helped Theophilus, the bishop of Alexandria, to destroy the Sarapeum;(527) or a confirmed pagan might try to check the work of destruction, as a governor of Antinoe summoned Schnoudi before him; but such interference of the civil power would be an exception. That the central government was not unwilling to use the old gods for diplomatic purposes, is shown by the treaty of Maximinus with the Nobatae in the reign of Marcian, one of the conditions of which was a yearly loan of the statue of Isis at Philae to the barbarians.(528)

41. The political importance of the divisions in the

Christian Churches of Egypt can hardly be overestimated. Egypt was the birthplace of the Arian heresy, which provided the first pretext for a definite breach between the Eastern and Western divisions of the Roman Empire, in the dispute between Constans and Constantius over the banishment of Athanasius by the latter; and the religious difference thus begun was thereafter, under varied forms, continued as the most marked outward sign in all the quarrels which led to the final severance of Rome and Constantinople. The growth of the antagonism between the imperial patriarchate of Alexandria (which represented the official creed of Constantinople) and the native Jacobite Church has already been traced. Its results were, first, the union of the civil and religious power in the persons of the prefect-patriarch, of Justinian, Apollinarius, and his successors, who furnished a precedent for the temporal dominion of the Popes in the Middle Ages; and, secondly, the subsequent dissensions which opened Egypt successively to the Persians and Arabs, and lost it to the Roman Empire.

42. The special existence of these divisions in Egyptian Christianity may be traced to the mixture of races in the country. The Greek ruling class had never amalgamated with their Egyptian subjects; and it was natural that each section should follow its own religious ideas. So long as the gods in question were pagan deities, whose accommodating attributes allowed them to be identified at the will of their worshippers with one another, no serious difficulties arose; the Greek and the Egyptian could worship each his own god in the same temple, and the priest was equally satisfied. But when the leaders of the Christian Church, partly, no doubt, from a desire to mark their separation from such loose theology, sought to enforce a cast-iron orthodoxy, set forth in creeds, each word of which must be literally believed on pain of everlasting damnation, the innate differences of the Greek and Egyptian mind began to be manifested. The philosophical subtleties of the Alexandrian school were quite unsuited to the

comprehension of the fellah; and, consequently, in the Arian and Monophysite controversies, the native Egyptian Church on each occasion held to the simpler form of belief.

43. The Christian Church in Egypt, however, was not uninfluenced by the older religion of the country. The importance of the Platonists of Alexandria in the early development of Christianity, particularly in the doctrine of the Logos, is well known. A more striking example of the debt of Christianity to paganism may be found in the worship of Mary as the mother of Jesus, the idea of which was probably, as the artistic representations were certainly, borrowed from the Egyptian conception of Isis with her child Horus.(529) And it is not improbable that the development of the doctrine of the Trinity, which formed no part of the original Jewish Christianity, may be traced to Egyptian influence; as the whole of the older Egyptian theology was permeated with the idea of triple divinity, as seen both in the triads of gods which the various cities worshipped, and in the threefold names, representing three differing aspects of the same personality, under which each god might be addressed.

44. But the most important contribution of Egypt to the life of the Christian Churches was the habit of monasticism. This has already been noticed in connection with the Jewish sect of the Therapeutai; and the custom of withdrawing from the world, for meditation in the solitude of the desert, was adopted also by the Christians. The earliest Christian hermits mentioned lived about the time of Constantine; and the rapidity with which the system spread may be judged from the fact that half a century later, in the reign of Valens, the monasteries were not only well established and recognised by law as bodies competent to hold property,(530) but were so popular as to present a serious difficulty to the government, on account of the number of men who claimed exemption from military service or liturgies on the ground of monastic vows.(531) A large number of the monasteries occupied the old temples,

156   RELIGIOUS INSTITUTIONS

or any other buildings, such as towers or pylons, which were at hand. Examples of such occupation were seen by Rufinus, about the end of the fourth century, at Oxyrhynchos; and the manner in which a military building could be adapted for monastic purposes may be seen in the Roman fortress of Babylon.(532) The desert monasteries were probably in most instances collections of separate cells, related only by their neigh-

FIG. 142.—The White Monastery: Old nave of church, now the courtyard. (Photo. by J. G. M.)

MONASTICISM

bourhood; but a few instances of convents were already to be found in the time of Rufinus, the largest being at Tabenna, which held three thousand monks. As the weakness of the central government increased, it became necessary for the monks to provide for their own safety against the desert tribes, who from time to time raided the country; and so the fortress type of monastery, the earliest example of which perhaps is the

FIG. 143.—The White Monastery: Walled-in columns of nave.
(Photo. by J. G. M.)

White Monastery, became common. This building may be dated to about the reign of Constantius, and presents outwardly a huge expanse of blank wall, broken only by windows high up, and by two small entrances which could easily be blocked. Such a monastery could stand a long siege against marauders, if sufficiently provisioned; and the extent of provision kept may be judged from the account in the Life of Schnoudi, of how his monastery maintained for three months twenty thousand men, as well as women and children, who had been rescued from the Blemmyes.(533) The district round had just been raided, and it is not probable that any large supplies could have been drawn thence; so that it must be supposed that the eighty-five thousand artabai of wheat, as well as the numerous other articles of food, with which the monks supplied their guests, must have been stored in the monastery. The military use of these Egyptian monasteries was, however, only a secondary one; but Justinian borrowed from them, doubtless, his idea when he erected a monastery to guard the passes under Mount Sinai against attacks from Northern Arabia.(534) In other countries, which were not exposed, like Egypt, to sudden raids from the desert, there was not the same incentive to conventual life; but nevertheless it was this system, rather than the eremitic, which finally spread throughout Europe, and moulded the ideas of the Christian Church of the Middle Ages.

CHAPTER X

LIFE IN THE TOWNS AND VILLAGES OF EGYPT

1. THE recent discoveries of papyri have thrown a considerable amount of light on the life of the inhabitants of Egypt during the period of Roman rule; and some points in particular may be noticed as of special interest. The most complete view of town life will doubtless be given by the Oxyrhynchos papyri, when they are all published; but even those which have already appeared, forming a comparatively small part of the whole mass, furnish an extremely interesting picture.

2. The public buildings of the town of Oxyrhynchos are catalogued, in a list of the watchmen who were distributed over the town at some date early in the third century.(535) There are found there temples of Sarapis, Isis, and Thoeris (the special deity of the town), which all had special watchmen assigned to them, six being placed in the temple of Sarapis, one in that of Isis, and seven in that of Thoeris, from which the relative sizes and importance of the temples may perhaps be conjectured. There was also a Cæsareum, which had no watchman; and a tetrastyle dedicated to Thoeris is mentioned. Two churches, the north and the south, come in the list; but these were not at the date regarded as public buildings, and only appear as giving their names to streets. Three watchmen were assigned to the theatre, two to the gymnasium, and one to the Nilometer. Besides these buildings, there is mention made of the Capitolium, of three sets of baths and of four gates.

3. This list of buildings can be taken as representative of the usual condition of an Egyptian town of the period. It shows that, in the religious life, the special local worship and that of Sarapis and Isis were still those recognised by the authorities; but that the Christians had made their appearance as an organised body, and were at any rate not ignored. The Cæsareum and the Capitolium marked the Roman supremacy; and the baths, the gymnasium, and the theatre supplied the needs which had been introduced into Egyptian life by the Greeks.

4. At Oxyrhynchos the gymnasium and its sports appear to have assumed considerable importance. The following proclamation, dated in 323, shows the popular feeling with regard to them:—

"Dioscorides, logistes of the Oxyrhynchite nome. The assault at arms by the youths will take place to-morrow, the 24th. Tradition, no less than the distinguished character of the festival, requires that they should do their utmost in the gymnastic display. The spectators will be present at two performances." (536)

The privileges which were granted to a victor in the games appears from another papyrus containing a copy of a letter sent in 292 by the senate of Oxyrhynchos to the strategos, the message of which is—

"At a meeting of our body a despatch was read from Theodorus, who was recently chosen in place of Areion the scribe to proceed to his highness the praefect and attend his immaculate court. In this despatch he explained that he is a victor in the games and exempted from inquiries.— We have therefore nominated Aurelius to serve, and we send you word accordingly, in order that this fact may be brought to his knowledge, and no time be lost in his departure and attendance upon the court. We pray for your health, dearest brother." (537)

5. In the Byzantine period, the gymnasium at Oxyrhynchos was apparently supplanted by the racecourse. In the sixth and seventh centuries, this, like most other things at Oxyrhynchos, apparently belonged to Flavius Apion; as a certain John, in a document addressed to

Apion, styles himself "by the help of God contractor of the racecourse belonging to your honourable house, and of the stable belonging to your said honourable house." (538) The spectators at Oxyrhynchos, as elsewhere, divided themselves into the factions of the Blues and the Greens; and each side seems to have kept its own starters, and to have provided funds for the maintenance of its horses: as receipts are preserved, one for $108\frac{3}{8}$ carats "paid by the most eminent Georgius the secretary to the two starters of the horses on the side of the Blues as their month's wages," (539) and another for a solidus less four carats "paid by the most eminent Anastasius the banker for the cost of an embrocation bought for the use of the horses of the public circus on the side of the Greens." (540) The violence of party spirit over the circus games was increased by the tendency to identify the two factions with the two sections of the Christian Church; and the extent to which the partisans indulged their quarrel is shown by the fact that, even while the Romans were shut up in Alexandria by 'Amr, there were open battles in the streets between the Blues, led by Domentianus, prefect of the Fayum, and the Greens, led by Menas the dux. (541)

6. The inhabitants of the villages would naturally ,ave to look to the metropolis of the nome for the provision of most of their amusements; but a record is preserved among the Fayum papyri showing that the chief men of the villages were not unmindful of the pleasures of their fellows. It runs as follows:—

"To Aurelius Theon, keeper of the training-school, from Aurelius Asclepiades, son of Philadelphus, president of the council of the village of Bacchias. I desire to hire from you Tisais the dancing girl and another, to dance for us in the above village for (fifteen?) days from the 13th Phaophi by the old calendar. You shall receive as pay thirty-six drachmæ a day, and for the whole period three artabai of wheat, and fifteen couples of loaves; also three donkeys to fetch them and take them back." (542)

7. Three brief letters from Oxyrhynchos are interesting, as showing the existence of "society" in the town. Apparently the fashionable hour for dinner-parties was the ninth, which would be early in the afternoon; and such dinner-parties could be held in one of the temples; while the festivals of the gods furnished opportunities for social displays. The invitations are—

"Chæremon requests your company at dinner, at the table of the lord Serapis in the Serapæum, to-morrow, the 15th, at 9 o'clock."[513]

"Herais requests your company at dinner, in celebration of the marriage of her children, at her house to-morrow, the 5th, at 9 o'clock."[544]

"Greeting, my dear Serenia, from Petosiris. Be sure, dear, to come up on the 20th for the birthday festival of the god, and let me know whether you are coming by boat or by donkey, in order that we may send for you accordingly. Take care not to forget. I pray for your continued health."[545]

8. There is, however, comparatively little evidence of luxury to be found either in the records of the life of Roman Egypt preserved in the papyri, or in the objects discovered in the excavation of Roman sites, Alexandria excepted. At Bacchias, the houses of which were probably as carefully investigated as any Roman town in Egypt, the catalogue of domestic articles found was "wooden bowls, platters, boxes, writing-tablets, styles, and reed pipes; bone dice, pins, and toilet implements; bronze rings and pins; combs, terra-cotta figurines, memorial prism-shaped shrines in wood (one in marble with four painted figures in relief), and so forth."[546] And other Roman sites have produced similar results.

9. The artistic products of Roman Egypt also show a low level of style, which gives ground for arguing that the general standard of life was likewise low. It is true that the painted portraits from the mummies of the Fayum show a fair amount of technical skill;[547] but these are the only objects, other than public monuments, which deserve the name of works of art. The pottery and terra-cottas of the Roman period are coarse,[548] and

the tombstones show an entire absence of taste.[549] Even in sculptures executed for public or semi-public purposes, though there is a certain amount of mastery of conventional technique to be found in some of the earlier stelai,[550] there is at the same time much extremely bad work;[551] and the style of art rapidly deteriorated in the second century. Statues of Caracalla seem to have been set up in many places in Egypt at the time of his visit to the country,[552] and those which have been discovered vie with each other in ugliness:[553] in one instance the artist could rise no higher than recutting the face of an older statue.[554] The few remains of the work of the later period are thoroughly debased. It is interesting to find among the Oxyrhynchos papyri a letter, dated in 357, from a logistes and the strategos of the nome, requesting Aurelius Sineeis, "in accordance with the directions of the letter, to construct a statue of our lord the most glorious prefect Pomponius Metrodorus."[555] It would be still more interesting to know what the statue was like when it was constructed.

10. But if the Egyptians were not luxurious, they were at any rate industrious. The "letter of Hadrian to Servianus," probably written in the third century, says that in Alexandria "no one is idle: some work glass, others make paper, others weave linen."[556] These three manufactures furnished the bulk of the Egyptian export trade,[557] if the supply of corn to Rome, which went rather by way of tribute than of trade, be left out of consideration: Aurelian, indeed, included them with corn in the contributions to be sent by Egypt to the capital.[558] Glass and paper were manufactured chiefly at Alexandria; but the weaving of linen cloth was an industry practised in all parts of the country; and no occupation, save that of husbandman, is as commonly mentioned in the papyri as that of weaver.[559] To this day excellent weaving is done in small villages, which are often renowned for special fabrics. The trades of each nome were organised in guilds, whose affairs were managed by presidents elected

each month; (560) and a series of declarations from various guilds of Oxyrhynchos—those of coppersmiths, bakers, beersellers, oilsellers, and beekeepers—has been found, in which each guild states the value of the goods in stock at the end of the month. As an example may be taken the declaration of the coppersmiths—

"To Flavius Eusebius, logistes of the Oxyrhynchite nome, from the guild of coppersmiths of Oxyrhynchos, through me, Aurelius Thonius, son of Macer. We declare that at our own assessment the value given below of the goods we have in stock is that for the present month, and we swear the divine oath that our statement is correct. The value is as follows, of malleable bronze six pounds, worth 1000 denarii, and of cast bronze four pounds. In the consulship of Flavius Ursus and Flavius Polemius the most illustrious, Athyr 30 (Signed) I, Aurelius Thonius, make the aforesaid declaration." (561)

These declarations serve to show how close a supervision was exercised by the local authorities over the tradesmen of their district; and another papyrus gives further evidence of the restrictions placed on business.

'To Flavius Thennyras, logistes of the Oxyrhynchite nome, from Aurelius Nilus, son of Didymus, of the illustrious and most illustrious city of Oxyrhynchos, an egg-seller by trade. I hereby agree, on the august, divine oath by our lord the Emperor and the Cæsars, to offer my eggs in the market-place publicly, for sale and for the supply of the said city, every day without intermission; and I acknowledge that it shall be unlawful for me in the future to sell secretly or in my house. If I am detected so doing (I shall be liable to the penalty for breaking the oath)." (562)

11. The main occupation of Egypt was, however, and always has been, agriculture. A special interest therefore attaches to the papyri which deal with farm work; and one long document, from Hermopolis, gives a general view of the occupations of the labourers on an Egyptian farm for several months of the year.(563) It appears from this that in Thoth (August–September)

the main work consisted in attending to the dykes, as the flood was then high; also men were employed in artificial irrigation of the lands uncovered by the water, in carting manure, and weeding: in the next month, Phaophi (September–October), the dykes still required attention, but less, as the river subsided; artificial irrigation was still carried on, and the breaking up of the ground was begun: in Athyr (October–November) the corn was sown, and the land had to be manured and watered: in Tybi (December–January) the growing crops only required watering and manuring, and hands were turned to vine-dressing and palm-cutting: while in Pharmouthi and Pachon (March–May) all were busy harvesting and thrashing the corn. Another papyrus, from Memphis, gives particulars of the work done in Mesore (July–August).[564] In this month there was a large body of men required to watch and repair the dykes; others were employed in clearing up after the thrashing of the harvest, and carrying away the chaff from the thrashing-floor to be used as fuel; while spare hands were put to the repair of farm implements.

12. The chief crops grown were corn and barley; but, in addition to these, lentils[565] and flax[566] were not infrequently sown; and garden grounds, with olives, figs, palms, and vines, are commonly mentioned. A considerable amount of land must also have been used as pasture,[567] which would be probably sown pasture, chiefly clover, as in modern times. The proportionate amount of land devoted to these various crops probably corresponded approximately with that of the present day, when over half of the total area under cultivation is employed for the growing of cereals. Cotton, rice, and sugarcane have been introduced, and between them occupy about one-sixth of the land, which may have resulted in a diminution in the amount of corn grown; and Indian corn has taken a place among the cereals of Egypt: but, with these exceptions, the crops now raised are much the same as those mentioned in the papyri.

13. A large number of leases of land are preserved,

and give information as to the rents usual in the country. They fall into two distinct classes.⁽⁵⁶⁸⁾ In the first, the rent paid was a stated number of artabai of corn, varying from one to seven and a half per aroura; in the second, it was a fixed proportion of the produce, the lowest rate being one-half and the highest four-fifths. The terms of the leases do not give any sufficient evidence for distinguishing between these two classes, which both occur in all parts of the country and at all periods.

14. The wages of the Egyptian labourers, so far as can be judged from the rather scanty records, show a tendency to rise steadily in nominal amount during the first three centuries. Thus, in 78 A.D., labourers at Hermopolis received from three to five obols a day;⁽⁵⁶⁹⁾ in the middle of the second century the ordinary day's wages of a workman in the Fayum were eight obols, to judge from the sum fixed for purchasing exemption from labour on dykes;⁽⁵⁷⁰⁾ in 215, bricklayers at Arsinoe were paid two and a half drachmæ, and a bricklayer's labourer two drachmæ;⁽⁵⁷¹⁾ and in 255 the rate at Memphis was from six to nine drachmæ daily.⁽⁵⁷²⁾ This rise, however, was due probably rather to the depreciation in the coinage than to any improvement in the position of the workmen, as the prices of all articles seem to show a corresponding advance.

15. In one way the papyri give a rather unfavourable impression of the Egyptians, on account of the number of complaints made to the local authorities of thefts and assaults. The impression is perhaps not quite a fair one, as the evil deeds were naturally chronicled, while the good ones went unrecorded; but the Romans, not without reason, regarded Egypt as a country specially liable to disturbance.⁽⁵⁷³⁾ Some of the cases may serve to show how quarrels arose in Egyptian villages; for instance, a formal complaint lodged with the strategos of the Herakleid district of the Arsinoite nome by Tarmouthis, a female seller of vegetables, sets forth that " on the fourth of this month, Taorsenouphis, wife of Ammonios Phimon, an elder of the village of Bacchias,

though she had no occasion against me, came to my house and made herself most unpleasant to me; besides tearing my tunic and cloak, she carried off sixteen drachmæ that I had put by, the price of vegetables I had sold. And on the fifth her husband Ammonios Phimon came into my house, pretending he was looking for my husband, and took my lamp and went up into the house; and he went off with a pair of silver armlets weighing forty drachmæ, my husband being away from home."(574) A more serious accusation is one addressed to the prefect from the Great Oasis by Syrus son of Petechon. He states: "I married a wife of my own tribe, Tsek . . ., a freeborn woman of free parents, and have children by her. Now Tabes, daughter of Ammonios, and her husband Laloi, and Psenesis and Straton their sons, have committed an act which disgraces all the chiefs of the town, and shows their recklessness; they carried off my wife and children aforesaid to their own house, calling them slaves, though they are free, and my wife has brothers living who are free; and when I remonstrated they seized me and beat me shamefully."(575) Perhaps the most curious commentaries on the state of Egypt, however, may be found in the life of Schnoudi. On one occasion a man came to him, and, on being told by the saint that he was a murderer, remembered an incident which had apparently passed out of his memory—how he had taken his sword, gone out, and killed a woman, no reason whatever being suggested for this.(576) At the same time the dux was on his way up the river; and, when a number of robbers were presented to him, he promptly put them to death without trial.(577) But the lawlessness of Egypt was unquestionably much greater in the latter half of the Roman period; and, as has already been seen, during the last fifty years before the Arab conquest, the country was practically in a state of anarchy.

APPENDIX I

THE ROMAN GARRISON IN EGYPT

UNDER Augustus, the Roman garrison of Egypt was furnished by three legions, one of which was stationed at Alexandria and a second at Babylon; together with nine cohorts, three being at Alexandria and three at Syene (Strabo, xvii. 1). But one legion had already been withdrawn by the time of Tiberius (Tac. Ann. iv. 5), and the garrison continued at this strength, the legions left being the iii Cyrenaica and the xxii Deiotariana, till the time of Trajan, who, not before the year 99 (cf. B.G.U. 140), withdrew these two and substituted for them a single new one, the ii Traiana Fortis, which continued to serve in Egypt for the rest of its history. There is no further account to be found of the Roman army in Egypt as a whole till that given by the Notitia Dignitatum, which mentions eight legions, eleven companies of cavalry, thirty alæ, and nineteen cohorts, as stationed in the province.

The Roman troops in Egypt were, as has been shown by Mommsen (Hermes, xix. p. 4), mainly recruited from Egypt; with the exception that, in the first century, when the iii Cyrenaica and xxii Deiotariana were in garrison, a large proportion of Galatians were found among the troops. He explains this circumstance by the supposition that, with the kingdoms of Egypt and Galatia, Augustus took over the Ptolemaic and Deiotarian armies (*ibid.* p. 51). In later times the Egyptian troops were never sent out of the country; and this fact, coupled with the constitution of the

Egyptian army, shows how the province was treated as a separate kingdom, and the forces raised there were used only for home service (Hermes, xix. p. 218). This rule was first broken by Valens, who, as already shown (ch. V. § 15), sent some of the Egyptian soldiers to serve in other provinces, and filled their places with Goths; and so, in the lists of the Notitia Dignitatum, the ala ii nova Ægyptiorum is found serving at Cartha in Mesopotamia, and the cohors ii Ægyptiorum at Vallis Diocletiana in Phœnicia.

The following tables give the references to the various legions, cohorts, alæ, and other troops which have been preserved in Egypt. [The legions whose names are bracketed were probably not stationed in Egypt.]

Legio i Illyrica. Dedication by priests at Koptos {315} (Rec. Trav. xvi. p. 44). Similar dedication, from Syene {323} (Inscr. App. iii. 8).
Legio i Maximiana. Stationed at Philæ {c. 425} (Not. Dign.).
Legio i Valentiniana. Stationed at Koptos {c. 425} (Not. Dign.).
Legio ii Flavia Constantia Thebæorum. Stationed at Cusæ {c. 425} (Not. Dign.).
Legio ii Trajana. A vexillus at Pselkis {109} (C.I.L. iii. 79). Graffito of a soldier at Thebes {127} (C.I.L. iii. 42). A centurion at Syene {c. 140} (Inscr. P.S.B.A. xviii. p. 107, No. 2). A veteran in Fayum {143} (B.G.U. 113). A soldier transferred into coh. i Aug. Præt. Lusitanorum {156} (B.G.U. 696). Soldiers {148, 161} (B.G.U. 265, 195). A centurion at Syene {162} (Inscr. P.S.B.A. xviii. p. 107, No. 3). A soldier {167} (B.G.U. 240). Dedication by tribune at Alexandria {176} (C.I.L. iii. 13). Veterans at Alexandria {194} (C.I.L. iii. 6580). Soldier {201} (B.G.U. 156). Restoration of camp under centurion {175} (M.A. 101). Equites promoti secundi at Tentyra {302} (G.G.P. ii. 74). Stationed at Parembole and Apollinopolis magna {c. 425} (Not. Dign.).

[Dates not fixed precisely.] Tombstones at Alexandria (C.I.L. iii. 6592, 6593, 6594, 6595, 6596, 6605, 6609, 6611, 6613; M.A. 92, 92A, 89A; Rev. Arch. 1891, p. 333, No. 9). Dedication at Alexandria (M.A. 14). Soldier (B.G.U. 378).
Legio ii Valentiniana. Stationed at Hermonthis {c. 425} (Not. Dign.).
[*Legio iii Augusta.*] Graffito by a tribune at Thebes {168} (C.I.L. iii. 67). Graffito by a soldier at Thebes {205} (C.I.L. iii. 52).

Legio iii Cyrenaica. Inscription of homage at Pselkis {33} (C.I.G. iii. 5101). Dedication at *Ekfas* {47/8} (C.I.L. iii. 6624). Sent to Jewish war {c. 70} (Tac. Hist. v. 1). Graffito by a soldier at Thebes {80/1} (C.I.L. iii. 34). Tombstone of soldier at Alexandria {80} (C.I.L. iii. 6603). Graffito at *Gebel-et-Ter* {under Domitian} (R.E.G. ii. p. 174 ff.). A soldier {95} (Pap. B.M. 142). In winter quarters {99 100 or 102/3} (B.G.U. 140).

[Undated.] Dedication by a centurion at Ptolemais (M.G. 301). Tombstones at Alexandria (C.I.L. iii. 6599, 6602, 6607). Graffito opposite *Girgeh* (R.E.G. i. p. 311).

Legio iii Diocletiana. Stationed at "Andros," "Præsentia," Ombos, and Thebes {c. 425} (Not. Dign.).

Legio iii Gallica. Statue dedicated by centurion at Alexandria {c. 105} (Inscr. M.A., Botti's Catalogue, p. 149). Dedication by priests at Koptos {315} (Rec. Trav. xvi. p. 44). Similar dedication from Syene {323} (Inscr. App. iii. 8).

Legio iv Flavia. Stationed at Oxyrhynchos {295} (G.O.P. i. 43).

Legio v Macedonica. Stationed at Memphis {c. 425} (Not. Dign.).

Legio vii Claudia Stationed at Oxyrhynchos {295} (G.O.P. i. 43).

Legio xi Claudia. Stationed at Oxyrhynchos {295} (G.O.P. i. 43).

[*Legio xii Fulminata.*] Graffito by a primipilaris at Thebes {65} (C.I.L. iii. 30). A veteran in Fayum {138} (B.G.U. 272).

Legio xiii Gemina. Stationed at Babylon {c. 425} (Not. Dign.).

[*Legio xv Apollinaris.*] A centurion in charge of works at Mons Claudianus {under Trajan} (C.I.L. iii. 25).

Legio xxii Deiotariana. A soldier {15} (Pap. B.M. 256R). Dedication at *Ekfas* {47/8} (C.I.L. iii. 6624). Graffito at Thebes {65} (C.I.L. iii. 30). Withdrawn for Jewish war {c. 70} (Tac. Hist. v. 1). Graffito at Thebes {84} (C.I.L. iii. 36. Reference to winter quarters {99 100 or 102/3} (B.G.U. 140). Graffiti at Thebes {147, 189} (C.I.G. iii. 4766, 4768).

[Undated.] Tombstones at Alexandria (C.I.L. iii. 6598, 6600, 6602, 6606, 6608, 6623, 6623 a; Rev. Arch. 1891, p. 333, No. 12). Graffiti at Thebes (C.I.L. iii. 56, 57, 58, 60). A soldier (B.G.U. 455).

Equites Stablesiani. Stationed at Pelusium {c. 425} (Not. Dign.).

Equites Saraceni Thamudeni. Stationed at Scenæ Veteranorum {c. 425} (Not. Dign.).

Equites Sagittarii indigenæ. Stationed at Tentyra, Koptos, Diospolis, Latopolis, and Maximianopolis {c. 425} (Not. Dign.).

Equites scutarii. Stationed at Hermopolis {c. 425} (Not. Dign.).

Equites felices Honoriani. Stationed at Asphynis {c. 425} (Not. Dign.).
Equites Mauri scutarii. Stationed at Lykopolis {c. 425} (Not. Dign.).
Equites cataphractarii. A vexillatio at Arsinoe {359} (B.G.U. 316).
Milites miliarenses. Stationed at Syene {c. 425} (Not. Dign.).
Ala i Abasgorum. Stationed at Hibis, in the Great Oasis {c. 425} (Not. Dign.).
Ala i Aegyptiorum. Stationed at Selle {c. 425} (Not. Dign.).
Ala ii Aegyptiorum. Stationed at Tacosiris {c. 425} (Not. Dign.).
Ala ii Ulpia Afrorum. Soldiers {159} (B.G.U. 142). {177} (B.G.U. 241). Stationed at Thaubastis {c. 425} (Not. Dign.).
Ala Apriana. Discharge of veterans {83} (C.I.L. iii. Const. Vet. xv.). A soldier {120} (B.G.U. 69). Graffito by prefect at Thebes {170} (C.I.L. iii. 49). Stationed at Hipponon {c. 425} (Not. Dign.). Inscription at Syene { ? } (C.I.L. iii. 6626).
Ala ii Arabum. Stationed at Terenuthis {425} (Not. Dign.).
Ala Arcadiana. [No station.] {c. 425} (Not. Dign.).
Ala ii Armeniorum. Stationed in Lesser Oasis {c. 425} (Not. Dign.).
Ala ii Assyriorum. Stationed at "Sosteos" {c. 425} (Not. Dign.).
Ala Augusta. Discharge of veterans {83} (C.I.L. iii. Const. Vet. xv.).
Ala iv Britonum. Stationed at Isium {c. 425} (Not. Dign.).
Ala i Jovia cataphractariorum. Stationed at Pampanis {c. 425} (Not. Dign.).
Ala Commagenorum. Discharge of veterans {83} (C.I.L. iii. Const. Vet. xv.). Graffito at Talmis {? 1st cent.} (C.I.G. iii. 5057).
Ala iii dromedariorum. Stationed at Maximianopolis {c. 425} (Not. Dign.).
Ala ii Herculia dromedariorum. Stationed at "Psinaula" {c. 425} (Not. Dign.).
Ala i Valeria dromedariorum. Stationed at "Prectis" {c. 425} (Not. Dign.).
Ala i Francorum. Stationed at Contra Apollinopolis {c. 425} (Not. Dign.).
Ala Gallica. Soldiers {191} (G.G.P. 1, 48; G.G.P. 2, 51).
Ala Antoniana Gallica. A sesquiplicarius {217} (B.G.U. 614).
Ala Veterana Gallica. Dedications at Alexandria {191} (C.I.L. iii. 14, 15). Stationed at Rhinocorura {c. 425} (Not. Dign.).
Ala Germanorum. Stationed at Pesela {c. 425} (Not. Dign.).
Ala i Herculia. Stationed at Scenae extra Gerrhas {c. 425} (Not. Dign.).
Ala i Iberorum. Stationed at Thmuis {c. 425} (Not. Dign.).

THE ROMAN GARRISON IN EGYPT 173

Ala Maurorum. Decurion in charge of quarries at Philæ {c. 203} (C.I.L. 370).
Ala Neptunia. Stationed at Chenoboskion {c. 425} (Not. Dign.).
Ala viii Palmyrenorum. Stationed at Phœnikon {c. 425} (Not. Dign.).
Ala v Prælectorum. Stationed at Dionysias {c. 425} (Not. Dign.).
Ala i Quadorum. Stationed in Lesser Oasis {c. 425} (Not. Dign.).
Ala v Rætorum. Stationed at Scenæ Veteranorum {c. 425} (Not. Dign.).
Ala vii Sarmatarum. Stationed at Scenæ Mandrorum {c. 425} (Not. Dign.).
Ala i Thracum Mauretana. A soldier {154/5} (B.G.U. 26). A decurion transferred into coh. i Aug. Præt. Lusitan. {156} (B.G.U. 696). Dedication at Alexandria {199} (C.I.L. iii. 14). Camp at *Qantarah* {288} (Inscr. E.E.F. Tanis, ii. p. 98).
Ala i Tingitana. Stationed at Thimanepsis {c. 425} (Not. Dign.).
Ala viii Vandalorum. Stationed at Neapolis {c. 425} (Not. Dign.).
Ala Vocontiorum. At Koptos {134} (B.G.U. 114). Dedication by duplicarius, opposite Koptos {164} (Inscr. in G.G.P. ii. p. 85). Graffito at *Gebel-et-Toukh* { ? } (R.E.G. i. p. 311, No. 6). A soldier {2/3c.} (B.G.U. 4).
Ala vii Herculia voluntaria. Stationed at Contra Latopolis {c. 425} (Not. Dign.).
Ala viii . Stationed at Abydos {c. 425} (Not. Dign.).
Ala Theodosiana. [No station] {c. 425} (Not. Dign.).
Cohors ix Alamannorum. Stationed at Burgus Severi {c. 425} (Not. Dign.).
Cohors i Apamæorum. A soldier {144} (B.G.U. 729). A soldier {145} (Pap. B.M. 178). A soldier {Antoninus} (B.G.U. 462). A libellarius {2nd cent.} (B.G.U. 243). Stationed at Silsilis {c. 425} (Not. Dign.).
Cohors ii Asturum. Stationed at Busiris {c. 425} (Not. Dign.).
Cohors xi Chamavorum. Stationed at Panopolis {c. 425} (Not. Dign.).
Cohors i Flavia Cilicum. Discharge of veterans {83} (C.I.L. iii. Const. Vet. xv.). A soldier exchanged into coh. i Aug. Præt. Lusitanorum {156} (B.G.U. 696).
Cohors i Flavia Cilicum equitata. Tribune at Mons Claudianus {118} (C.I.G. 4713), Prefect (C.I.R. 18). Built basilica at Syene {c. 140} (C.I.L. iii. 6625). Erected altar at Syene {c. 140} (Inscr. P.S.B.A. xviii. p. 107, No. 2). Erected altar at Syene {162} (Inscr. P.S.B.A. xviii. p. 107, No. 3) [probably = coh. i equitata {154/5} (B.G.U. 26) and coh. i Flavia {158} (Inscr. App. iii. 10)].

Cohors i Damascenorum. Prefect {135} (B.G.U. 73, 136).
Cohors i Epireorum. Stationed at Castra Judaeorum {c. 425} (Not. Dign.).
Cohors vii Francorum. Stationed at Diospolis {c. 425} (Not. Dign.).
Cohors iii Galatarum. Stationed at Cephro {c. 425} (Not. Dign.).
Cohors vii Hyrcanorum. Graffito by prefect at Thebes { ? } (C.I.L. iii. 59).
Cohors i Hispanorum. Discharge of veterans {83} (C.I.L. iii. Const. Vet. xv.).
Cohors i Hispanorum equitata. Erected altar at Syene {98} (Inscr. P.S.B.A. xviii. p. 107, No. 1).
Cohors ii Hispanorum. Graffiti at Talmis {84} (C.I.G. iii. 5043, 5044, 5045, 5046, 5047). Stationed at Oxyrhynchos {295} (G.O.P. i. 43).
Cohors ii Hispanorum equitata. Graffito by prefect at Thebes {195} (C.I.L. iii. 50).
Cohors Ityraeorum. Erected altar at Syene {39} (Inscr. P.S.B.A. xviii. p. 107, No. 1).
Cohors ii Ityraeorum. Discharge of veterans {83} (C.I.L. iii. Const. Vet. xv.). Graffito at Pselkis {136} (C.I.G. iii. 5081). Graffito at Talmis {147} (C.I.G. iii. 5050). Stationed at Aiy {c. 425} (Not. Dign). Graffito at Hiera Sykaminos {probably 1st or 2nd cent.} (C.I.G. iii. 5110).
Cohors ii Ityraeorum equitata. Erected altar at Syene {98} (Inscr. P.S.B.A. xviii. p. 107, No. 1).
Cohors iii Ityraeorum. Discharge of veterans {83} (C.I.L. iii. Const. Vet. xv.). Graffito at *Gebel-et-Toukh* { ? } (R.E.G. i. p. 311, No. 7).
Cohors iv Juthungorum. Stationed at Aphroditopolis {c. 425} (Not. Dign.).
Cohors i Augusta Praetoria Lusitanorum. Camp at Hierakonpolis {288} (C.I.L. iii. 22). Stationed at same place {c. 425} (Not. Dign.).
Cohors i Augusta Praetoria Lusitanorum equitata. In winter quarters at Contrapollonopolis major: strength, 6 centurions, 3 decurions, 114 horse, 19 camel-riders, 363 foot {156} (B.G.U. 696).
Cohors iv Numidorum. Stationed at Narmunthis {c. 425} (Not. Dign.).
Cohors i (Augusta) Pannoniorum. Discharge of veterans {c. 83} (C.I.L. iii. Const. Vet. xv.). Stationed at Thmuis {c. 425} (Not. Dign.).
Cohors scutata civium Romanorum. A soldier {143/4} (B.G.U. 741). Stationed at Muthis {c. 425} (Not. Dign.). Tombstone at Alexandria { ? } (C.I.L. iii. 6610).
Cohors i Sagittariorum. Stationed at "Naisiu" {c. 425} (Not. Dign.).
Cohors v Syenensium. Stationed at Syene {c. 425} (Not. Dign.).

Cohors vi Sugambrorum. Stationed at Castra Lapidariorum {c. 425} (Not. Dign.).
Cohors i Thebæorum. Discharge of veterans {83} (C.I.L. iii. Const. Vet. xv.). Soldier at Cortis {116} (Rivista Egiziana, 1894, p. 529). Graffiti at Talmis { ? } (C.I.G. iii. 5052, 5053, 5054, 5055), at Hiera Sycaminos { ? } (C.I.G. iii. 5117).
Cohors i Thebæorum equitata. Erected altar at Syene {98} (Inscr. P.S.B.A. xviii. p. 107, No. 1).
Cohors ii Thebæorum. Discharge of veterans {83} (C.I.L. iii. Const. Vet. xv.). Graffito of prefect at Thebes {95} (C.I.L. iii. 37).
Cohors i Felix Theodosiana. Stationed at Elephantine {c. 425} (Not. Dign.).
Cohors i Flavia Thracum. Graffito at *Wady Hammamat* {Domitian} (Letr. Rech. 427).
Cohors ii Thracum. Ostrakon at Thebes {c. 200} (R.E. ii. p. 346). Stationed at Muson {c. 425} (Not. Dign.).
Cohors ix Tzanorum. Stationed at "Nitnu" {c. 425} (Not. Dign.).
Numerus Transtigritanorum. A soldier at Arsinoe {498} (B.M. Pap. 113, 5a).
Numerus Auxiliariorum Constantianorum. A soldier {359} (B.G.U. 316).
Numerus Hermonthitorum {525} (B.G.U. 673).
Scythi Justiniani. Stationed at Hermopolis Magna {6th cent.} (G.G.P. 2, 95).
Bucolia. At Scenæ Mandræ {2nd/3rd cent.} (B.G.U. 625).
Sagittarii Hadriani Palmyreni Antoniniani. A vexillarius at Koptos {216} (Petrie, Koptos, vi. 5).
Classis Alexandrina. Soldier {1st cent.} (B.G.U. 455). A soldier {143/4} (B.G.U. 741). Prefect {159} (B.G.U. 142, 143).
Classis prætoria Misenarum. Discharge of veterans {143} (B.G.U. 113). Veterans {176, 189} (B.G.U. 327, 326).
Classis Syriaca. Discharge of veterans {143, 148} (B.G.U. 113, 265).

APPENDIX II

PREFECTS OF EGYPT

C. CORNELIUS GALLUS .	B.C. 30 (Strabo, xvii. 1) (Dio C. li. 9, lii. 23). B.C. 29, Apl. 15 (Inscr. Sitzungsb. d. k. Preuss. Akad. 1896, p. 469).
C. Petronius .	B.C. 26 (Strabo, xvii. 1) (Dio C. liv. 5).
Ælius Gallus .	B.C. 25 (Strabo, xvi. 3, xvii. 1) (Dio C. liii. 29).
C. Petronius, *it*. [*a*]	B.C. 24 (Strabo, xvii. 1).
P. Rubrius Barbarus .	B.C. 13 (Inscr. Bull. dell' Ist. 1866, p. 44). B.C. 12 (C.I.L. iii. 6588).
C. Turranius	B.C. 7 (C.I.G. iii. 4923). ? (Pap. B.M. 354).
P. Octavius .	A.D. 1, Sept. 23 (C.I.G. iii. 4715). 3, Feb. 25 (Inscr. Brugsch Geogr. i. 136).
'M. Maximus	[under Augustus] (Philo, adv. Flacc. 1).
Aquila .	[under Augustus] (Josephus, Ant. Jud. xix. 5. 2).
Vitrasius Pollio	16/17 (C.I.G. 4963).
C. Galerius .	21 (C.I.G. 4711). ? (Plin. N.H. xix. 3).
Vitrasius Pollio, *it*.	to *circa* 31 (Seneca, Cons. ad Helv.). (Dio C. lviii. 19).
Ti. Julius Severus .	*circa* 32 (Philo, adv. Flacc. 1) (Dio C. lviii. 19).
A. Avillius Flaccus	32–37 (Philo, adv. Flacc. 1). ? (C.I.G. 4716).
Æmilius Rectus	[under Tiberius] (Suetonius, Tib. 32) (Dio C. lvii. 10).
L. Seius Strabo	[under Tiberius] (Dio C. lvii. 19).

PREFECTS OF EGYPT

Nævius Sertorius Macro [b]	[under Caligula] (Dio C. lix. 10).
C. Vitrasius Pollio	39, Apl. 28 (Inscr. P.S.B.A. xviii. p. 107 = Acad. des Inscr. et B.L. 1896, p. 39). 40/1 (Pap. B.M. 177).
L. Æmilius Re[ctus]	41/2 (Inscr. Bull. corr. hell. 1895, p. 524).
C. Julius Postumus	*circa* 47 (C.I.G. iii. 4957).
Cu. Vergilius Capito	47/8 (C.I.L. iii. 6024). 49, Feb. 1 (C.I.G. iii. 4956). 49/50 (G.O.P. i. 38). 52, Apl. 24 (G.O.P. i. 39).
L. Lusius	54, Apl. 5 (Inscr. App. iii. 5).
M. Metius Modestus	[under Claudius] (Suidas, *s.v.* 'Επαφρόδιτος)
Ti. Claudius Balbillus	56 (Tacitus, Ann. xiii. 22). ? (C.I.G. iii. 4699). ? (Plin. N.H. xix. 3). ? (C.I.G. iii. 4957).
L. Julius Vestinus	59/60 (Inscr. R.E.G. vii. p. 284). 60, 1 (Inscr. Petrie, Illahun, p. 32). 61/2 (B.G.U. 112). ? (C.I.G. iii. 4957).
Cæcina Tuscus	67 (Dio C. lxiii. 18) (Tac. Ann. xiii. 20). (Tac. Hist. iii. 38).
Ti. Julius Alexander	68, Sept. 28 (C.I.G. iii. 4957). 69, July 1 (Tac. Hist. i. 11, ii. 79) (Sueton. Vesp. 6) (Josephus, Bell. Jud. ii. 18).
Ti. Julius Lupus	71 (Josephus, Bell. Jud. vii. 10). ? (Plin. N.H. xix. 11).
Paulinus	[succeeded Lupus] (Josephus, Bell. Jud. vii. 10).
Stettius Africanus	82, Feb. 2 (C.I.L. iii. 35).
C. Septimus Vegetus	86 (C.I.L. iii. 2, p. 856). 88, Feb. 26 (Inscr. B.C.H. 1896, p. 167). ? (Suet. Dom. 4).
Mettius Rufus [c]	90, Apl. 10 (G.O.P. i. 72). 90, May 10 (Inscr. Petrie, Koptos, c. vi. No. 4). 90 (Inscr. Petrie, Koptos, c. vi. No. 3). ? (Inscr. R.E.G. iv. p. 46, No. v. 1). ? (Suetonius, Domitian, 4).
T. Petronius Secundus	95, March 14 (C.I.L. iii. 37).
C. Pompeius Planta	98 (Inscr. P.S.B.A. xviii. p. 107 = Acad. des Inscr. et B.L. 1896, p. 40) (Plin. Ep. ad Traj. 7, 10). 99, Feb. 26 (B.G.U. 226). ? (Inscr. R.A. 1889, i. p. 70).

V—12

PREFECTS OF EGYPT

C. Vibius Maximus	103, Aug. 29 (Inscr. M.A. 70). 104, Feb. 16 (C.I.L. iii. 38). ?(B.G.U. 329).
C. Minicius Italus [d]	105 (C.I.L. v. 875). ?(Inscr. M.A. Botti's Catalogue, p. 149).
C. Sulpicius Similis	108/9 (C.I.L. iii. 24). 109, May 10 (C.I.G. iii. 4713 e). 109, May 14 (C.I.G. iii. 4714). ?(B.G.U. 140).
M. Rutilius Lupus	115/6 (Eusebius, Hist. Eccl. iv. 2). 116, May 24 (C.I.G. iii. 4948). 117, Jan. 5 (B.G.U. 114). ?(C.I.G. iii. 4843). ?(G.O.P. i. 97). ?(Pap. Bull. dell' Ist. di diritto romano, 1895, p. 155).
Q. Marcius Turbo [e]	117 (Dio C. lxix. 18) (Hist. Aug. Hadrian, 7).
Rhammius Martialis	118, Apl. 23 (C.I.G. iii. 4713).
T. Haterius Nepos	121, Feb. 18 (C.I.L. iii. 39). 122, Apl. 21 (B.G.U. 742). 124, Apl. 13 (C.P.R. 18).
T. Flavius Titianus	126, March 20 (C.I.L. iii. 41). 127, Aug. 20 (G.O.P. i. 34^v). 130/1 (B.G.U. 420). 131, Aug. 2 (B.G.U. 459).
Sex. Petronius Mamertinus	134, Feb. 25 (B.G.U. 114). 134, March 10 (C.I.L. iii. 44). 135, Feb. 11 (B.G.U. 19). ?(C.I.L. iii. 77).
Valerius Eudæmon	[under Hadrian] G.O.P. i. 40.
C. Avidius Heliodorus	139, March 30 (B.G.U. 729). 140, Aug. 12 (C.I.G. iii. 4955). 142, Aug. 26 (Pap. Bull. dell' Ist. di diritto romano, 1895, p. 155). 143 (B.G.U. 113) (B.G.U. 256). ?(C.I.L. iii. 6025). ?(Inscr. P.S.B.A. xviii. p. 107 = Acad. des Inscr. et B.L. 1896, p. 41).
M. Petronius Honoratus	148, Jan. 12 (B.G.U. 265). ?(Pap. B.M. 358).
L. Munatius Felix	150 (Justin Martyr, Apol.). ?(Inscr. R.A. 1894, p. 402). ?(C.I.G. iii. 4863). ?(B.G.U. 161). ?(B.G.U. 613). ?(Pap. B.M. 358).
M. Sempronius Liberalis [f]	154, Aug. 29 (B.G.U. 372). 155 (B.G.U. 26). 156, Jan. 1 (B.G.U. 696).
[Vol]usius Mæcianus [g]	about 159 (B.G.U. 613).

PREFECTS OF EGYPT

L. Valerius Proculus . . [under Antoninus] (C.I.L. ii. 1970) (B.G.U. 288).

M. Annius Syriacus 162/3 (B.G.U. 198) (G.G.P. ii. 56). 163, Jan. (Pap. B.M. 328). ?(Inscr. P.S.B.A. xviii. p. 107).
Domitius Honoratus . . 165, Jan. 6 (G.O.P. i. 628).
T. Flavius Titianus . . 166, May 10 (C.I.G. iii. 4701).
M. Bassæus Rufus [*h*] . . *c*. 167 (C.I.L. vi. 1599).
C. Calvisius Statianus . . 175, Oct. 26 (M.A. 101). *c*. 176 (Dio C. lxxi. 28).
T. Pactumeius Magnus between 177 and 180 (C.I.G. iii. 4704) (B.G.U. 525).
Flavius Priscus . . . 181 (B.G.U. 12).
P. Mænius Flavianus . . between 180 and 183 (C.I.G. iii. 4683).

M. Aurelius Papirius Dionysius [under Commodus] (Dio C. lxxii. 14).

L. Mantennius Sabinus . 193, March 6 (B.G.U. 646). 194, April 21 (Borghesi, Œuvres, iv. 441).
M. Ulpius Primianus . . 194/5 (C.I.G. iii. 4863). 196, Feb. 24 (C.I.L. iii. 51).
Æmilius Saturninus [*i*] . . 197, July 11 (B.G.U. 15 II).
Mæcius Lætus . . . 201/2 (Euseb. H. E. vi. 2).
Subatianus Aquila . . 201/2 (B.G.U. 484). 204 (Euseb. H. E. vi. 3). 207, Oct. 11 (Pap. Gen. 16). ?(C.I.L. iii. 75).
Septimius Heracleitus . . 215, March 16 (B.G.U. 362).
Valerius Datus [*k*] 216, June 5 (B.G.U. 159). 217, Feb. 17 (B.G.U. 614). 216/7 (B.G.U. 266).
Basilianus . . . . 217/8 (Dio C. lxxviii. 35).
Geminius Chrestus . . 219, Aug. 13 (Inscr. App. iii. 13). 220/1 (G.G.P. i. 49).
Mævius Honorianus . . 232, June (C.I.G. iii. 4705).

—idinius Julianus . . . [under Severus Alexander] G.O.P. i. 35.
Epagathus . . . . [under Severus Alexander] (Dio C. lxxx. 2).

Appius Sabinus . . . 250, July 17 (C.P.R. i. 20). ?(Euseb. H. E. vi. 40, vii. 11).

Æmilianus . . . . [under Gallienus] (Hist. Aug. Trig. Tyr.) (Euseb. H. E. vii. 11).

PREFECTS OF EGYPT

Firmus .	[under Aurelian?] (Hist. Aug. Firmus, 3).
Celerinus [?] .	[under Carus] (Claudian, Epithal. Pall. 72).
Pompeius [*m*]	*c.* 302 (C.I.G. iii. 4681).
Culcianus	303, Feb. 28 (G.O.P. i. 71). ? (Euseb. H.E. ix. 11).
Satrius Arrianus .	307 (G.G.P. ii. 78).
Sabinianus .	323, Aug. 17 (G.O.P. i. 60).
Fl. Antonius Theodorus	338, March 28 (G.O.P. i. 67).
Longinianus .	354, Feb. 26 (Cod. Theod. xvi. 2. 11).
Parnasius .	*c.* 357 (Amm. Marc. xix. 12).
Pomponius Metrodorus	357, July 2 (G.O.P. i. 66).
Artemius	360 (Amm. Marc. xxii. 11).
Ecdicius	362, Dec. 2 (Cod. Theod. xv. 1. 8). *c.* 362 (Julian, Ep. ad Ecd.).
Tatianus	365/8 (Chron. Putean.). 367, May 10 (Cod. Theod. xii. 18. 1).
Publius .	369/70 (Chron. Put.).
Tatianus, *il.* .	371/3 (Chron. Put.). ? (John of Nikiou, 82).
Ælius Palladius .	374 (Chron. Put.) (Inscr. App. iii. 15). ? (Theod. H.E. iv. 19).
Tatianus *tert.*	375 (Chron. Put.).
Hadrianus .	376/7 (Chron. Put.).
Julianus	380, March 17 (Cod. Theod. xii. 1. 80). 380 (Chron. Put.). ? (C.I.G. iii. 5071).
Paulinus	380 (Chron. Put.).
Bassianus	381 (Chron. Put.).
Palladius	382, May 14 (Cod. Theod. viii. 5. 37). 382 (Chron. Put.).
Hypatius	383, May 8 (Cod. Theod. xi. 36. 27). 382/3 (Chron. Put.).
Antoninus	383/4 (Chron. Put.).
Florentius	384, Dec. 18 (Cod. Theod. ix. 33. 1). 384/5 (Chron. Put.).
Paulinus, *il.* .	385, July 25 (Cod. Theod. xi. 39. 10). 385, Nov. 30 (Cod. Theod. xii. 6. 22).
Florentius, *il.*	386, Feb. 17 (Cod. Theod. i. 14. 1). 386, May 17 (Cod. Theod. xii. 1. 112).
Erythrius	388, Apl. 30 (Cod. Theod. ix. 11. 1).
Alexander	390, Feb. 18 (Cod. Theod. xiii. 5. 18).
Evagrius	391, June 16 (Cod. Theod. xvi. 10. 11). ? (Soz. H.E. vii. 15).

PREFECTS OF EGYPT 181

Potamius	392, March 5 (Cod. Theod. i. 20. 2).
Hypatius, *it.* . . .	392, Apl. 9 (Cod. Theod. xi. 36. 31).
Potamius, *it.* . .	392, June 22 (Cod. Theod. xii. 1. 126). 392, July 18 (Cod. Theod. xvi. 4. 3). 392, July 30 (Cod. Theod. viii. 5. 51).
Cl. Septimius Eutropius	between 384 and 392 (Inscr. App. iii. 16)..
Charmosynus . . .	395 (Theophanes, Chronogr. 83).
Gennadius . . .	396, Feb. 5 (Cod. Theod. xiv. 27. 1).
Remigius . .	396, March 30 (Cod. Theod. iii. 1. 7).
Archelaus .	397, June 17 (Cod. Theod. ix. 45. 2). 397, Nov. 26 (Cod. Theod. ii. 1. 9).
Orestes .	415 (Socr. H.E. vii. 13).
Cleopater	435, Jan. 29 (Cod. Theod. vi. 28. 8).
Florus . .	453 (Priscus, Frag. 22).
Eustathius .	501 (Eutych. ii. 132).
Theodosius .	[under Anastasius](John of Nikiou, 89) (Malala, xvi. 401).

(MILITARY PREFECTS, acting with Patriarch as Civil Prefect.)

Johannes	[under Maurice] (John of Nikiou, 97).
Paulus	[under Maurice] (John of Nikiou, 97).
Johannes, *it.* .	[under Maurice] (John of Nikiou, 97).
Menas . . .	[under Maurice] (John of Nikiou, 97) Paulus, Diac. xvii.).
Theodorus . .	639 (John of Nikiou, 111).

NOTES.

[*a*] The grounds for supposing C. Petronius to have been twice prefect are set forth in Note X. App. IV.

[*b*] Macro was only nominated as prefect, and never took office.

[*c*] The Oxyrhynchos papyrus shows that D. G. Hogarth was right in restoring the name of Mettius Rufus in the erasures of the two Koptos inscriptions published in Petrie, Koptos, c. vi.

[*d*] The reason given by P. Meyer (Hermes, xxxii. p. 214) for supposing an otherwise unknown Dioscurus to have been prefect of Egypt in 105/6—that his name appears with that of an architect on a stone pedestal, apparently as the person in charge of the quarry from which the stone was taken—is hardly worth discussion.

[*e*] Marcius Turbo was titular prefect of Egypt only. He was placed in this position that he might enjoy the special privileges it accorded, while he held command in Dacia.

[*f*] P. Meyer (Hermes, xxxii. p. 224) has shown good reasons for supposing Sempronius Liberalis to have been the prefect mentioned by Malala (Chronogr. xi. 367) as killed by the mob in the reign of Antoninus.

[*g*] Volusius Maecianus is dated by Pap. B.M. 376, compared with B.G.U. 613: see Kenyon, Catalogue of Greek Papyri, ii. p. 77. A. Stein (Arch. epigr. Mittheilungen aus Oesterreich, 1896, p. 151, and Hermes, xxxii. p. 663) had already arrived at virtually the same date.

[*h*] As to the dating of Bassaeus Rufus, see Meyer (Hermes, xxxii. p. 226).

[*i*] P. Meyer (Hermes, xxxii. p. 483) is probably right in supposing that the rescript B.G.U. 15 II. was issued by Saturninus as prefect.

[*k*] Flavius Titianus was, according to Dio Cassius (lxxvii. 21), a procurator only; and it is unnecessary to suppose him to have been prefect, though this view has been generally taken. See Note XV. App. IV.

[*l*] A. Stein (Hermes, xxxii. p. 65) is here followed in placing Celerinus as prefect under Carus.

[*m*] J. P. Mahaffy (Athenæum, Feb. 27, 1897, and Cosmopolis, April 1897) reads the name of the prefect on "Pompey's pillar" as Posidius.

APPENDIX III

INSCRIPTIONS IN THE GHIZEH MUSEUM

THE following inscriptions are all in the Ghizeh Museum, and are, for the most part, unpublished. Some have been published, but are in periodicals not readily accessible: I have therefore added them here. The readings given are from my own copies:—

1.

ΎΠΕΡ ΚΑΙΓΑΡΟΓΑΥΤΟΚΡΑ

ΤΟΡΟΓΘΕΟΥΕΚ ΘΕΟΥ Η ΟΙΚΟΔΟΜΗ

ΤΟΥ ΠΕΡΙΒΟΛΟΥ ΤΩ ΘΕΩΙ ΚΑΙΚΥΡΙ

Ω ΓΟΚΝΩΠΑΙΩΙ ΠΑΡΑΤΩ / ΕΚΝΕΙΛΟΥ

ΠΟΛΕΩΓ ΠΡΟΒΑΤΟΚΤΗΝΟΤΡΟΦΗΝ

ΚΑΙ ΤΩΝ ΓΥΝΑΙΚΩΝ ΚΑΙ ΤΩΝ ΤΕΚΝ

ΩΝ   ΕΥΧΗΝ ς 'ΚΑΙΓΑΡΟΓ ΦΑ.Μ.Κ

Ὑπὲρ Καίσαρος Αὐτοκρά-
τορος θεοῦ ἐκ θεοῦ ἡ οἰκοδομή
τοῦ περιβόλου τῷ θεῷ καὶ κυρί-
ῳ Σοκνοπαίῳ παρὰ τῶ[ν] ἐκ Νειλου-
πόλεως προβατοκτηνοτρόφ{ω}ν
καὶ τῶν γυναικῶν καὶ τῶν τέκν-
ων εὐχὴν (ἔτους) ϛ΄ Καίσαρος Φαμ(ένωθ) κ΄.

A stele from Dîmeh (Soknopaiou Nesos), with a rough relief of a ram-headed figure, representing the

shepherds of Nilopolis, adoring Sebek. Published by F. Krebs in transcript, Zeitschrift für Ægypt. Sprache, xxxi. p. 31. See fig. 87.
Date: 24 B.C., March 16.

2.

(a) ΥΠΕΡΤΙΒΕΡΙΟΥΚΑΙϹΑΡΟϹϹΕΒΑϹΤΟΥ

ΙϹΙΔΙΚΑΙΑΡΠΟΧΡΑΤΗΚΑΙΠΑΝΙΘΕΟΙϹ

ΜΕΓΙϹΤΟΙϹ ΤΟΝΠΕΡΙΒΟΛΟΝΠΑΜΕΝΙϹ

ΠΑΡΘΕΝΙΟΥΚΑΙΠΑΡΘΕΝΙΟϹΥΙΟϹ

ϹΗΤΙΒΕΡΙΟΥ ΚΑΙϹΑΡΟϹϹΕΒΑϹΤΟΥ

(b.) ΕΤΟΥϹΙΒΑΝΤΩΝΙΝΟΥΚΑΙϹΑΡΟϹΤΟΥΚΥΡΙΟΥΔΥΟΤ·ΚΑΘΟΙΚΟ·

ΕΠΙΠΑΝΙϹΚΟΥΠΤΟΛΛΙΔΟϹΠΡΟϹΤΑΤΗΕΙϹΙΔΟϹΘΕΑϹΜΕΓΙϹΤΗϹ

(a) Ὑπὲρ Τιβερίου Καίσαρος Σεβάστου
Ἴσιδι καὶ Ἁρπο{κ}ράτῃ καὶ Πᾶνι Θεοῖς
μεγίστοις τὸν περίβολον Πάμενις
Παρθενίου καὶ Παρθένιος υἱός
(ἔτους) ἡ΄ Τιβερίου Καίσαρος Σεβάστου.

(b) Ἔτους ιβ΄ Ἀντωνίνου Καίσαρος τοῦ Κυρίου δύο τ(ε)ίχ(η) καθ(αιρεθέντα) {ᾠ}κοδομήθη
ἐπὶ Πανίσκου Πτολλίδος προστάτ{ου} Ἴσιδος θεᾶς μεγίστης.

A stele, probably from Qus (Apollinopolis Parva) (to judge by comparison with the next inscription), with adoration by the emperor of Isis and Harpokrates. See fig. 17.

The first inscription was cut in 20/21; the second, squeezed in at the bottom, in 148/9.

3.

ΥΠΕΡΤΙΒΕΡΙΟΥΚΑΙϹΑΡΟϹϹΕΒΑϹΤΟΥ

ϹΗΕΠΕΙΦΙΑ ΚΡΟΝΩΙΘΕΩΙΜΕΓΙϹΤΩΙ

·ΙΡΟϹΠΙΟϹΠΑΜΝΕΩϹΠΡΟϹΤΑΤΗϹΙϹΙΔΟϹ

Ὑπὲρ Τιβερίου Καίσαρος Σεβαστοῦ
(ἔτους) ιη´ Ἐπεὶφ ια´ Κρόνῳ θεῷ μεγίστῳ
Παρθένιος Παμνέως προστάτης Ἴσιδος.

A stele from Qus (Apollinopolis Parva), with adoration by the emperor; below, an inscription in demotic.
Date: 31, July 5.

4.
ᴸΙΑΤΙΒΕΡΙΟΥΚΛΑΥΔΙΟΥΚΑΙΣΑΡΟΣ

ΣΕΒΑΣΤΟΥΓΕΡΜΑΝΙΚΟΥ

ΑΥΤΟΚΡΑΤΟΡΟΣ   ΧΟΙΑΚ Ξ

ΣΤΟΤΟΥΗΤΙΟΣ ΑΡΠΑΗΣΙΟΣ ΑΝΕΘΗΚΕΝ

ΤΟΙΣΔΙΟΣΚΟΡΟΙΣΥΠΕΡΑΥΤΟΥΕΙΑΓΑΘΩ

(ἔτους) ια´ Τιβερίου Κλαυδίου Καίσαρος
Σεβάστου Γερμανικοῦ
Αὐτοκράτορος Χοίακ ς´
Στοτο{ν}ῆτι{ο}ς Ἁρπαήσιος ἀνέθηκεν
τοῖς Διοσκόροις ὑπὲρ αὐτοῦ ἐ{ι̣π}´ ἀγαθᾷ

A stele in form of a pylon, from Dîmeh (Soknopaiou Nesos); the inscription is at the foot.
Date: 50, Dec. 2.

5.
ΛΟΥΣΙΟΣ ///////// ΚΛΑΥΔΙΩΙΛΥΣΑ

ΝΙΑΣΤΡΑΤΗΓΩΙΑΡΣΙΝΟΕΙΤΟΥ

ΧΑΙΡΕΙΝΤΟΥΠΟΓΕΓΡΑΜΜΕΝΟΝ

ΕΚΘΕΜΑΠΡΟΘΕΣΕΝΟΙΣΚΑΘΗΚΕΙ

ΤΟΥΝΟΜΟΥΤΟΠΟΙΣΙΝΑΠΑΝΤΕΣ

ΙΔΩΣΙΤΑΥΠΕΜΟΥΚΕΛΕΥΟΜΕΝΑ

ΕΡΡΩΣΟ

ΛΟΥΚΙΟΣ ΛΟΥΣΙΟΣ ////////// ΛΕΓΕΙ

ΕΠΕΙ ΑΡΣΙΝΟΕΙΤΟΥ ΙΕΡΕΙΣ ΘΕΟΥ

ΣΟΚΝΟΠΑΙΟΥ ΕΝΕΤΥΧΟΝ ΜΟΙ

ΛΕΓΟΝΤΕΣ ΕΙΣ ΓΕΩΡΓΙΑΣ ΑΓΕΣΘΑΙ

ΤΟΥΤΟΥΣ ΜΕΝ ΑΠΟΛΥΩ Ι ΕΑΝ

ΔΕ ΤΙΣ ΕΞΕΛΕΓΧΘΗ ΙΤΑΥΠ ΕΜΟΥ

ΑΠΑΣ ΚΕΚΡΙΜΕΝΑ Η ΠΡΟΣΤΑ

ΧΘΕΝΤΑ ΚΕΙΝ ΗΣΑΣ Η ΒΟΥΛΗΘΕΙΣ

ΑΜΦΙΒΟΛΑ ΠΟΙΗΣΑΙ ΚΑΤΑ ΙΑΝ

Η ΑΡΓΥΡΙΚΩΣ Η ΣΩΜΑΤΙΚΩΣ

ΚΟΛΑΣΘΗΣΕΤΑΙ Ꝉ ΔΙ ΤΙΒΕΡΙΟΥ

ΚΛΑΥΔΙΟΥ ΚΑΙΣΑΡΟΣ ΣΕΒΑΣΤΟΥ

ΓΕΡΜΑΝΙΚΟΥ ΑΥΤΟΚΡΑΤΟΡΟΣ

ΦΑΡΜΟΥΘΙ ι'

Λούσιος [ἔπαρχος] Κλαυδίῳ Λυσανίᾳ στρατηγῷ Ἀρσινοείτου χαίρειν. Τὸ ὑπογεγραμμένον ἔκθεμα πρῦτες ἐν οἶς καθήκει τοῦ νομοῦ τόποις, ἵνα πάντες ἴδωσι τὰ ὑπ' ἐμοῦ κελευόμενα· Ἔρρωσο.
Λούκιος Λούσιος [ἔπαρχος] λέγει· ἔπει Ἀρσινοείτου ἱερεῖς θεοῦ Σοκνοπαίου ἐνέτυχόν μοι λέγοντες εἰς γεωργίας ἄγεσθαι,

INSCRIPTIONS IN THE GHIZEH MUSEUM

τούτους μεν ἀπολύω· ἐὰν
δέ τις ἐξελέγχθη τὰ ὑπ' ἐμοῦ
ἅπαξ κεκριμένα ἢ προστα-
χθέντα κ[ε]ινήσας ἢ βουληθεὶς
ἀμφίβολα ποιῆσαι κατὰ πᾶν,
ἢ ἀργυρικῶς ἢ σωματικῶς
κολασθήσεται. (Ἔτους) ιδ' Τιβερίου
Κλαυδίου Καίσαρος Σεβαστοῦ
Γερμανικοῦ Αὐτοκράτορος,
Φαρμοῦθι ί.

A limestone slab from the Fayum, carefully cut. The word following the name Lusius has been erased in ll. 1 and 8; it was probably a title, and that of ἔπαρχος fits the erasure. The only other official who could have issued such a rescript was the epistrategos, and his title is too long for the lacuna.

Date: 54, April 5.

6.

```
       ϳΟ ΚΡΑΤΟ ΡΟϹ ΤΙΤΟΥ Κ ΑΙϹ...

     ...ΥΕϹΠΑϹΙΑΝΟΥ ϹΕΒΑϹΤΟΥ ΚΑΙ

  ////////////// ΚΑΙϹΑΡΟϹ     ΚΑΙ Τ;

   ΠΑΝΤΟϹΑΥΤΩΝΟΙΚΟΥ    ΤΙΚΛΑ

   ΑΠΟΛΛΙΝΑΡΙΟϹ ΚΥΡΙΝΑ ΔΙΑΦΡΟ

   ΤΟΥ ΠΑΤΡΟϹ · ΤΙ · ΚΛΑΥΔΙΟΥΧΡΗϹΙΜΟΥ

   ΑΠΟΛΛΩΝΙ ΘΕΩΜΕΓΙϹΤΩ ΚΑΙ ΤΟΙϹ
```

Ὑπὲρ Αὐτ]οκράτορος Τίτου Καίσαρο[ς
Οὐεσπασιάνου Σεβάστου καὶ
[Δομιτιάνου] Καίσαρος καὶ το[ῦ
παντὸς αὐτῶν οἴκου Τι(βέριος) Κλα[ύδιος
Ἀπολλινάριος Κυρίνα, διὰ φρο[ντίσ-
του πατρὸς Τι(βερίου) Κλαυδίου Χρησίμου [ἀνέθηκε?
Ἀπόλλωνι θεῷ μεγίστῳ καὶ τοῖς [συννάοις θεοῖς.

A block, broken at edges: provenance not stated. In line 3 the name of Domitian has been erased.

Date, 79/81.

NEXOYBHCΠETENIOYH[...] ANEΘHKENCTHAHNICIΔOCΘEAC

MEΓICTHC ΠAΘYPAC L ΙΒ ΤΡΑΙΑΝΟΥ ΤΟΥ ΚΥΡ.

Νεχούβης Πετελίου . . . . ἀνέθηκεν στήλην Ἴσιδος θεᾶς
μεγίστης Παθυρᾶς (ἔτους) ιβ′ Τραιάνου τοῦ κυρ[ίου.

A stele from Gebelên (Pathyra).
Date: 108/9.

3.

(a.) YTOKPATOPOCKAICAPOC
     ΘIKOYΓEPMANIKOYMEΓICTOY

(b.) MEΓAΛHTYXHIOY   Υ
     ωNANICΛωNTHC   PE
     NEωΘHKAI EKOCMHΘH
     ΠΙΟΥ IKTωAN ΟΥΠΠ ΛΕΓ
     ΓAΛΛIKHC KAI ΔΙΛΛΥΡIK
     NC ΑΓΙΠΤΑΡΙωN ΤΗ ΠΡΟ   Jω
     ΑΤΟC ΑΡΧΙΕΡΕωC ΚΑΙ ΧΑ   ΕΡΕ

ωC ΛΕΓ ΓΑΛΛ ΚΑΙ ΓΑΤΑΝΟΥ Ι[...] ωC ΛΕΓ

ΔΙΛΛΥΡΙΚΗC ΚΑΙ ΑΖΙΖΟΥ ΙΕΡΕωC ΕΝΥ

ΠΑΤΙΑ ΛΙΚΙΝΝΙΟΥ CEB΄ ΤΟ ϛ΄ ΚΑΙ ΛΙΚΙΝΙΟΥ

[...] ΦΚΑΙCΑΡΟC ΤΟ Β ΜΗΝΟC ΛωΟΥ Α

ΚΑΙ Ε[..] ΑΝΝΟΥ [...] ΚΑΙ λ. ΑΡΧΧ = ΚΑΙ

ΠΡΙ

(*a*) Ὑπὲρ Ἀ[ὐ]τοκράτος Καίσαρος [Τραιάνου
. . Παρ[θικοῦ Γερμανικοῦ Μεγίστου [. . .
(*b*) Μεγάλη τύχη τοῦ [. . .] ο[. . . . .
τ]ῶν ἀ[γ]γέλων τη[. . .]ρει[. . . . .
ἐ]νεώθη καὶ ἐκοσμήθη[. . . . .
ἐ]πὶ Οὐικτωρίνου π(ραι)π(οσίτου) λεγ[εώνων
γ´] Γαλλικῆς καὶ α´ Ἰλλυρικ[ῆς . . . . . .
? τῶ]ν σαγιτταρίων τῇ προ[νοίᾳ (? . . . . . .]ω
.]ατος ἀρχιερέως καὶ χα[. . . . . ἱ]ερέ-
ως λεγ(έωνος) γ´ Γαλλ(ικῆς) καὶ Γατάνου ἱ[ερέ]ως λεγ(έωνος)
α´ Ἰλλυρικῆς καὶ Ἀζίζου ἱερέως, ἐν ὑ-
πατίᾳ Λικιννίου Σε[β(άστου) τὸ ϛ´ καὶ Λικιν{ν}ίου
. . . Καίσαρος τὸ β´, μῆνος Λώου α´·
καὶ ἐ[πὶ -]αννοι[. . .]καὶ [. . .] ἀρχ(ιερέων) καὶ
. . . .]πρ[. . . . .

A block from Assuan (Syene), originally part of an architrave; subsequently turned over and re-used.

With the second inscription should be compared the inscription from Koptos published in Recueil de Travaux, xvi. 44, No. xcv., which was set up for the safety of the same legions iii Gallica and i Illyrica—under the command of Victorinus.

Date: original inscription, 116/7; second, 323.

4.

ΥΠΕΡΤΗΣΑΥΤΟΚΡΑΤΟΡΟΣΚΑΙΣΑΡΟΣΤΙΤΟΥ

ΑΙΛΙΟΥΑΔΡΙΑΝΟΥΑΝΤΩΝΙΝΟΥΣΕΥΑΣΤΟΥ

ΕΥΣΕΒΟΥΣΤΥΧΗΣΑΡΠΟΧΡΑΤΗΙΘΕΩΙ

ΜΕΓΙΣΤΩΙ ΤΕΙΧΗ ΤΠΕΡΙΒΟΛΟΥΠΑΛΑΙΩ

ΘΕΝΤΑΚΑΘΗΡΕΘΗΚΑΙΟΙΚΟΔΟΜΗΘΗ

ΕΠΙΠΑΝΙΣΚΟΥΠΤΟΛΛΙΔΟΣΠΡΟΣΤΑΤΟΥΙΣΙΔ

ΘΕΑΣΜΕΓΙΣΤΗΣ   ΕΤΟΥΣΙΒΑΝΤΩΝΙΝ

ΚΑΙΣΑΡΟΣΤΟΥΚΥΡΙΟΥΦΑΜΕΝΩΘΙ Κ

Ὑπὲρ τῆς Αὐτοκράτορος Καίσαρος Τίτου
Αἰλίου Ἀδριανοῦ Ἀντωνίνου Σε[β]άστου.

Εὐσεβοῦς Τύχης Ἁρπο{κ}ράτῃ θεῷ
μεγίστῳ τείχη τοῦ περιβόλου παλαιω-
θέντα καθῃρέθη καὶ {ᾠ}κοδομήθη
ἐπὶ Πανίσκου Πτολλιδος προστάτου ᾿Ἰσιδ[ος
θεᾶς μεγίστης· ἔτους ιβ´ Ἀντωνίν[ου
Καίσαρος τοῦ κυρίου Φαρμοῦθι κ[?

A stele, probably from Qus (Apollinopolis Parva).
Compare Nos. 2, 3, and 11.
Date: 149, April 15 (?).

10

ΘΕΑΙΜΕΓΙΣΤΗΙΙΣΙΔΙΠΛΟΥΣΙΑ

ΤΙΒ ΙΟΥΛΙΟΣ ΑΛΕΞΑΝΔΡΟΣ

ΓΕΝΑΜΕΝΟΣ ΕΠΑΡΧΟΣ ΣΠΕΙΡΗΣ Α

ΦΛΑΟΥΙΑΣΤΩΝΑΓΟΡΑΝΟΜΗΚΟΤΩΝ

ΟΕΠΙΤΗΣΕΥΘΥΝΙΑΣ ΤΟΥ ΒΓΡΑΜΜΑΤΟΣ

ΤΟΝΑΝΔΡΙΑΝΤΑΣΥΝΤΗΙΒΑΣΕΙΑΝΕΘΗΚΕ

L ΚΑ ΑΥΤΟΚΡΑΤΟΡΟΣΚΑΙΣΑΡΟΣΤΙΤΟΥΑΙΛΙΟΥ

ΑΔΡΙΑΝΟΥΑΝΤΩΝΕΙΝΟΥΣΕΒΑΣΤΟΥΕΥΣΕΒΟΥΣ

ΜΕΣΟΡΗ ΕΠΑΓΟΜΕΝΩΝ Γ

Θεᾷ μεγίστῃ Ἴσιδι Πλουσίᾳ
Τιβ(έριος) Ἰούλιος Ἀλέξανδρος,
γενάμενος ἔπαρχος σπείρης α´
Φλαουίας, τῶν ἀγορανομηκότων,
ὁ ἐπὶ τῆς εὐθ{η}νίας τοῦ β´ γράμματος,
τὸν ἀνδριάντα σὺν τῇ βάσει ἀνέθηκε
(ἔτους κα´ Αὐτοκράτορος Καίσαρος Τίτου Αἰλίου
Ἀδριάνου Ἀντων{ε}ίνου Σεβάστου Εὐσεβοῦς
Μεσόρη ἐπαγομένων γ´.

Base of a statue, from Alexandria. Published by
Néroutsos Bey, Bulletino dell' Instituto Egiziano,
xii. p. 77.
Date: 158, Aug. 26.

11

ΑΥΤΟΚΡΑΤΟΡΟΣ ΚΑΙΣΑΡΟΣ ΤΙ

ΑΙΛΙΟΥΑΔΡΙΑΝΟΥΑΝΤΩΝΙΝΟΥ

ϹΕΒΑϹΤΟΥ ΕΥϹΕΒΟΥϹΕΤΟΥϹ

ΑΘΥΡΚᾹ   ΕΠΙ ΠΑΝΙϹΚΟΥ

ΠΟΛΛΙΔΟϹ Π   ΑΤΟΥΙϹΙΔ

ΘΕΑϹ   ΤΟΚΚ

Αὐτοκράτορος Καίσαρος Τί[του
Αἰλίου Ἀδριάνου Ἀντωνίνου
Σεβάστου Εὐσεβοῦς ἔτους[. .
Ἄθυρ κα΄. ἐπὶ Πανίσκου
Π{τ}όλλιδος π[ροστ]άτου Ἰσιδ[ος
θεᾶς [μεγίστης καὶ Ἁρ]ποκ{ρ}ά[του
. . . .

Stele, probably from Qus (Apollinopolis Parva), with bas-relief of emperor adoring Isis. Compare Nos. 2, 3, and 9.

Date: Nov. 17, in same year of reign of Antoninus Pius.

12

ΥΤΟΚΡΑΤΟΡΟϹ ΜΑΡΚΟΥ ΑΥΡΗΛΙΟΥϹΕΟΥΗΡΟΥ

ΝΤΩΝΙΝΟΥΕΥΤΥΧΟΥϹ ΕΥϹΕΒΟΥϹ ϹΕΒΑϹΤΟΥ

ΑΙΟΥΛΙΑϹΔΟΜΝΗϹϹΕΒΑϹΤΗϹΜΗΤΡΟϹΑΝΕΙΚΗΤΩΝ

ΤΡΑΤΟΠΕΔΩΝϹΕΡΗΝΟϹΑΛΕΞΑΝΔΡΟΥ ΠΑΝΤΑΡΧΗϹΑϹ

ΗϹΟΜΒΕΙΤΩΝΠΟΛΕΩϹΕΥϹΕΒΕΙΑϹΧΑΡΙΝΑΝΕΘΗΚΕΝ

ΑΓΑΘΩΙ ΕΤΕΙ ΚΒ = ΦΑΡΜΟΥΘΙ ΕΝΑΤΗ

Α]ὐτοκράτορος Μάρκου Αὐρηλίου Σεουήρου
Ἀ]ντωνίνου Εὐτυχοῦς Εὐσεβοῦς Σεβάστου

κ]αὶ Ἰουλίας Δόμνης Σεβάστης μητρὸς ἀν{ε}ικήτων
στ]ρατοπίδων Σέρηνος Ἀλεξάνδρου πανταρχήσας
τ]ῆς Ὀμβείτων πόλεως εὐσεβείας χάριν ἀνέθηκεν
ἐ]π' ἀγαθῷ, ἔτει κβ' φαρμοῦθι ἐνάτῃ.

Probably from Ombos; a block of stone, apparently used as a door-lintel, broken to left.

Date: 214, March 4.

B.   ΤΟΙCΕΥΤΥΧΕCΤΑΤΟΙCΚΑΙ

ΟΥΚΥΡΙΟΥΗΜΩΝΑΥΤΟΚΡΑΤΟΡΟ

ΜΑΡΚΟΥΑΥΡΗΛΙΟΥΑΝΤΩΝΕΙΝΟΥ

ΕΥΤΥΧΟΥCΕΥCΕΒΟΥCCΕΒΑCΤΟΥ

LΒ϶   ΜΕCΟΡΗ   Κ   ΕΠΙ

ΓΕΜΙΝΙΩΧΡΗCΤΩΕΠΑΡΧΩΑΙΓΥΠΤΟΥ

ΚΑΙΟΥΑΛΕΡΙΟΥΑΠΟΛΙΝΑΡΙΟΥΕΠΙΤΡΟ

ΠΟΥΟΡΟΥC ΜΑΥΡΗΛΙΟCΑΠΟΛΛΩ

ΝΙΟCΤΟΝΚΗΠΟΝΕΚΘΕΜΕΛΙΟΥΑΝΩ

ΚΟΔΟΜΗCΕΝΚΑΙΕΖΩΓΡΑΦΗCΕΝCΥΝΤΟΙC

ΦΥΤΟΙCΕΠΟΙΗCΕΝΕΚΤΟΥΙΔΙΟΥ

ΕΠΑΓΑΘΩΙ

Ἐπὶ] τοῖς εὐτυχεστάτοις καί[ροις
τ]οῦ κυρίου ἡμῶν Αὐτοκράτορο[ς
Μάρκου Αὐρηλίου Ἀντων{ε}ίνου
Εὐτυχοῦς Εὐσεβοῦς Σεβάστου
(ἔτους) β' Μεσόρη κ', ἐπὶ
Γεμινί{ου} Χρήστ{ου} ἐπάρχ{ου} Αἰγύπτου
καὶ Οὐαλερίου Ἀπολ{λ}ιναρίου ἐπιτρό-
που ὄρους, Μ(άρκος) Αὐρήλιος Ἀπολλα
νιος τὸν κῆπον ἐκ θεμελίου ἀνῳ-
κοδόμησεν καὶ ἐζωγράφησεν σὺν τοῖς
φύτοις· ἐποίησεν ἐκ τοῦ ἰδίου
ἐπ' ἀγαθῷ.

A slab of limestone, roughly cut; provenance unknown.
Date: 219, Aug. 13.

4   ΥΡΗΛΙΟCΙCΙΔѠPOC

    CYNTOICTEKNOICKTOIC

    ΙΔΙΟΙCΥΠΕΡΕΥΧΑΡΙCΤΙΑC

    ΑΝΕΘΗΚΕΝΕΠΑΓΑΘѠ

    ΕΤΟΥCΓΟΥΑΛΕΡΙΑΝΟΥ

    ΚΓΑΛΛΙΗΝΟΥCΕΒΒ

    ΜΕCΟΡΗ Θ

Α]ὐρήλιος Ἰσίδωρος
σὺν τοῖς τέκνοις κ(αὶ) τοῖς
ἰδίοις ὑπὲρ εὐχαριστίας
ἀνέθηκε⟩ ἐπ' ἀγαθῷ
ἔτους γ΄ Οὐαλεριάνου
κ(αὶ) Γαλλιήνου Σεβ(άστων)
Μεσόρη θ΄.

A round block, perhaps base of a statue, from Alexandria.
Date: 256, Aug. 2

15 ϹΥΠΑΝ.... ϹΙϹΤΘΕΟΥΘΕΛΗCΑΝΤΟCΚΑΙ

    ΤΟΥΧΡΙCΤΟΥΑΥΤΟΥΕΠΙΤΗCΠΑΝΕΥΔΑΙΜΟΝΟC

    ΒΑCΙΛΕΙΑCΤѠΝΤΑΠΑΝΤΑΝΕΙΚѠΝΤѠΝΔΕCΠΟΤѠΝ

    ΗΜѠΝΟΥΑΛΕΝΤΙΝΙΑΝΟΥΚΑΙΟΥΑΛΕΝΤΟC

    ΚΑΙΓΡΑΤΙΑΝΟΥΤѠΝΑΙѠΝΙѠΝΑΥΓΟΥCΤѠΝ

    ΕΝΤΗΕΥΤΥΧΕCΤΑΤΗΑΥΤѠΝΔΕΚΑΕΤΗΡΙΔΕΙΤΕΤΡΑ

ΠΥΛΟΝΕΠΩΝΥΜΟΝΤΟΥΘΕΙΟΤΑΤΟΥΒΑCΙΛΕΩCΗΜΩΝΟΥΑΛΕΝΤΟC

ΕΚΘΕΜΕΛΙΩΝΕΚΤΙCΘΗΕΠΙΤΗCΕΠΑΡΧΗCΤΟΥΚΥΡΙΟΥ·

ΛΑΜΠΡΟΤΑΤΟΥΕΠΑΡΧΟΥΑΙΓΥΠΤΟΥΑΙΛΙΟΥ

ΠΑΛΛΑΔΙΟΥΛΟΓΙCΤΕΥΟΝΤΟCΚΑΙΕΠΙΚΕΙΜΕΝΟΥ

ΤΩΚΤΙCΘΕΝΤΙΤΕΤΡΑΠΥΛΩΦΛΑΟΥΙΟΥ

ΚΥΡΟΥΠΟΛΙΤΕΥΟΜΕΝΟΥ   ΕΠΑΓΑΘΩ

Τ]οῦ Παν[τοκράτορ]ος υεοῦ θελησάντος καὶ
τοῦ Χρίστου αὐτοῦ ἐπὶ τῆς πανευδαίμονος
βασιλείας τῶν τὰ πάντα ν{ε}ικώντων δεσποτῶν
ἡμῶν Οὐαλεντινιάνου καὶ Οὐαλέντος
καὶ Γρατιάνου τῶν αἰωνίων Αὐγούστων,
ἐν τῇ εὐτυχεστάτῃ αὐτῶν δεκαετηριδ{ε}ι, τετρά-
πυλον ἐπώνυμον τοῦ θειοτάτου βασιλέως ἡμῶν Οὐαλέντος
ἐκ θεμελίων ἐκτίσθη, ἐπὶ τῆς ἐπάρχης τοῦ κυρίου
λαμπροτάτου ἐπάρχου Αἰγύπτου Αἰλίου
Παλλαδίου, λογιστεύοντος καὶ ἐπικειμένο
τῷ κτισθέντι τετραπύλῳ Φλαουίου
Κύρου πολιτευομένου ἐπ' ἀγαθῷ.

Inscribed on a XXVIth dynasty altar from Athribis.
Published in R.A. 1847, 15th Aug.

Date: 374.

16 a

ΑΝΤΙΝΟΩΙ

ΕΠΙΦΑΝeΙ

ΦΕΙΔΟCΑΚΥΛΑC

ΕΠΙCΤΡΑΤΗΓΟC

ΘΗΒΑΙΔΟC

Ἀντινόῳ
Ἐπιφάνει
Φεῖδος Ἀκύλας
Ἐπιστράτηγος
Θηβαίδος.

INSCRIPTIONS IN THE GHIZEH MUSEUM

A granite altar from Sheikh-Abâdeh (Antinoopolis). Date: probably about the middle of the second century.

16. b
```
ΤΟΥΣΤΗΣΥΦΗΛΙΩΓΗΣΑΥΤΟΚΡΑ

ΤΟΡΑΣΚΑΙΤΡΟΠΑΙΟΥΧΟΥΣΔΕΣΠΟΤΑΣ

ΗΜΩΝΟΥΑΛΕΝΤΙΝΙΑΝΟΝΘΕΟΔΟΣΙΟΝ

ΑΡΚΑΔΙΟΝΤΟΥΣΑΙΩΝΙΟΥΣΑΥΤΟΥΡ

ΓΟΥΣΚΑΙΦΛΑΥΙΟΝΟΝΩΡΙΟΝΤΟΝ

ΕΠΙΦΑΝΕΣΤΑΤΟΝΦ///////////////

ΤΑ///////ϹϹΟΛΑΜΠΡΟΤΑΤΟΣΕΠΑΡΧΟΣ

ΤΟΥΙΕΡΟΥΠΡΑΙΤΩΡΙΟΥΤΗΣΣΥΝΗΘΕΙ

ΚΑΘΟΣΙΩϹΕΙΑΦΙΕΡΩϹΕΙΕΠΙΚΛΑΥΔΙΟΥ

ϹΕΠΤΙΜΙΟΥΕΥΤΡΟΠΙΟΥΤΟΥΛΑΜΠΡΟΤΑΤΟΥ

ΗΓΕΜΟΝΟϹ
```

Τοὺς τῆς ὑφ' ἡλίῳ γῆς αὐτοκράτορας καὶ τροπαιούχους δεσπότας ἡμῶν Οὐαλεντινιανὸν Θεοδόσιον Ἀρκάδιον τοὺς αἰωνίους αὐτούργους καὶ Φλα[ο]υίον Ὀνώριον τὸν ἐπιφανέστατον . . . .
. . . . . . ὁ λαμπρότατος ἔπαρχος τοῦ ἱεροῦ πραιτωρίου τῇ συνήθει καθοσιώσει ἀφιερώσει ἐπὶ Κλαυδίου Σεπτιμίου Εὐτροπίου τοῦ λαμπροτάτου ἡγεμόνος.

Inscribed on the back of the altar, 16 a.
Date: between 384 and 392.

APPENDIX IV

NOTES

Note I.—Position of the Archidikastes.

The office of archidikastes was one which existed under the Ptolemies, when he was president of the chrematistai, or circuit judges; and Strabo (xvii. 1. 12) definitely states that the Ptolemaic archidikastes was continued as a Roman official. At the same time he describes him as a local Alexandrian judge; and, to meet the difficulty thus created, Mommsen (Roman Provinces, vol. ii. p. 247, note 1, English trans.) supposes that the Alexandrian archidikastes was distinct from the president of the chrematistai, and that the latter had perhaps been set aside before the Roman period. This supposition, however, is met by the references to the archidikastes in papyri as πρὸς τῇ ἐπιμελείᾳ τῶν χρηματιστῶν καὶ τῶν ἄλλων κριτηρίων (B.G.U. 455, 614), which shows that the Roman officer was the successor, in title, at any rate, of the Ptolemaic archidikastes for the whole of Egypt.

The situation, however, was complicated by the fact that the chrematistai had been abolished by the Romans, and the circuits were held by the prefect and dikaiodotes in their stead. Both these officials were superior in rank to the Roman archidikastes; and consequently his original duty of revising the decisions of the judges on circuit necessarily elapsed, as there could be no appeal from a superior to an inferior.

There are several references in the published papyri

to the archidikastes and his functions; and a brief summary of these may assist in clearing up his position in Roman times.

B.G.U. 73. A letter from the archidikastes to the strategos of the Herakleid division of the Arsinoite nome, enclosing a document, the character of which is not specified, for deposit in the local archives by their keepers.

B.G.U. 136. A note of the entry of an action, relative to the administration of the property of a minor by her guardians, before the archidikastes at Memphis; the action was referred by him to the local strategos for trial.

B.G.U. 241. A document sent from Karanis in the Arsinoite nome to the archidikastes, stating the division made by two sons of property left by their father.

B.G.U. 455. A letter to the archidikastes, conveying the acknowledgment of the sale of a certain piece of land to the writer, a legionary.

B.G.U. 578. A letter from the archidikastes to the strategos of the Herakleid division of the Arsinoite nome, conveying a copy of a petition, enclosing the formal acknowledgment of a loan, which had not been repaid; the lender therefore wished copies of the documents to be filed in both archives (*i.e.* presumably at Alexandria, and in the nome), and the strategos to inform the borrower of this step, which was the preliminary to an action for recovery of the money; the archidikastes accordingly sent the copy for the local archives, and directed the strategos to inform the borrower that it had been filed.

B.G.U. 614. Copies of documents in a suit, beginning with a petition to the prefect, relative to an action for the recovery of a loan; after the suit had been authorized by the prefect, the plaintiff, a soldier, applied to the archidikastes, setting forth that he was unable, on account of his military duties, to visit the place where the defendants resided, and therefore wished them to be summoned before the archidikastes. The archidikastes, as a necessary preliminary, ordered copies of the plaints to be delivered to the defendants; and the plaintiff asked the archidikastes to write to the strategos of the Herakleid district of the Arsinoite nome and enclose copies for delivery.

B.G.U. 729. An acknowledgment, addressed to the archidikastes, by a soldier, of the deposit with him of certain articles.

B.G.U. 741. A copy of an acknowledgment, addressed to the archidikastes, of a loan on the security of property in the Arsinoite nome, from one soldier to another.

These cases, taken with B.G.U. 455 and 614, suggest that the court of the archidikastes at Alexandria was the most convenient place for the deposit of agreements to which soldiers were parties: as their military duties would be apt to take them away from the place at which the agreement was concluded.

G.G.P. ii. 71. An authorisation from parties concerned, to a man, to prove a will from Kysis in the Great Oasis before the archidikastes at Alexandria.

R.E.G. 1894, vii. p. 301, No. I. An authorisation from the parties concerned, to a man, to present to the archidikastes at Alexandria documents relative to the cession of a share in a certain business at Kysis in the Great Oasis.

R.E.G. 1894, vii. p. 302, No. III. Similar to last.

G.O.P. i. 34ᵛ. An order for the deposit of the records of the διαλογὴ τῶν κατὰ καιρὸν ἀρχιδικαστῶν in the archives at Alexandria.

The first point to be decided with reference to the archidikastes is, whether he sat at Alexandria only, or travelled round the nomes. The three documents from the Great Oasis are clearly on the side of the former alternative; and there is nothing against it in the other papyri, except in B.G.U. 136. It is important, however, to notice that in this case, in which alone the archidikastes is found with certainty sitting elsewhere than at Alexandria, the court was held at Memphis; and F. Krebs (Philologus, liii. p. 577 ff.) has pointed out that the high priest of all Egypt similarly appears as sitting at Alexandria and Memphis. Further, the terms of the petitions in B.G.U. 578 and 614, both relating to places in the Fayum, show that the archidikastes held his court somewhere outside the immediate neighbourhood of these places; which would hardly apply to Memphis, only a day's journey away from the Fayum. There is also a small point to be noted in the terms of B.G.U. 73, which seems to show an ignorance of local circumstances; the archidikastes writes to Archias, who is known from G.G.P. ii. 45 to have been strategos of the Herakleid division of the Arsinoite nome, addressing him as strategos of the Arsinoite nome; which he would hardly have done, if he had visited the nome and learned its peculiar division into districts. And the reference in G.O.P. i. 34 to the διαλογή of the archidikastes does not imply that he went on circuit. On the whole, the evidence seems to show that the archidikastes sat at Alexandria, possibly with power to remove his court to Memphis. It may be remarked that there is no authority for the completion of the lacuna in B.G.U. 614, l. 7, as ἱερ[εὺς καὶ ἀρχιδικαστὴς τῆς τοῦ Ἀρσινοί]του Ἡρακλείδου μερίδος, so far as I can see.

What the precise duties of the archidikastes were, do not appear very clearly. He seems to have had a special charge of the archives at Alexandria, in which copies of all documents deposited in the various local archives throughout the country had also to be placed (G.O.P. i. 34); this function is shown by the three Oasis papyri, which refer to various documents to be presented to him; and the cases in B.G.U. 241 and 455 appear to be similar.

The three instances in which the archidikastes appears as a judge are all civil cases, and in all three there is no reference to any delegation of authority to him from the prefect, which shows that he was legally competent to try such suits. The circumstances under which the suits were brought before him, rather than before the prefect or dikaiodotes on circuit, are shown by B.G.U. 614, wherein the plaintiff desired the defendants to be summoned before the archidikastes, presumably at Alexandria, because he himself was a soldier, and therefore unable to go to the local court. In B.G.U. 578, also, the plaintiff was a citizen of Antinoe, while the defendant resided in the Fayum; and possibly it was more convenient for him to go to Alexandria, where copies of the documents preserved in the archives of both his own district and the defendant's would be at hand, than to visit the Fayum and bring his case before the circuit judges, only to find that he had to send back to Antinoe for some written evidence.

It may be concluded that the archidikastes sat at Alexandria as a permanent judge, before whom the plaintiff, and probably the defendant also, in any civil case, both parties to which did not reside in the same district, could elect to have their dispute tried.

The instance of the archidikastes holding his court at Memphis must be left, until further evidence as to the reason for his presence there is discovered. B.G.U. 136 unfortunately only contains the official notes of the trial, which gave, no doubt, all necessary particulars at the time, but are not full enough to show any reason why there should, in this case, be an apparent departure from the usual rule as to the duties of the archidikastes.

NOTE II.—STRATEGOI AND ROYAL SCRIBES OF THE HERAKLEID DIVISION OF THE ARSINOITE NOME.

The exceptionally large proportion of the papyri hitherto published which come from sites in the Herakleid division of the Arsinoite nome, furnish a fairly complete list of the strategoi and royal scribes for that division, at any rate during the second century. A catalogue of the known names and dates may therefore serve usefully to illustrate the tenure of these appointments.

STRATEGOI.

Name.	Date.	Reference.
Oiax	19th Nov. 11	Pap. B.M. 256 ^{R}e.
[Dionysodorus (A)	14/15	Pap. B.M. 357.]
[Claudius Lysanius (A)	5th April 54	App. III. 5.]
[G. Julius Asinianus (A)	15th June 57	B.G.U. 181.]

STRATEGOI AND ROYAL SCRIBES

Name.	Date.	Reference.
Ti. Claudius Arcius-	26th Feb. 99 before 14th Jul. 101	B.G.U. 226. G.G.P. ii. 44.
Asclepiades	9th Jan. 108	B.G.U. 103.
(Sara)pion	1st April 114	B.G.U. 22.
Protarchus	22nd Aug. 130	B.G.U. 647.
Archias	20th June 135 28th Jan. 136	B.G.U. 73. G.G.P. ii. 45.
Vegetus Sarapion	29th Jan. 137	B.G.U. 352; G.G.P. ii. 45 a.
Claudius Cerealis	15th Feb. 139	G.G.P. ii. 46 a.
Apollinaris	Jan. 141	B.G.U. 353, 354, 355, 357.
Ælius Sarapion	31st Jan. 143 144/5	B.G.U. 51. B.G.U. 52, 133.
Archibius	26th Jan. 146	Pap. B.M. 309.
Maximus Nearchus	3rd May 146 146/7 24th July 147	Pap. Gen. 6. B.G.U. 137. B.G.U. 95.
[Herakleides (B)	30th Jan. 151	B.G.U. 358.]
Theodorus	14th Feb. 159	Pap. B.M. 376.
Hierax	159/60 28th Jan. 161 28th July 161 28th Jan. 162	B.G.U. 16, 239, 524. B.G.U. 629. B.G.U. 224, 410. Pap. B.M. 327.
Stephanus	29th Jan. 163	Pap. B.M. 328.
Ælius Eudæmon	before 10th Aug. 169	B.G.U. 168.
[Serenus (B)	10th Aug. 169 26th Nov. 169	B.G.U. 18. B.G.U. 168.]
[Alexander (c)	11th April 170	B.G.U. 347.]
Sarapion	3rd Oct. 170 (E)	B.G.U. 347.
Potamon	173/4 26th Nov. 174 174/5 Aug. 175	B.G.U. 598. B.G.U. 26. B.G.U. 59. B.G.U. 55, ii.
Flavius Apollonius	28th Oct. 177 Jan.-Feb. 179	B.G.U. 194. Pap. B.M. 368.
Apollonius	26th May 184	B.G.U. 361, ii.
Ptolemæus	between 180 and 193	B.G.U. 242.
Ammonius	188/9	B.G.U. 430.
Dioscorus	17th Aug. 190	B.G.U. 432.
Didymus	22nd Feb. 191	B.G.U. 72.
Artemidorus	19th May 193 26th July 194	B.G.U. 15. B.G.U. 46.
[Philoxenus (D)	17th Sept. 194	B.G.U. 199ʳ.]
Hierax Nemesion	between 194 and 198	G.G.P. ii. 61.

Name.	Date.	Reference.
Demetrius	7th March 199	Pap. B.M. 474.
	10th Oct. 199	B.G.U. 41.
	25th June 200	B.G.U. 25.
	25th Feb. 202	B.G.U. 139.
Agathos Dæmon	21st April 202	B.G.U. 577.
	202/3	B.G.U. 97.
	23rd June 203	B.G.U. 663.
	6th Oct. 203	B.G.U. 203.
Dionysius	10th Nov. 207	B.G.U. 652.
	207/8	B.G.U. 392, 653.
Apollophanes Sarapammon	23rd Jan. 209	B.G.U. 2.
Aur. Hierax Ammonius	May–June 213	B.G.U. 145.
Aur. Dionysius	7th Nov. 216	B.G.U. 534.
	216/7	B.G.U 266.
	24th Feb. 217	B.G.U. 64.
	7th April 217	B.G.U. 614.
Aur. Didymus	8th Oct. 222	B.G.U. 35.
	April–May 225	B.G.U. 42.
	May–June 225	Pap. B.M. 176.
[Aur. Herakleides (A)	between 257 and 261	B.G.U. 244.]

(A) Strategoi of the whole Arsinoite nome.
(B) Royal scribes acting for the strategos.
(C) Gymnasiarch acting for the strategos.
(D) Strategos of divisions of Themistos and Polemon acting for the division of Herakleides also.
(E) See as to this date in Note III.

ROYAL SCRIBES.

Name.	Date.	Reference.
Asclepiades	19th Nov. 11	Pap. B.M. 256 Re.
Evangelus	before 76	B.G.U. 583.
Claudius Julianus	14th July 101	G.G.P. ii. 44.
	21st Dec. 101	Pap. B.M. 173.
Herminus	29th Jan. 137	B.G.U. 352; G.G.P. ii. 45 a.
	July 138	Pap. B.M. 208 a.
Sarapion	Jan. 141	B.G.U. 353, 354, 355.
	30th Jan. 141	B.G.U. 357.
	June–July 142	B.G.U. 17.
	Jan.–Feb. 143	B.G.U. 51.
	31st Jan. 144	Pap. B.M. 304.
	144/5	B.G.U. 52.
Heracleides	28th Jan. 146	Pap. B.M. 309.
	24th July 147	B.G.U. 95.
	30th Jan. 151	B.G.U. 358.

Name.	Date.	Reference.
Timagenes	14th Feb. 159	Pap. B.M. 376.
	159/60	B.G.U. 16, 524, 629.
	28th July 161	G.G.P. ii. 55.
	28th Jan. 162	Pap. B.M. 327.
Zoilus	162/3	G.G.P. ii. 56.
	29th Jan. 163	Pap. B.M. 328.
Serenus	10th Aug. 169	B.G.U. 18.
	26th Nov. 169	B.G.U. 168.
Asclepiades	26th Nov. 174	B.G.U. 26.
	174/5	B.G.U. 298.
	Aug. 175	B.G.U. 55, ii.
	175/6	B.G.U. 79.
Apollonius	Jan. 179	Pap. B.M. 368.
Harpocration Hierax	188/9	B.G.U. 60, 126, 138, 430.
	May–June 189	B.G.U. 115, i. ii.
	20th Aug. 189	B.G.U. 117.
	28th Aug. 189	B.G.U. 116.
	193	Pap. B.M. 345.
Canopus Asclepiades	25th Feb. 202	B.G.U. 139.
	202/3	B.G.U. 97.
	21st April 203	B.G.U. 577.
(Sarapa)mmon	June–July 208	B.G.U. 639.
Monimus Gemellus	27th Oct. 212	Pap. B.M. 350.
Aur. Isidorus Origenes	216/7	B.G.U. 266; Pap. B.M. 452.
Aur. Cassius Dionysius	218	C.P.R. 32.

Note III.—The Delegation of Functions during Vacancies in Office.

There is a phrase, occasionally found in papyri, the exact force of which does not seem to have been definitely settled, though P. Meyer (Hermes, xxxii. p. 227, note 3) has correctly classified most of its uses. Various individuals are mentioned at different times as διαδεχόμενοι τὴν στρατηγίαν, while in one instance the dikaiodotes is described as διαδεχόμενος καὶ τὰ κατὰ τὴν ἡγεμονίαν. A review of the known instances will serve to show that the word διαδεχόμενος is not employed in its usual classical sense as referring to a strategos-elect or prefect-elect, but has an exceptional meaning.

(A.) *Prefect.*

B.G.U. 327. A petition addressed to C. Caecilius Salvianus, dikaiodotes, as διαδεχόμενος καὶ τὰ κατὰ τὴν ἡγεμονίαν, with reference to the non-payment of a legacy, on 1st April 176.

The circumstances of the government in Egypt just about this time were peculiar. The prefect, who is named by Dio Cassius (lxxi. 28. 3) Flavius Calvisius, but who appears on an Alexandrian inscription (M.A. 101) as C. Calvisius Statianus, had joined the rebellion of Avidius Cassius, which was put down by the emperor Marcus Aurelius in 176, and for a punishment was banished. The emperor probably had no one ready to take the place of the banished prefect; and so his duties would devolve upon the next in rank, the dikaiodotes— an unusual event, as it was the rule that each prefect in Egypt held his office until his successor entered Alexandria (Ulpian, Dig. i. 17). It does not seem necessary to suppose, with P. Meyer (Hermes, xxxii. p. 227), that the delay in filling the vacancy was due to the presence of the emperor in Egypt, which rendered the appointment of a prefect, as his representative, superfluous.

(B.) *Strategoi.*

B.G.U. 18. A list of men nominated for liturgies published by Serenus, royal scribe of the Herakleid district of the Arsinoite nome, διαδεχόμενος τὰ κατὰ τὴν στρατηγίαν, on 10th Aug. 169.

B.G.U. 82. A priest, desiring to have his son circumcised, produced evidence of his lineage to the royal scribe, διαδεχόμενος τὴν στρατηγίαν (18th Sept. 185).

B.G.U. 168. A petition to the epistrategos, setting forth that certain property in dispute had been awarded to the petitioner by the late strategos of the Herakleid division, Ælius Eudæmon; but the defendant in the case, ἐπιγνοῦσα τὴν τοῦ Εὐδαίμονος ἔξοδον, did not hand over the property: the epistrategos was then addressed, and he ordered the case to be brought before the royal scribe, διαδεχόμενος τὰ κατὰ τὴν στρατηγίαν. This was done, the scribe in question being Serenus, on 26th November (probably in the year 169. See 18, above).

B.G.U. 199. A return from the tax-collectors, addressed to Philoxenus, strategos of the divisions of Themistos and Polemon, also διαδεχόμενος καὶ (τὰ) κατὰ τὴν στρατηγίαν for the Herakleid division, on 17th Sept. 194.

B.G.U. 347. A letter, written by Sarapion, strategos of the Herakleid division διὰ Ἀλεξάνδρου γυμνασιάρχου διαδεχομένου τὴν στρατηγίαν, and dated 11th April 170, produced before the high priest.

B.G.U. 358. A census-return of camels, made to the royal scribe Heracleides, διαδεχόμενος τὴν στρατηγίαν, on 30th Jan. (apparently in the year 151).

B.G.U. 529. A return made by the corn collectors to Aurelius Isidorus, royal scribe of the Herakleid division, διαδεχόμενος τὰ κατὰ τὴν στρατηγίαν, in July 216.

G.G.P. ii. 61. A petition addressed to Hierax Nemesion, strategos of the Herakleid division, δι' Ἀνυβίωνος ἀγορανομήσαντος γυμνασιαρχήσαντος διαδεχομένου τὴν στρατηγίαν. (Date, about 194.)

G.O.P. i. 56. A request from a woman, addressed to Maximus, a priest, exegetes, and senator of Oxyrhynchos, asking him as a matter of urgency, in the absence of the royal scribe, who was διαδεχόμενος τὴν στρατηγίαν, to sanction the appointment of a man to act as her guardian for the purposes of a loan required at once. (Date, 27th Oct. 211.)

G.O.P. i. 62ᵛ. A letter to Syrus, διαδεχόμενος στρατηγίαν (of Oxyrhynchos), relative to the lading of corn (third century).

Of the above ten cases, it will be seen one refers to a strategos of another district, six to the royal scribe of the district, two to holders of minor offices, and one to an individual not definitely stated to have any rank. It would appear, therefore, that the person chosen διαδέχεσθαι τὴν στρατηγίαν was not necessarily, but was usually, the next in official standing to the strategos—the royal scribe.

There may also be quoted, as probably having reference to the same custom, the following papyrus:

G.O.P. i. 59. A letter sent by the council of Oxyrhynchos to Aurelius Apollonius the strategos, through Aurelius Asclepiades, an ex-hypomnematographos, διάδοχος, where διάδοχος may be taken to mean διαδεχόμενος τὴν στρατηγίαν.

Three of the Berlin papyri—18, 168, 347—refer to events happening in the same district within a few months; and a comparison of them will serve to elucidate somewhat the relationships of the strategoi and the διαδεχόμενοι. In the first place, however, it should be remarked that the date in B.G.U. 347, i. 12, is almost certainly wrong. Letters are said to have been written by Alexander on 3rd Oct. 169, when he is described as an ex-gymnasiarch, and on 11th April 170, when he is described as a gymnasiarch. As it was contrary to the usual rule for a man to be chosen to serve as gymnasiarch a second time, it seems natural to suppose that the date of the first-mentioned letter is wrongly given, and that it should have been 3rd Oct. 170, shortly before which Alexander had resigned his office of gymnasiarch. In further support of this view, it may be noticed that, if this date is correct, the letter which was addressed to the high priest, and presented to him on his visit to Memphis, was only about three months old when presented; but if the date given in the papyrus is right, fifteen months had elapsed between the writing and the delivery of the letter. As the high priest must have visited Memphis at least once a year, and as the matter in question was the circumcision of a boy, so long a delay seems improbable.

Assuming that the date should be corrected as stated, it is possible to reconstruct the series of changes which took place in regard to the duties of the strategos of the Herakleid division in the years 169 and 170.

Ælius Eudæmon had been strategos of the division; but he died (this seems to be the meaning of ἔξοδος in B.G.U. 168) some time before 10th August 169, on which date Serenus the royal scribe acted as strategos (B.G.U. 18). Serenus was still so acting on 26th Nov. 169 (B.G.U. 168). But on 11th April 170 Sarapion had been appointed strategos. Alexander, a gymnasiarch, however, wrote a letter for him as διαδεχόμενος (B.G.U. 347, ii.). On 3rd Oct. 170, Alexander again wrote a letter for Sarapion; but on this occasion as copyist merely, to all seeming, since he is no longer described as διαδεχόμενος τὴν στρατηγίαν. The explanation would appear to be that, on the death of the strategos, the royal scribe naturally did his work until a new strategos was appointed. For some reason, however, the new strategos when chosen was unable to undertake the duties at once, and got a man of position to do them for him; and this man subsequently continued to help him.

This theory supposes that the term διαδεχόμενος has slightly different shades of meaning when applied to the royal scribe who was acting strategos during a vacancy, and the gymnasiarch who was acting strategos on behalf of another man. The other cases noted tend to support this. There is no reference, in the instances where a royal scribe is named as διαδεχόμενος τὴν στρατηγίαν, to the existence of a strategos at the same time; on the other hand, in each case where the holder of some minor office is so named, there is also a strategos mentioned. In the devolution of the duties of the strategos on the royal scribe during a vacancy in the former office, there is a parallel to the arrangement already shown to have been made for the performance of the work of the prefecture by the dikaiodotes on the sudden removal of the prefect. It appears that the royal scribe, under these circumstances, possessed the full powers of the strategos: he could be named as a judge (B.G.U. 168), could nominate to liturgies (B.G.U. 18), and received the tax returns (B.G.U. 529). It is probable, then, that it was the rule for the royal scribe, in case of any casual vacancy in the office of strategos, to assume all the duties; and the one instance (B.G.U. 199), in which the strategos of a neighbouring district acted for that in which there was a vacancy, may be regarded as exceptional.

The position of the διαδεχόμενοι in the other cases cited (B.G.U. 347; G.G.P. ii. 61; G.O.P. i. 59) is quite different. They occur simply as agents for the transmission of letters to and from the strategos. What official standing they had may be gathered from a comparison of the two letters in B.G.U. 347 with the petition in G.O.P. i. 56. From the two former it appears that Alexander the gymnasiarch wrote letters at different times on behalf of Sarapion the strategos on practically identical subjects; but one was written by him as διαδεχόμενος τὴν στρατηγίαν, while the other was written without any such authority. The circumstances under which he was entitled to assume any of the functions of the strategos may be explained by the Oxyrhynchos papyrus, in which a person of some rank is requested to sanction the appointment of a guardian,— an act which really lay in the province of the strategos, —because the matter was urgent, and the royal scribe, who was also διαδεχόμενος τὴν στρατηγίαν, was away. Therefore it would seem that, when a strategos was absent from his district, he could appoint some person to perform the ordinary routine business of his office, and this person was entitled to subscribe himself as διαδεχόμενος τὴν στρατηγίαν or διάδοχος.

Individual instances occur of substitutes for other officials—a procurator usiacus διαδεχόμενος τὴν ἀρχιερωσύνην (B.G.U. 362, vii. 26); elders διαδεχόμενοι for the village scribe of Nilopolis (B.G.U. 15, i. 8); and a senator of Hermopolis for the prytaneus (C.P.R. i. 20, 3): but only in the second case does the evidence show clearly that they acted with full powers during a vacancy in office. The other two cases may simply refer to a delegation of functions by an absent officer.

NOTE IV.—THE REGISTRY OF DEEDS.

L. Mitteis (Hermes, xxx. p. 564 ff.) has discussed the methods of registry exemplified by the Fayum papyri. He concludes that the agoranomos was probably originally a Greek official, and the Hellenes brought with them the custom of making contracts before him; while the γραφεῖον was introduced for the purpose of registering Egyptian documents, especially those written in demotic characters. In course of time the distinction between the nations disappeared, and the official functions became concurrent. Still, there was a certain difference: the agoranomos had notarial duties, concerned with the completion of contracts; while the grapheion, though on one side similar, as the place where the contracts were made (B.G.U. 86, 191, 251, 252, 297, 394), is also in some cases only the place of registry (B.G.U. 50, 153; C.P.R. i. 4, 5), the documents being executed privately.

This statement meets all the instances recorded in the Fayum papyri; but those from Oxyrhynchos show that the customs prevailing there were somewhat different. In them the agoranomos is all-important, and the grapheion disappears. It is to the agoranomoi that notices of the transfer or sale of land are sent (G.O.P. i. 45, 46, 47, 100); in their presence, or at their office, the agoranomeion, the contracts were written (G.O.P. i. 73, 75, 96, 99); they had the custody of the deeds when executed (G.O.P. i. 106, 107); and, in the case of the emancipation by purchase of slaves, it apparently fell to them to announce the completion of the necessary formalities (G.O.P. i, 48, 49, 50).

The formula employed in describing the completion of contracts of sale differs again in the Vienna papyri from the Herakleopolite nome. In these (C.P.R. 6, 7, 8) the contract is said to be executed δι' ἐπιτηρητῶν ἀγορανομίας; and here, as at Oxyrhynchos, no mention is made of the grapheion.

In a single contract of sale from Elephantine (N. et E. 17), the same formula is used as at Oxyrhynchos, stating that the deed was drawn up before the agoranomoi.

It would appear, therefore, that, on the evidence now published, the grapheion was an institution peculiar to the Arsinoite nome, where it relieved the agoranomoi of many of their duties with regard to the execution and registration of contracts. The word grapheion occurs once in the Oxyrhynchos papyri (G.O.P. i. 44); but the name here appears to be applied to a tax, payable at the agoranomeion.

Note V.—The Police Administration.

A large number of officials, connected in various ways with police duties, are mentioned in papyri. The only attempt hitherto made for their classification is one by Hirschfeld (Sitzungsberichte d. Kaiserl. Akademie zu Berlin, 1892, p. 815), on the basis of a Paris papyrus from Panopolis. This mentions (*a*) two εἰρηνοφύλακες; (*b*) three ἐπὶ τῆς εἰρήνης; (*c*) two ἀρχινυκτοφύλακες; (*d*) eight or more φύλακες αὐτῶν; (*e*) ten more ἐπὶ τῆς εἰρήνης; (*f*) two εἰρηνάρχαι; (*g*) eight φύλακες αὐτῶν; (*h*) four πεδιοφύλακες; (*i*) some ὀρεοφύλακες ὁδοῦ ᾿Οασέως; (*j*) some ἰβιω(φύλακες). These he arranges in three classes: (1) the officers named under (*a*), (*b*) and (*e*), and (*f*); (2) those under (*c*), (*d*), and (*g*); (3) those under (*h*), (*i*), and (*j*). The individuals are all Egyptians, and between the ages of 30 and 35, except one who is 48, and the two eirenarchs, who are respectively 60 and 85 years old.

The evidence of other papyri, however, tends to upset this classification in some respects; although it is not yet possible to definitely settle the exact rank of many of the officers mentioned. A comparison of the evidence gives the following results:—

Εἰρηνάρχαι. There were two of these officials both at Panopolis (see above) and Oxyrhynchos (G.O.P. i. 80), and an eirenarch is mentioned in the correspondence of Flavius Abinnæus from Dionysias in the Fayum (Pap. B.M. 240, 242). The Oxyrhynchos papyrus shows them to have been the chief police officers, holding jurisdiction over the nome; it contains a declaration on oath, made to them by the archephodos of a village, that certain individuals "wanted by the police of the village of Armenthæ in the Hermopolite nome are not in our village or in Armenthæ itself."

᾿Αρχέφοδοι. These officers are the ones most frequently mentioned in connection with the maintenance of order in the country.

For each village one or two archephodoi were appointed (B.G.U. 321, 375; Pap. B.M. 199; G.G.P. ii. 66; G.O.P. i. 80, are instances of one; B.G.U. 6, of two); there is no evidence of more than two in any case. They are most commonly named in orders to present criminals for trial (B.G.U. 147, 148, 374, 375, 376; G.G.P. ii. 66), which during the first three centuries of Roman rule were always addressed to them, though sometimes other officials are added in the address; and it was to them that evidence was given to help in the discovery of a criminal (G.O.P. i. 69). They were superior to the phylakes, who received their pay from them (G.G.P. ii. 43), and may reasonably be regarded as the heads of the police in the villages.

Πρεσβύτεροι. The elders were not, in the first instance, police officers; but they are named in conjunction with the archephodoi and phylakes in two official lists (B.G.U. 6; Pap. B.M. 199), and once are associated with the archephodoi as the recipients of an order to present a criminal at the court (B.G.U. 148). They were, as the governing body of the village, generally responsible for its peace and order, which explains their association with their regular police.

Εὐσχήμονες. The same explanation applies to the association of the euschemones with the archephodoi in orders of arrest (B.G.U. 147, 376); as they, like the elders, were not in strictness members of the police administration.

Εἰρηνοφύλακες. The eirenophylakes, who are mentioned in the Panopolis list (see above), may perhaps be considered as equal in rank with the archephodoi, in view of the fact that, in a list of the officials of Soknopaiou Nesos (Pap. B.M. 199), the sums entered against the names of the archephodos and eirenophylakes, of whom there are two, are the same—in each case 600 drachmae. This sum F. G. Kenyon (in his note on this papyrus, p. 158, Catalogue of Greek Papyri, ii.) takes to be the salary paid to the officers in question.

Φύλακες. The physical work of arrest of malefactors was done by the phylakes, who were apparently classed at Panopolis (see the papyrus quoted above) under different names according to their special duties. Of the Panopolite names the only one found elsewhere is the πεδιοφύλαξ (Pap. B.M. 189). That they were required to be young men has been noticed in connection with the Panopolis list. Their salary at Soknopaiou Nesos is given as 300 drachmae (Pap. B.M. 199; see reference to Kenyon's note above), and there were four of them in this village. There is an interesting record from Oxyrhynchos (G.O.P. i. 34ʳ), which details the names and stations of the phylakes in that town: one appears to have been placed in each street, while six guarded the temple of Serapis, seven that of Thoeris, one that of Isis, three the theatre, and two the gymnasium.

Λῃστοπιασταί. The lestopiastai are mentioned in a special order, by which five were sent to assist the village officers in the search for certain criminals (B.G.U. 325). It is possible that they were men detailed from headquarters for special service, as they were evidently distinct from the regular local force.

Δημόσιοι. The police officers of a village are sometimes referred to in a body as the demosioi. That this name includes all the ranks is shown by the phrase ὁ τῆς κώμης ἀρχέφοδος καὶ οἱ ἄλλοι δημόσιοι (G.O.P. i. 69), and by a list embracing under this title elders, archephodoi, and phylakes (B.G.U. 6).

Κωμάρχαι. In the beginning of the fourth century the place of the archephodoi is taken, in orders for arrest, by the Komarchs (G.O.P. i. 64, 65; B.G.U. 634).

Ἐπιστάτης εἰρήνης. In one instance the name of this officer is coupled with the Komarchs (G.O.P. i. 64).

Note VI.—Senates in Egypt.

The withdrawal from Alexandria by Augustus of the privilege of self-government by a senate is stated by Dio Cassius (li. 17). Mommsen (Roman Provinces, ii. p. 236, note 1) doubts this statement, on the ground that it is improbable that Augustus would have so slighted Alexandria in comparison with the other Egyptian communities, to which he left their existing organisation. But Alexandria stood in a very different position to any other Egyptian town. A senate at Ptolemais or Naukratis could not be a source of any serious danger to the Roman government: in both towns the citizenship was probably confined to the descendants of the original Greek settlers, whose interest it would be to keep on good terms with the Romans, surrounded as they were by a people of a different race, whose natural instincts would make them hostile to the specially privileged Greeks planted among them; and even if the senate in either place had desired to head a revolt, they controlled only a small body of citizens, of no great wealth. But in Alexandria the Greek and Egyptian elements had coalesced to a considerable extent; and there was a large population, of notoriously turbulent disposition, amongst whom the senate could have found a body of supporters sufficient to meet the Roman garrison with a reasonable prospect of success in an attempt to seize the city. And the loss of Alexandria meant to the Romans the loss of Egypt; not only was the machinery of government centred there, but it was the only port by which reinforcements from Rome could enter Egypt. At Alexandria, too, were stored the supplies of corn on which the city of Rome largely depended for its subsistence. It was consequently of the greatest importance that there should not be a body in Alexandria which might serve as a focus for revolutions. And that Augustus would not have been moved by any consideration for the feelings of the Alexandrians, is shown by his proposal to remove the seat of government from Alexandria to Nikopolis. The wisdom of his action in abolishing the senate was shown not long after its re-establishment by Severus, when it headed the revolt which was finally crushed by Aurelian (Eusebius, Hist. Eccl. vii. 32).

The senate at Ptolemais Hermiou can only be inferred to have existed under the early empire from the words of Strabo (xvii. 1. 42), who says that the town had a σύστημα πολιτικὸν ἐν τῷ Ἑλληνικῷ τρόπῳ; but this would certainly mean to any Greek the inclusion in the organisation of a senate. The only mention of a senator of Ptolemais is in 295 (G.O.P. i. 43, iii. 3, 8).

At Naukratis, likewise, the existence of a senate is only a probability as regards the earlier period of Roman rule. But, if Ptolemais retained its senate, there was no reason for abolishing that of Naukratis; and the statement of Dio (li. 17) is sufficient ground for believing in the continuance of the latter. There was certainly a senate at Naukratis in 323 (Pap. Gen. 10).

The senate at Antinoopolis appears very shortly after the foundation of the city (C.I.G. iii. 4679); and there is no reason to doubt that it existed from the first.

Senates or senators at other towns are mentioned in the following years:—

Arsinoe: 205 (Pap. B.M. 348), 214 (C.P.R. 45), 216 (B.G.U. 362), 345 (Pap. B.M. 233).

Herakleopolis: 216 (C.P.R. 35), 263 (B.G.V. 554).

Hermopolis magna: 250 (C.P.R. 20, i.), 266 (C.P.R. 39), 271 (C.P.R. 9), 321/2 (C.P.R. 10), 330 (C.P.R. 19).

Oxyrhynchos, 211 (G.O.P. i. 56), 223 (G.O.P. i. 77), 238 44 (G.O.P. i. 80), 283 (G.O.P. i. 55), 292 (G.O.P. i. 59), 316 (G.O.P. i. 103), 323 (G.O.P. i. 60), 342 G.O.P. i. 87).

A proclamation made in 288 (G.O.P. i. 58) refers to the senates in the various nomes in the Heptanomis and Arsinoite nome.

Note VII.—The Archons of Thebes.

It has been supposed by A. Wiedemann (R.E. ii. p. 346) that there were independent kings of the Thebaid in the second century; and he supports his theory by finding on an ostrakon the name Petronius as that of the ruler by whose regnal year the document is dated. It is difficult, however, to imagine that such a kingdom of the Thebaid could have existed unmentioned by historians, and unnoticed in the inscriptions of Upper Egypt belonging to that period; and it seems more reasonable to suppose that the ostrakon has been misread by Wiedemann. This view is supported by his transcript of another ostrakon, which he deciphers as a letter from Κλαυδιος Ποσιδωνιος Χεπειρης Βθρακων ; and he regards the Χ (= in) and β (prefixed for formation of genitive) as evidence of the influence of the Ethiopico-Meroitic language; whereas the right reading is certainly Χ (= ἑκατόνταρχος) σπείρης β΄ Θράκων. It is true that a "king" of Thebes is mentioned (Hist. Aug. Niger, 12) as having presented to Pescennius Niger a portrait statue of himself; but the Thebaid was certainly not independent in the reign of Commodus, and the "king" was doubtless one of the archons mentioned as existing at Thebes in the time of Hadrian (C.I.G. iii. 4822, 4823, 4824).

Note VIII.—The Dux Ægypti and other Byzantine Officials.

F. G. Kenyon (Catalogue of Greek Papyri in B.M. ii. p. 270, note) has pointed out that the arrangement of authority given in the Notitia Dignitatum, where there is a comes limitis Ægypti, commanding the divisions of Middle and Lower Egypt, a dux Thebaidis, and a dux Libyarum, is of later origin than the time of Constantius II.; and that the supreme military officer in Lower and Middle Egypt is always, in documents of the first half of the fourth century, the dux. This is borne out by an inscription on an altar in the temple at Luxor (published in the Bull. de la Soc. des Antiq. de France, 1888, p. 273), dedicated to Constantine by the dux Ægypti et Thebaidis utrarumque Libyarum, which shows that the divisions of the province, though recognised, were under one commander, who bore the title of dux.

The date of the change to the arrangements described by the Notitia may be very nearly fixed by the addresses of the imperial rescripts. In 384, Merobaudes is addressed as dux Ægypti (Cod. Theod. xi. 30. 43); but in 391, Romanus is styled comes limitis Ægypti (Cod. Theod. xvi. 10. 11); and this title is the one subsequently used. The dux Libyarum appears in a rescript of 417 (Cod. Theod. viii. 1. 16).

It is noticeable that the change from the style of præfectus Ægypti to that of præfectus Augustalis came almost at the same time. In 380 a rescript was addressed to Julianus by the former title (Cod. Theod. xii. 1, 80), which is the one found in all previous documents; while in 382, Palladius was entitled præfectus Augustalis (Cod. Theod. viii. 5, 37), which was the name always subsequently used.

Note IX.—Comparison of Ancient and Modern Local Government of Egypt.

The system of local government in Egypt, as it existed before the introduction of European ideas to any large extent, offers some interesting points of comparison with the Roman organisation. Clot Bey (Aperçu Général sur L'Égypte, ii. p. 141) gives an account of the officials under the rule of Mehmet-Ali, from which the following is summarised:—

Under the Vali were seven mudirs, who were placed in charge of the seven provinces into which Egypt was divided. Under them were the mamours, who presided over the departments of these provinces. The districts of these departments were managed by nazirs. Finally, each village had at its head the sheik-el-beled.

The duties of the mudir corresponded to those of the epistrategos. He had to visit the departments of his province, and see to the execution of the orders of the Vali, just as the epistrategos had done in his circuits of the nomes.

The mamour was chiefly concerned with agriculture and taxation, especially that payable in kind. He was also charged with the supervision of public works, and with levying men for their execution and for military service. In the former aspect of his office he resembled the Roman toparch, while his other duties were rather those of the strategos.

The nazir had inherited other functions of the strategos, in the arrangement of the work of his district and the delegation of authority from his superiors.

The sheik-el-beled filled the place of the elders of the village. He had a certain amount of authority as a minor police magistrate, and was responsible for the taxes of his village.

There was also in each village a special official known as the kholy, charged with the management of the cultivation of the land, who therefore corresponded to the sitologos; and a seraf, who, like the praktor, collected taxes, and paid them to the mamour, as the praktor had done to the strategos.

It is interesting to note that the mudirs were always Turks, as the epistrategoi were always Romans; while the mamours and lower officials, like their predecessors in Roman times, were, as a rule, natives.

Note X.—The Prefecture of Petronius.

It seems necessary to suppose that Petronius was reappointed prefect after the failure of Ælius Gallus in Arabia. From Strabo (xvii. 1. 53) it is evident that he succeeded Cornelius Gallus, and was followed in office by Ælius Gallus. Then, while Ælius Gallus was in Arabia, the Æthiopians took advantage of the absence of the Roman troops from Egypt to invade the country. Petronius then marched up and drove them back from the frontiers, subsequently pursuing his conquests up to the capital of Æthiopia. Pliny (N.H. vi. 181) expressly states that he made this expedition as prefect; so it would appear that Ælius Gallus was removed from office as soon as the news of his defeat in Arabia reached Rome, and Petronius, who had probably been left in command of Egypt, was reinstated as prefect.

Note XI.—The Coinage of the Early Roman Emperors.

Coins of Augustus and Tiberius of the Alexandrian mint are comparatively rare, while none are known of Caligula.

The manner in which hoards of coins, when found in Egypt, have usually been scattered by the dealers into whose hands they passed, has prevented any exact comparison of the numbers of coins put into circulation under the different emperors being formulated. Three hoards of some size—two, containing 4605 and 62 specimens respectively, from Bacchias, and one containing 91, from Karanis—were discovered in 1895–6 by D. G. Hogarth and B. P. Grenfell, when they were excavating sites in the Fayum on behalf of the Egypt Exploration Fund; and these came intact to me for examination. The subjoined table will serve to illustrate the comparative issues of the first century and a half of Roman rule in Egypt. It may be premised that the condition of the coins shows them to have been collected about the same time, and not gradually hoarded—the oldest being also the most worn; so that the figures prove generally the number of each issue in circulation at the time when the hoards were deposited:—

	Bacchias I.	Bacchias II.	Karanis.
Ptolemaic	2	...	...
Claudius	359	5	3
Nero	2947	44	49
Galba	190	2	2
Otho	54	1	...
Vitellius	19	...	...
Vespasian	237	6	4
Titus	30	...	...
Domitian	1	...	...
Nerva	22	...	...
Trajan	89	1	4
Hadrian	560	3	18
Sabina	6	...	...
Ælius	5	...	...
Antoninus	75	...	7
Aurelius	8	...	2
Verus	1	...	2

All these coins, with two exceptions—one Ptolemaic

bronze and one large bronze of Antoninus—are debased silver tetradrachms of the Alexandrian mint

NOTE XII.—THE HADRIANON AT ALEXANDRIA.

There has been a certain amount of difficulty in explaining the references made to a building at Alexandria known as the Hadrianon. On coins of Hadrian (B.M. Cat. 875, 876) there is represented a portico, having within it a standing statue of Sarapis, which may be certainly accepted as representing the Sarapeion; and by the statue there stands the emperor, touching with his right hand a shrine inscribed ΑΔΡΙΑΝΟΝ. This would suggest that Hadrian gave his name to a chapel attached to the Sarapeion, which may have existed before his time, as a similar shrine inside the portico with statue of Sarapis, but without the inscription, is shown on coins of Trajan (B.M. Catalogue, 534-539). But, as pointed out by R. S. Poole (Introduction to B.M. Catalogue of Coins, Alexandria, p. xcii), the relation of the chapel to the Sarapeion could not have been very close, as Epiphanius mentions that the building formerly known as the Hadrianon, and subsequently as the Licinian gymnasium, was rebuilt as a church under Constantius II. (adv. Hær. II. ii. 69). As the worship of Sarapis was not overthrown till the time of Theodosius. I., the appropriation of a chapel attached to his temple for the purposes of a Christian church was out of the question in the reign of Constantius.

The difficulty, however, may perhaps be solved by the evidence afforded by two lately-discovered documents. In a papyrus from Oxyrhynchos (G.O.P. 34$^\mathrm{v}$) there is contained an edict of the prefect Flavius Titianus with reference to the deposit of copies of archives in the Ἁδριανὴ βιβλιοθήκη at Alexandria. As the Sarapeion was the great library of Alexandria, it would be only natural for a chapel attached to it to be appropriated for the storage of archives; and the building represented on coins may be supposed to be this library of Hadrian.

There is also an inscription preserved in the Museum at Alexandria (M.A. 108), in which, among a long list of local officers, there are three times mentioned high priests of the Hadrianeion. This must have been a temple appropriated to the worship of Hadrian, whose deification is paralleled in the same inscription by that of Antoninus and Trajan, who likewise had a high priest. This temple would naturally be one of the earliest to be appropriated by the Christians, as it would not have anything like the same force of sanctity to preserve it as the Sarapeion or other temples of the older gods; and it would appear that, the worship of Hadrian having already fallen into disuse in the time of Licinius, the building had been turned to the more secular purposes of a gymnasium.

It seems reasonable, therefore, to suppose that the Hadrianon represented on the coins was the library of Hadrian mentioned in the decree of Titianus, and was a chapel attached to the Sarapeion; while the Hadrianon which, according to Epiphanius, was turned into a church in the time of Constantius II., was a distinct temple, and was the Hadrianeion whose priests are named in the Alexandrian inscription.

Note XIII.—The Death of Antinous.

The mystery which surrounds the death of Antinous was possibly not unintentional on the part of those concerned. The authorities on the question are, unfortunately, all comparatively late in date; and the nearest approach to contemporary evidence is found in Dio Cassius (lxix. 11), who quotes a statement of Hadrian that Antinous fell into the Nile. At the same time Dio states his own belief that the boy was sacrificed. F. Gregorovius, in his discussion of the matter (Hadrian, p. 172, 2nd ed.), inclines to think that the Egyptian priests professed to have discovered in the stars some mischance which threatened the emperor, and could only be averted by the death of his most cherished favourite; and thereupon Antinous devoted himself to save his master, with the prospect that his death would bring him the honours of deification. This theory is not out of consonance with the spirit of the Egyptian religion of the period; but perhaps it is unnecessary to suppose that the death of Antinous was other than accidental. Hadrian, in order to cover his passionate grief at the loss of his favourite (Hist. Aug. Hadrian, 14), and to justify himself in building a city to his memory, may have countenanced the elaboration of the story of his self-sacrifice. It is interesting, however, to compare with the commonly-received account a papyrus from Bacchias (discovered by Hogarth and Grenfell in 1896, and shortly to be published), which contains a copy of a letter of Hadrian, in which he moralises on the prospect of the continuation of life.

Note XIV. The Bucolic Revolt.

The Bucolic revolt is treated by Mommsen (Roman Provinces, ii. p. 261) as originally a rising of the criminals who had found a refuge in the marshes to the east of Alexandria. But this theory somewhat misapprehends the significance of the disturbance. The revolt began among the Bucolic troops (Hist. Aug. Aurelius, 21), who were Egyptians, recruited for home service, as appears from a letter (B.G.U. 625) written by a man who had been chosen by conscription for the corps, and was going to Skenai Mandrai to take up his military duties. It was therefore a much more serious matter than an outbreak on the part of a body of banditti; it was a mutiny on the part of the native auxiliaries, who were so far representative of the feeling of the country that they were joined by the neighbouring population. The leader of the revolt, Isidorus, appears to have been exalted into the position of a national martyr; as, in a papyrus (G.O.P. i. 33) which is almost certainly connected with the revolt of Avidius Cassius, his name is quoted by Appianus, an Alexandrian gymnasiarch, as one of his predecessors in death on behalf of their country.

Note XV.—Aurelius Theocritus.

The interesting papyrus published by J. Nicole (Pap. Gen. 1, and R.A. 1893, p. 225) probably refers to the events mentioned by Dio Cassius under the reign of Caracalla. It contains a letter written by Aurelius Theocritus to the strategoi of the Arsinoite nome, referring to the esteem in which Titanianus (a high official, since he is given the epithet κράτιστος) was held by the emperor, and ordering them "to treat his people well, not to injure his property or disturb his labourers, and to give him every assistance," on pain of the severest displeasure.

The emperor is mentioned as Antoninus simply; but the name Aurelius Theocritus shows that it is Caracalla rather than Antoninus Pius who is in question, as a freedman of the latter would have had the gentile name of Ælius; and the tone of the letter distinctly suggests that it was written by one of the freedmen, who habitually acted as secretaries of the emperors. In these considerations, there is strong ground for identifying the writer of the letter with the freedman of Caracalla, Theocritus, mentioned by Dio. It is then very tempting to attempt to find in the Titanianus of this letter the procurator Titianus, who is reported to have been assassinated by order of Theocritus for insulting him; and the letter itself becomes additionally interesting, as it may have been a prelude to the assassination. The date of the letter is, on this theory, 9th June 214.

NOTE XVI.—THE EGYPTIAN "TYRANTS."

Mommsen (Roman Provinces, ii. p. 251, note 1) doubts the existence of the alleged Egyptian tyrants Æmilianus, Firmus, and Saturninus; and he assumes the disturbances which are described as having taken place in Alexandria during the middle of the third century, beginning in the reign of Gallienus, to have all belonged to the period of the Palmyrene occupation of Egypt. There is, however, reason to suppose that the accounts given by the ancient historians are more nearly correct than Mommsen would allow them to be, and that there were two distinct wars in Egypt during this period: one, during the reign of Gallienus, connected with the revolt of Æmilianus; and a second, beginning perhaps in the last year of Gallienus and continuing till after the accession of Probus, which was waged by the Romans against the Palmyrene invaders.

The fullest account of the first struggle is to be found in the Historia Augusta (Gallienus, 4; Triginta Tyranni, 22). But more important evidence is contained in a letter of Dionysius, bishop of Alexandria, who died in 265: he describes how the two factions had divided the town into two hostile parts, and rendered the space between their halves a desert (Eusebius, Hist. Eccl. vii. 21). This is a definite proof of civil war in Alexandria before the Palmyrene invasion, as in 265 the Palmyrene government was still on terms of friendship with Rome. Further, the existence of Æmilianus as a claimant to the rule of Egypt is attested by coins, which R. S. Poole gives good reasons for attributing to him (B.M. Catalogue of Coins—Alexandria, Introduction, p. xxiv.); and the fact of his striking coins is sufficient to show him to have held possession of Alexandria, where alone there was a mint. On these grounds there seems to be a reasonable amount of contemporary support for the account of the revolt of Æmilianus given in the Historia Augusta.

Of the Palmyrene invasion there is a detailed and

reliable account in Zosimus (i. 44, 61). The details of the part taken by Firmus in the war are to be found in the Historia Augusta (Firmus; Aurelianus, 32); and, in the absence of any evidence to support his theory, it is difficult to see why Mommsen should reject the whole account, as there is nothing intrinsically improbable in the existence of an Egyptian leader acting in alliance with the Blemmyes and Palmyrenes. He did not rise to the importance of a "tyrant" of Egypt till after the defeat of the Palmyrenes; but when they were driven out of Alexandria he became the leader of the opposition to the Romans, although there is no evidence that he was proclaimed emperor. Vopiscus, the writer of the lives of Aurelian and Firmus in the Historia Augusta, contradicts himself upon this point: in one place (Aurelianus, 32) stating that Firmus ruled Egypt without the insignia of empire; in another (Firmus, 2), that he wore the purple, called himself emperor in his edicts, and struck coins. In the absence, however, of edicts or coins of Firmus, it may be justifiable to doubt whether he did assume the title of emperor.

NOTE XVII.—GEORGE THE MUKAUKIS.

The Arab account of the conquest of Egypt names the most important actor on the Roman side as Al-Muḳauḳis, or, more fully, as George son of Menas the Muḳauḳis (Abû Ṣâliḥ, 23 a). He is represented as the governor of Egypt, as having invited the Arabs into the land, and finally as the betrayer of the country to the invaders. There are, however, some intrinsic improbabilities in the tale which have called for explanation.

Professor Karabacek has discussed (in Mittheilungen aus der Sammlung der Papyrus Erzherzog Rainer, i. 1) the position of the Muḳauḳis, and concludes that the name was a transference of the Greek honorary title μεγαυχής, and that the position of George son of Menas was probably that of pagarch.

The evidence of John of Nikiou, however, which is much earlier and more reliable than that of any Arab writer, throws a good deal of light on the question. He states that, after the battle of Heliopolis (about July 640), when 'Amr was preparing to besiege Babylon, he sent to George the prefect, and ordered him to build a bridge over the canal of Kalyoub, north of Babylon; and George then began to co-operate with him (John of Nikiou, 113). In this fact may be found the origin of the Mukaukis story. George was probably prefect of Augustamnica, as his province is not specified, and the names of the prefect of the province of Egypt and the prefects of Lower Egypt and Arcadia at this time are given elsewhere by John. His post on the eastern frontier of Egypt would make him the first person of high rank to whom the messengers of Mahomet came; and thus it came to pass that the earliest communications between the Mahometans and the Romans in Egypt were carried on through him; and he naturally assumed a position of importance in the eyes of the Arab chroniclers. Subsequently, when he went over to the Mahometan side, he was able, by commanding from his province the communications between Babylon and Alexandria, to render most valuable assistance to 'Amr: and thus his importance was further enhanced. The prominence given to him in the Arab accounts is doubtless due to these circumstances.

Note XVIII.—Village Lands and the Corn Tax.

A papyrus from Soknopaiou Nesos, published by J. Nicole (Pap. Gen. 16, with commentary in R.A. 1894, ii. p. 34), shows that, in one instance at least, common land of the village existed in Egypt. It is a complaint from twenty-five farmers, and in the course of the narrative it is stated that there were "a number of arourai of land, belonging to the village," on the shore of the lake Moeris. "When this land is uncovered" after the yearly flood, "it is let for cultivation, and the rent of corn paid by the lessees is deposited in the imperial granaries, for the purpose of defraying all charges on the village. By means of this rent the village has been able to meet all its liabilities, both public and private," and thereby had been free from the distress common in Egypt at the time.

This interesting document throws considerable light on the method of payment of the tax of corn in Egypt. 'Al-Makrizi (xxvi.) gives a description of the general rule laid down by the Romans: the imperial officials decided the amount to be paid by each village, after considering its condition of prosperity, and notified the local authorities. These thereupon met, and divided their assessment among the inhabitants of the village. The papyrus shows that the amount assessed by the representatives of the government was regarded as the common liability of the village; and in such a case as that of Soknopaiou Nesos, where the village had certain common property, could be wholly or partially met out of the proceeds of that property. It was in accordance with this principle that the persons responsible for the payment of the full amount of the tax assessed were the elected representatives of the district,—the elders, or, in the case of a town which had been granted the privilege of self-government by a senate, the prytaneus, —who were liable to have their property impounded till the tax was paid (B.G.U. 8).

Two Oxyrhynchos papyri (G.O.P. i. 127, 142) bear out the statement of 'Al-Makrizi, that the towns or villages were required to pay their assessed proportion of the corn tax to the authorities at Alexandria. In these it is recorded how the towns of Oxyrhynchos and Kynopolis and the village of Koma had sent their quota down the river, bearing the cost of freight.

That the village of Soknopaiou Nesos was not unique in having lands which belonged to the village as a community, is shown by a contract for leasing village land at Obthis in the Hermopolite nome (C.P.R. i. 41), and a proposal to rent from the senate of Hermopolis certain land owned by the city (C.P.R. i. 39).

Note XIX.—Annona.

The occasional references to payments of corn as annona, found in the papyri, do not furnish any definite information upon this tax. It appears that it ranked with the other charges on land, δημόσια and σιτικά (B.G.U. 94), and that it was collected, like them, in corn by the sitologoi (B.G.U. 336, 529, 534). The rate, however, at which it was assessed upon the land cannot at present be determined. Its purpose may possibly be conjectured from a reference in the Coptic panegyric of Victor the son of Romanus (Mémoires d. l. Mission Archéologique Franç. viii. 2, p. 190), where it is stated that Victor received sixteen annonæ. This suggests that the annona was the allowance of corn made by the government to the inhabitants of Alexandria, which had apparently been made continuously from the time of the Greek rulers of Egypt, and was increased by Diocletian (Procopius, Arcan. 26). The manner in which the annona is coupled with the epibole, or supply of corn for the use of Constantinople, in the recital of burdens on the land in a lease, supports this view (B.G.U. 519). And it further appears, from the recitals in leases (compare B.G.U. 289 and 519), that the three taxes which were imposed specially on the land were δημόσια, σιτικά, and annona. The first is known to refer to the payments of corn into the public granary for the supply of the next year's seed ; the second, to the contributions levied for the support of Rome, and afterwards of Constantinople. There is no third object recorded to which the government turned the corn they collected in Egypt, except that of the grant to Alexandria. It is probable, therefore, that this was the purpose to which the annona was put.

Note XX.—Stephanikon.

The object of the tax known as the stephanikon has been discussed by F. G. Kenyon (Catalogue of Greek Papyri in B.M. ii. p. 107), who concludes that it was a continuation of the στέφανος,—a special present to the king,—collected under the Ptolemies; or possibly a revival of it by Caracalla, as the earliest receipts for it (B.G.U. 62; Pap. B.M. 474) are dated in 199. It may also be observed that, of the nine extant documents referring to this tax, seven fall within the years 199 to 222,—that is, from the association of Caracalla in the empire to the death of Elagabalus; while the other two, which are undated, may be taken, on palæographical grounds, as belonging to the same period. If, therefore, the tax may be supposed to have been revived by Caracalla, it may also be supposed to have been abolished by Severus Alexander.

All entries for payments of the tax are in sums of four drachmæ, or multiples of that amount, with one exception (B.G.U. 535); and this perhaps gives some support to the theory that the pretext of the impost was a special present,—the usual gift required being a single tetradrachm, which was the only coin of a higher standard than copper struck in Egypt, and was the commonest coin current in the country. The payments of the tax, however, were apparently not calculated on an annual basis; for instance, one man paid thirteen tetradrachms in the course of twenty-one months (B.G.U. 452).

Note XXI.—Rents paid for Land.

In the following list are classified the various records of rents paid in Egypt during the Roman period. The cases (1) in which the rent is fixed by a rate per aroura, and those (2) in which it is a certain proportion of the produce, are separated. Where no remark is added as to the nature of the crop, the land may be presumed to have been corn land; the rent was paid in corn, unless otherwise stated:—

I.

Reference.	Date.	Nome.	Amount of Land.	Rent.
B.G.U. 644	69	Arsinoite	20 ar.	2 art. per ar.
B.G.U. 538	100	do.	10 ar.	72½ art.
B.G.U. 661	140	do.	5 ar.	20 art.
G.O.P. i. 101	142	Oxyrhynchite	38 ar.	190 art. and 12 drach.
Pap. B.M. 314	149	Arsinoite	7 ar.	14 art.
B.G.U. 227	151	do.	1 ar.	6 art.
C.P.R. 31	154	do.	3 ar.	10 art. and 23 choinices of bread.
B.G.U. 708	165	do.	3 ar.	21 art.
B.G.U. 39	186	do.	5 ar.	22½ art.
Pap. B.M. 350	212	do.	150 ar.	2 art. per ar.
C.P.R. 33	215	do.	93 ar.	2½ art. per ar.
C.P.R. 35	216	Herakleopolite	6 ar.	20 art.
C.P.R. 32	218	Arsinoite	12 ar.	2 art. per ar.
B.G.U. 633	221	do.	2 ar.	10 art.
C.P.R. 36	225	Herakleopolite	1 ar.	5 art. barley.
C.P.R. 37	251	do.	5 ar.	32 art.
C.P.R. 38	263	Arsinoite	2 ar.	6 art.
C.P.R. 39	266	Hermopolite	6 ar.	18 art. and 72 drach.
C.P.R. 40	301	Herakleopolite	50 ar. pasture	250 drach. per ar.
C.P.R. 41	305	Arsinoite	9 ar.	5¼ art. per ar.
G.O.P. i. 102	306	Oxyrhynchite	9 ar. flax	1 tal. 3500 dr. per ar.
B.G.U. 408	307	Arsinoite	½ ar.	1½ art.
B.G.U. 349	313	do.	2 ar.	2 art. per ar.
B.G.U. 411	314	do.	5 ar.	12½ art.
G.G.P. i. 54	378	do.	40 ar.	3 art. and ½ art. barley per ar.
B.G.U. 586	4th cent.	do.	13 ar.	1½ art. per ar.
G.G.P. i. 56	536	Hermopolite	4 ar.	20 art. for watered part, 10 for unwatered.

2.

Reference.	Date.	Nome.	Amount of Land.	Rent.
B.G.U. 197	17	Arsinoite	2 ar.	$\frac{2}{3}$ produce.
Pap. B.M. 163	88	do.	$4\frac{1}{2}$ ar. vineyard	$\frac{2}{3}$ produce.
B.G.U. 237	165	do.	$\frac{3}{4}$ ar.	$\frac{1}{2}$ produce.
G.O.P. i. 103	316	Oxyrhynchite	1 ar. flax	$\frac{1}{2}$ produce.
G.G.P. i. 58	561	Hermopolite	$3\frac{3}{4}$ ar.	$\frac{1}{3}$ produce, less 18 carats.
Pap. B.M. 113, iv.	595	Arsinoite	$3\frac{3}{4}$ ar.	$\frac{3}{4}$ produce and $\frac{5}{8}$ hay.
Pap. B.M. 113, iii.	6th cent.	do.	$3\frac{3}{4}$ ar.	$\frac{3}{4}$ produce and $\frac{5}{8}$ hay.
B.G.U. 308	Byzantine	do.	40 ar. pulse	$\frac{2}{3}$ pulse and $\frac{1}{8}$ hay.
C.P.R. 42	do.	Herakleopolite	$22\frac{2}{3}$ ar.	$\frac{1}{2}$ crop.

APPENDIX V

REFERENCES

CHAPTER I.

(1) Letronne, Recueil, p. 140.
(2) Tacitus, Hist. i. 11, gives this side of the question.
(3) *Ibid*. iii. 48.
(4) Philo, adv. Flaccum, 13 (see ch. II. § 11), illustrates the difficulty.
(5) See Dio Chrysostom, or. xxxii. ad Alexandrinos.
(6) See ch. III. § 7 for examples.
(7) Tacitus, Ann. ii. 59.
(8) *Ibid*. Hist. i. 11.
(9) Dio Cass. lviii. 19 (Severus).
(10) Tac. Hist. i. 11 (Ti. Julius Alexander).
(11) Philo, adv. Flac. 1.
(12) Dio Cass. lvii. 17.
(13) C.I.G. iii. 4956, 4957 (edicts against extortion); compare G.O.P. i. 44 (advice to lighten burden of tax-farmers).
(14) C.I.G. iii. 4957; B.G.U. 176, 648; Appendix III. 5 (orders as to exemptions).
(15) B.G.U. 378 (delegation to dikaiodotes), 613 (to præfectus alæ); G.O.P. i. 67 (to an ex-magistrate).
(16) B.G.U. 113, 114 (as to legality of marriage of soldiers), 614; C.P.R. 18; Pap. B.M. 177 (disputes as to inheritance); G.O.P. i. 38 (lawsuit as to identity of a child), i. 67, 71; Pap. B.M. 358 (concerning property), 354 (as to wrongful imprisonment).
(17) B.G.U. 19 (reference on a point of legal interpretation from royal scribe), 195 (case to be referred by epistrategos); G.O.P. i. 97 (reference from strategos).
(18) B.G.U. 347 (prefect at Memphis), 362 (at Arsinoe), 525 (at Nilopolis).
(19) B.G.U. 325 (negligent lestopiastai to be sent bound to prefect).
(20) B.G.U. 159, 372 (proclamations to those who had fled to escape liturgies), 256; C.P.R. 20; G.O.P. i. 40 (petitions to prefect against nominations to liturgies).
(21) B.G.U. 198, 420; G.G.P. ii. 56; G.O.P. i. 72 (orders for

returns as to property); B.G.U. 484; Pap. B.M. 260 (for census); G.O.P. i. 34ᵛ (order as to keeping of records).

(22) B.G.U. 696 (exchanges and enlistments sanctioned by prefect), 113, 114, 195 (soldiers' grievances); G.O.P. (release from service granted).

(23) See Appendix II. for a list of known prefects and their dates.

(24) Seneca, Cons. ad Helv. xvii. 4.

(25) B.G.U. 288.

(26) The position of the dikaiodotes is discussed by Wilcken (Observationes ad historiam Ægypti prov. Rom.) against Marquardt, and by Mitteis (Herm. xxx. p. 564 ff.); see also Strabo, xvii. 1, and B.G.U. 378 (which proves the superior authority of the prefect).

(27) B.G.U. 327, and Note III. App. IV.

(28) B.G.U. 361; Pap. B.M. 196 (cases referred from strategos).

(29) See Note I. App. IV. as to the position of the archidikastes.

(30) Strabo, xvii. 1.

(31) G.G.P. ii. 71 (a case from Kysis in the Oasis), and others cited in Note I.

(32) B.G.U. 136.

(33) See Simaika (La Prov. Rom. d'Egypte, part iv. ch. 1) as to the provinces and authority of the epistrategoi.

(34) B.G.U. 19, 168, 340, 462.

(35) B.G.U. 15, 194, 235.

(36) B.G.U. 43; G.G.P. i. 49; Pap. B.M. 376.

(37) Wilcken (Hermes, xxvii. p. 287 ff.) has collected and discussed most of the evidence as to the strategoi.

(38) Letronne, Rech. 129; C.I.G. iii. 4722, 4732, 4736 (union of Hermonthite and Latopolite nomes), 5077 (Ombite and Hermonthite nomes and district of Thebes); M.A. Inscr. 108 (Apollonopolite and Sethroite nomes).

(39) B.G.U. 2, 6, etc. (Arsinoite nome divided into districts of Herakleides and Themistos with Polemon; united, B.G.U. 181, 244); see Note II. App. IV.

(40) B.G.U. 2, 72, 589 (complaints of trespass), 22, 45, 181, 242 (of assault), 46, 321, 663 (of robbery); G.G.P. ii. 61 (of embezzlement); Pap. Gen. 6; Pap. B.M. 357 (of debt); B.G.U. 361, 448; Pap. B.M. 171 b (for opening of will).

(41) N. et E. 69 (discussed by Wilcken, Philologus, liii. Ὑπομνηματισμοί); B.G.U. 245.

(42) B.G.U. 136 (powers delegated by archidikastes), 245 (by dikaiodotes).

(43) B.G.U. 647 (evidence of a surgeon as to a wound taken); compare G.O.P. i. 51 (report of a physician on a suicide).

(44) Pap. B.M. 309, 328, 376; B.G.U. 26, 53, 55, 59, 60, etc.; Pap. Gen. 5; G.G.P. ii. 45, 45 a; G.O.P. i. 74; see introduction to G.G.P. ii. 55, and Kenyon, Cat. of Greek Papyri, ii. 18.

(45) C.I.G. iii. 4957; compare G.O.P. i. 57 (responsibility of strategos for payment of taxes); B.G.U. 598; G.G.P. ii. 44 (assessment of taxes); B.G.U. 8, 462 (recovery of debts).

REFERENCES

(46) B.G.U. 6, 91, 235.
(47) C.I.G. iii. 4957; see also Note II. App. IV.
(48) B.G.U. 473; G.O.P. i. 82.
(49) C.I.G. iii. 4957; compare G.O.P. i. 61.
(50) B.G.U. 26, 51, 52, 53, 55, 59, 60, etc.
(51) B.G.U. 17, 79.
(52) B.G.U. 18, 168, 358, 529; see also Note III. App. IV.
(53) See Note II.
(54) The office of nomarch is discussed by Viereck (Hermes, xxvii. p. 516 ff.).
(55) G.G.P. ii. 44 50 a, b.
(56) B.G.U. 220, 221, 345, 356, 463; Pap. B.M. 297 b.
(57) B.G.U. 8.
(58) B.G.U. 8.
(59) B.G.U. 8 (προεστῶτες τῶν νομαρχικῶν ἀσχολημάτων).
(60) B.G.U. 73; C.P.R. 18.
(61) B.G.U. 184, 240, 379; Pap. B.M. 299, 300.
(62) B.G.U. 112, 420, 536.
(63) B.G.U. 184, 240, 420, 459, 536; Pap. B.M. 299, 300 (βιβλιοφύλακες ἐγκτησέων).
(64) B.G.U. 478, 480 (βιβλιοφύλακες δημοσίων λόγων).
(65) B.G.U. 6 (at Mouches in the Arsinoite nome); Pap. B.M. 199 (at Soknopaiou Nesos); but see Kenyon, Cat. of Papyri in B.M. ii. p. 158, on the question of income.
(66) B.G.U. 214, 345, 381, 382, 431; G.G.P. i. 48; Pap. B.M. 255.
(67) B.G.U. 148, 195; compare Pap. B.M. 342.
(68) G.G.P. ii. 67.
(69) B.G.U. 53, 59, 95, 97, 524, 537, 577; G.G.P. i. 45; Pap. Gen. 5 (census returns collected by village scribe); B.G.U. 20, 139; Pap. B.M. 131 (returns as to lands and crops); B.G.U. 84, 330, 457, 659 (as to taxes); B.G.U. 6, 18, 91, 194, 235 (names supplied for liturgies).
(70) B.G.U. 53, 59, 95, 97, 154, 225, 484, 524, 577.
(71) The powers of the agoranomos are discussed by Mitteis (Hermes, xxx. p. 564 ff.); see also Note IV. App. IV.
(72) B.G.U. 177, 193; N. et E. 17; C.P.R. 6, 7, 8; G.O.P. i. 73, 75, 96, 99, 106, 107.
(73) G.O.P. i. 45, 46, 47, 48, 49, 50, 100.
(74) B.G.U. 86, 191, 196, 234, 297, 350, 394, 514, 542; Pap. B.M. 142, 334, 341, 348.
(75) B.G.U. 153; C.P.R. i. 4; Pap. B.M. 142, 143, 154, 293.
(76) The police administration of Egypt is treated by Hirschfeld (Sitzungsb. d. Kaiserl. Akad. zu Berlin, 1892, p. 815); see also Note V. App. IV.
(77) G.O.P. i. 80.
(78) B.G.U. 6, 147, 148, 321, 374, 375, 376; G.G.P. ii. 43, 66; Pap. B.M. 199; G.O.P. i. 69, 80.
(79) B.G.U. 147, 376 (associated with euschemones), 148 (with archephodoi).

(80) B.G.U. 147, 376 (euschemones); Pap. B.M. 199 (eirenophylakes).
(81) B.G.U. 325 (lestopiastai); Pap. B.M. 199; G.O.P. i. 43ᵛ (phylakes).
(82) B.G.U. 98, 157, 515.
(83) B.G.U. 388 (inventory taken by exegetes of property of a dead man, probably a State debtor); G.O.P. i. 54 (exegetes asked to pay an account on behalf of the city), 56 (acting for strategos).
(84) B.G.U. 147, 376 (euschemones ordered to present a criminal in court), 194 (supplied names for liturgies), 381 (received payment of taxes).
(85) C.P.R. 20 (money spent on office of kosmetes).
(86) B.G.U. 347 (gymnasiarch acting as strategos); G.O.P. i. 54, 88.
(87) Strabo, xvii. 1; B.G.U. 250.
(88) B.G.U. 15, 25, 41, 42, etc.; G.G.P. ii. 52, 62 a; Pap. B.M. 166 a, 258, 306, etc. (πράκτορες ἀργυρικῶν).
(89) B.G.U. 414, 425, 457, 515; Pap. B.M. 171 a (πράκτορες σιτικῶν).
(90) B.G.U. 362 (πράκτορες βαλανείου).
(91) B.G.U. 62, 362, 542, 458, 518; Pap. B.M. 474, 477 (πράκτορες στεφανικοῦ).
(92) B.G.U. 194; compare B.G.U. 15.
(93) Pap. B.M. 306.
(94) B.G.U. 10, 478, 479, 480.
(95) B.G.U. 81, 425 (σίτου), 381 (κρίθης).
(96) B.G.U. 25, 41, 42; Pap. B.M. 255.
(97) B.G.U. 15, 67, 81, 188, etc.
(98) B.G.U. 7 (dekaprotoi sent in returns as to cultivators), 552, 553, 554, 556, 557, 579, 743, 744 (measured corn in granary).
(99) C.I.G. iii. 4867, 4868, etc. (Syene); Petrie, Koptos, c. vi. No. 4 (Koptos); Pap. B.M. 318, 320 (Prosopite nome).
(100) G.O.P. i. 44.
(101) G.I.G. iii. 4957; G.O.P. i. 44.
(102) Compare C.I.G. iii. 4867, 4876, 4877, 4882, 4885 (tax collected by farmers), with C.I.G. iii. 4870, 4875, 4879, 4880, 4883 (same tax collected by praktores).
(103) B.G.U. 8.
(104) B.G.U. 8 (epitropos inquired into property of State debtor), 156 (received rent for State land), 620 (collected fines due to the imperial treasury), 648 (issued order as to work on royal lands); C.P.R. 1 (sold confiscated land).
(105) Dio Cassius, li. 17; see also Note VI.
(106) Strabo, xvii. 1.
(107) C.I.G. iii. 4957 (exemption of Alexandrians from taxation); Eusebius, Hist. Eccl. vii. 21 (their sharing in corn distribution); Philo, adv. Flacc. 10 (privilege as to scourging); Pliny, Ep. ad Traj. 6 (attainment of Roman citizenship).
(108) Dio Cassius, li. 17; Hist. Aug. Sev. 17.

REFERENCES

(109) C.I.L. viii. 8934.
(110) Strabo, xvii. 1 ; see Note VI. App. IV.
(111) See Note VI. App. IV. ; Pap. Gen. 10.
(112) C.I.G. iii. 4679.
(113) B.G.U. 362, 586; C.P.R. 34, 45 ; Pap. B.M. 233, 348.
(114) B.G.U. 554; C.P.R. 35.
(115) C.P.R. 8, 9, 10, 35, 39.
(116) G.O.P. i. 55, 56, 59, 60, 77, 80, 87, 103.
(117) C.I.G. iii. 4822, 4823, 4824 ; see Note VII. App. IV.
(118) See Notitia Dignitatum and Hieroclis Synecdemus as to the higher officers of the Byzantine government in Egypt; see also Note VIII. App. IV.
(119) Pap. B.M. 234.
(120) B.G.U. 305, 320, 366, 396, 403 ; Pap. B.M. 113^{10}; see also Wilcken (Hermes, xxvii. p. 287 ff.).
(121) B.G.U. 21.
(122) G.O.P. i. 42, 52, 53, 66, 83, 84, 85, 86, 87 ; see editor's note on 42.
(123) G.O.P. i. 66.
(124) Pap. B.M. 113^{10}, 408.
(125) B.G.U. 21 (ephor and quadrarius); Codex Theod. xii. 6, 22 (exactores).
(126) Pap. B.M. 240, 241, 242, 245, 406, 411, 412.
(127) Pap. B.M. 408.
(128) G.O.P. i. 125.
(129) G.O.P. i. 126.
(130) G.O.P. i. 142, 143.
(131) G.O.P. i. 133 (see also 134-139) ; Codex Theod. xi. 24. 1, 3.

CHAPTER II.

(132) See ch. I. § 23.
(133) Josephus, Antiq. xiv. 7. 2, xix. 5. 2 ; compare Strabo, xvii. 1, and Philo, leg. ad Gaium, 10.
(134) Dio Cass. li. 18.
(135) Strabo, xvii. 1. 53.
(136) Strabo, xvii. 1. 53 ; inscription of Gallus from Philæ, published by Lyons and Borchardt (Sitzungsb. d. Kaiserl. Preuss. Akad. d. Wissensch. zu Berlin, 1896, p. 469).
(137) Dio Cass. liii. 23 ; Ammianus Marcell. xvii. 4.
(138) Strabo, xvii. 1. 53.
(139) Suetonius, Aug. 17, 18.
(140) Strabo, xvi. 4. 22 ; see also Mommsen, Roman Provinces, ii. p. 290 ff. (English trans.), [whom I have followed here].
(141) See Note X. App. IV.
(142) Strabo, xvii. 1 ; Pliny, Nat. Hist. vi. 181 : Dio Cass. liii. 29.
(143) See for illustrations the numerous military inscriptions of the first, second, and third centuries A.D., found in the towns of the Dodekaschoinoi, in C.I.G. iii. 5042-5117.

(144) C.I.G. iii. 5080 ; see on this inscription Wilcken in Hermes, xxviii. p. 154.
(145) Tacitus, Ann. iv. 5, compared with Strabo, xvii. 1.
(146) Dio Cass. lvii. 10.
(147) Tacitus, Ann. ii. 59, 60, 61 ; Pliny, Nat. Hist. viii. 185.
(148) Philo, adv. Flacc. and legatio ad Gaium, and Josephus, Antiq. xviii. 8, are the authorities for the events described in §§ 9–12. Their accounts have been discussed by Wilcken (Hermes, xxx. p. 481 ff.).
(149) Josephus, Antiq. xix. 5. 2 ; Zonaras, vi. 11.
(150) B.G.U. 511 ; see Wilcken, l.c.
(151) Pliny, N.H. vi. 84.
(152) Periplus, 26 ; see Mommsen, Rom. Prov. ii. p. 294, note 1.
(153) See Note XI. App. IV.
(154) Josephus, Bell. Jud. ii. 18.
(155) Pliny, N.H. vi. 181.
(156) Tacitus, Hist. i. 31.
(157) B.M. Catalogue of Greek Coins—Alexandria, p. 21.
(158) Suetonius, Nero, 47 ; Plutarch, Vit. Galbæ.
(159) B.G.U. 189 (dated 7 A.D.).
(160) Pap. B.M. 277 (23 A.D.) ; B.G.U. 713 (41/2 A.D.).
(161) C.I.G. iii. 4699.

CHAPTER III.

(162) Tacitus, Hist. i. 31.
(163) Tacitus, Hist. ii. 6.
(164) Catalogue of Greek Coins of Alexandria in B.M. p. 25 ; Pap. B.M. 260, 261.
(165) Tacitus, Hist. ii. 79 ; Suetonius, Vesp. 6.
(166) Tacitus, Hist. iii. 8.
(167) Suetonius, Vesp. 7.
(168) Dio Cass. lxvi. 1 ; Tacitus, Hist. iii. 48.
(169) Suetonius, l.c. ; Tacitus, Hist. iv. 81 ; Dio Cass. lxvi. 8.
(170) Dio Cass. lxvi. 8.
(171) Tacitus, Hist. v. 1.
(172) Suetonius, Tit. 5.
(173) See R. S. Poole in introduction to Catalogue of Greek Coins in B.M.—Alexandria, p. xcvii.
(174) Juvenal, Sat. xv. ; and see Petrie, Nagada and Ballas, p. 65 (as to the identification of Ombos).
(175) Plutarch, de Iside, 72.
(176) Cassiodorus Chron.
(177) See App. I. p. 16 .
(178) Pliny, Panegyr. 31, 32.
(179) Eusebius, H.E. iv. 2 ; Dio Cass. lxviii. 32 ; John of Nikiou, 72 ; see also Butler, Coptic Churches, ch. iv. p. 178.
(180) Dio Cass. lxix. 11 ; Cassiodorus, Chron. See also Gregorovius, der Kaiser Hadrian, p. 473 ; and Note XII. App. IV.
(181) Historia Augusta, Hadr. 20.

REFERENCES

(182) Philostratus, Vit. Sophist. ii. 37. See Gregorovius, *op. cit.* p. 313.
(183) See R. S. Poole, Catalogue of Greek Coins in the B.M.—Alexandria, p. 31.
(184) See Petrie and C. Smith in Petrie, Hawara, cc. iii. and vi.
(185) Dio Cass. lxix. 11; Historia Augusta, Hadr. 14. See Note XIII. App. IV.
(186) Inscription in G.M., published in R.A. 1870, p. 314. See Mommsen, Rom. Prov. ii. p. 297, note; and Mahaffy, Empire of the Ptolemies, p. 185 and note.
(187) C.I.G. iii. 4725-4730.
(188) Malala, Chron. xi. p. 280 (ed. Niebuhr); John of Nikiou, 74; see P. Meyer in Hermes, xxxii. p. 224.
(189) See R. S. Poole, in Catalogue of Greek Coins in B.M.—Alexandria, p. 31.
(190) Dio Cass. lxxi. 4; Historia Augusta, Aurel. 21. See Note XIV. App. IV.
(191) Dio Cass. lxxi. 22; Historia Augusta, Aurel. 25; compare G.O.P. i. 33.
(192) Historia Augusta, Aurel. 26; Dio Cassius, lxxi. 28.
(193) Historia Augusta, Cassius.
(194) See Mommsen, Rom. Prov. ii. p. 302.
(195) Pliny, N.H. vi. 101.
(196) B.G.U. 68 (rate, 10 per cent.; date, 113 A.D.), 272 (12 per cent., 138), 301 (12 per cent., 157), 578 (12 per cent., 187); Pap. B.M. 311 (12 per cent., 149), 336 (12 per cent., 167).
(197) B.G.U. 372.
(198) B.G.U. 15 (dated 194); Pap. Gen. 16 (207); B.G.U. 159 (215).
(199) Historia Augusta, Comm. 17.
(200) B.G.U. 417.

CHAPTER IV.

(201) B.G.U. 646.
(202) B.G.U. 46.
(203) Historia Augusta, Niger, 10; Zosimus, Hist. i. 8; Eutropius, viii. 18.
(204) Historia Augusta, Severus, 8.
(205) A papyrus is dated by the reign of Niger on 3rd December 193 (G.G.P. ii. 60); another by the reign of Severus on 21st February 194 (B.G.U. 326).
(206) Dio Cassius, li. 17, lxxv. 31; Historia Augusta, Severus, 17.
(207) Dio Cassius, lxxvii. 22; Historia Augusta, Caracalla, 6.
(208) Dio Cassius, lxxvii. 21. See Note XV. App. IV.
(209) Dio Cassius, lxxviii. 35.
(210) *Ibid.*
(211) Dio Cassius, lxxx. 2.
(212) Catalogue of Greek Coins in the B.M.—Alexandria, pp. 235-239.

(213) Zosimus, i. 20; B.G.U. 8. See also Viereck on the latter in Hermes, xxvii. p. 516.
(214) Eusebius, H.E. vi. 41; B.G.U. 287.
(215) Catalogue of Greek Coins in the B.M.—Alexandria, pp. 298, 299; inscription in Petrie, Koptos, ch. vi. No. 7; G.G.P. i. 50.
(216) Historia Augusta, Gallienus, 4; Triginta Tyranni, 22; Eusebius, H.E. vii. 21. See Note XVI. App. IV.
(217) Zosimus, i. 44; Historia Augusta, Claudius, 11.
(218) Historia Augusta, Firmus, 2, 3. See Hogarth in Petrie, Koptos, p. 34, and Note XVI. App. IV.
(219) Catalogue of Greek Coins in the B.M.—Alexandria, pp. 309, 310.
(220) Zosimus, i. 61; Ammianus Marcellinus, xxii. 16; Eusebius, Hist. Eccl. vii. 32.
(221) Historia Augusta, Aurelianus, 32; Firmus, 5.
(222) Zosimus, i. 71; Historia Augusta, Probus, xvii.
(223) B.G.U. 475.
(224) Historia Augusta, Probus, 9.
(225) B.G.U. 8.
(226) B.G.U. 200 (price of corn, 8 drachmæ an artaba in 183), 14 (16 drachmæ in 255); G.G.P. i. 51 (19 drachmæ in latter part of third century).
(227) B.G.U. 362 (wages 1¾-3 drachmæ a day in 215), 14 (6 drachmæ in 255).

CHAPTER V.

(228) Procopius, de Bell. Pers. i. 19; see also Letronne, Recueil, ii. p. 205, and Revillout, R.E. iv. p. 156.
(229) Malala, Chronogr. xii. p. 308 (ed. Niebuhr); Eutropius, ix. 22, 23; Paulus Diaconus, x. 297; John of Nikiou, 77.
(230) See Poole in Catalogue of Greek Coins in B.M.—Alexandria, pp. xxv, xxvi.
(231) Procopius, Arcana, 26.
(232) C.I.G. iii. 4681; see J. P. Mahaffy in Athenæum, 27th February 1897, and Cosmopolis, April 1897; and in reply to him, W. M. F. Petrie in Athenæum, 10th April 1897.
(233) See Gibbon, Decline and Fall of the Roman Empire, ch. xiii.
(234) Eusebius, H.E. viii. 8; Coptic Panegyric of Victor in Mémoires de la Mission Archéologique Française, viii. 2.
(235) Lactantius, de mort. persecut.
(236) Zosimus, ii. 17.
(237) Zosimus, ii. 22.
(238) Socrates, H.E. i. 5; Sozomen, H.E. i. 15; Theodoret, H.E i. 1.
(239) Socr. i. 9; Soz. i. 21; Theod. i. 8.
(240) Socr. i. 27; Soz. ii. 22; Theod. i. 25.
(241) Socr. ii. 3; Soz. iii. 2; Theod. ii. 1.
(242) Socr. ii. 9; Soz. iii. 5; Theod. ii. 3.

(243) Socr. ii. 22; Soz. iii. 20; Theod. ii. 6.
(244) Socr. ii. 26; Soz. iv. 9; Theod. ii. 10.
(245) Ammianus Marcellinus, xxii. 11; Socrates, H.E. iii. 2; Sozomen, H.E. v. 7; Theodoret, H.E. iii. 14.
(246) Socrates, H.E. iii. 4. 15; Sozomen, H.E. v. 7, 15; Theodoret, H.E. iii. 2. 5; Julian, Ep. ad Ecdicium.
(247) Theodoret, H.E. iv. 2; Sozomen, H.E. vi. 5.
(248) Socrates, H.E. iv. 13. 20; Sozomen, H.E. vi. 12, 19, 20; Theodoret, H.E. iv. 18.
(249) Codex Theodos. xii. 1. 63.
(250) Socrates, H.E. iv. 37; Theodoret, H.E. 420.
(251) Socrates, H.E. i. 19; Athanasius, Apol. i. 21; Philostorgius, iii. 4.
(252) Codex Theodos. xi. 24. 1.
(253) Codex Theodos. xii. 18. 1, xii. 1. 63.
(254) Codex Theodos. xi. 2.

CHAPTER VI.

(255) Zosimus, iv. 30.
(256) See Mommsen, Hermes, xix. p. 218.
(257) Codex Theodos. xvi. 1. 2.
(258) Socrates, H.E. v. 16; Sozomen, H.E. vii. 15; Zosimus, iv. 37.
(259) Socrates, H.E. vi. 7.
(260) Socrates, H.E. vii. 7.
(261) Eutychius, Annales, i. 548 (ed. Migne); Theophanes, Chronogr. 70.
(262) Socrates, H.E. vii. 13.
(263) Socrates, H.E. vii. 15; Theophanes, Chronogr. 71.
(264) Evagrius, H.E. i. 7; Coptic Life of Schnoudi (in Mémoires de la Mission Archéol. Française, iv.), fol. 53 r.
(265) Priscus, frag. 21 (ed. Müller); Jordanes, de success regn.; with Letronne's comments in Recueil, ii. p. 205 ff. See also L. Stern in R.E. ii. p. 240, on a fragment of an epic poem relating to this war.
(266) Priscus, frag. 22 (ed. Müller); Eutychius, Ann. ii. 96; Evagrius, H.E. ii. 5.
(267) Evagrius, H.E. ii. 8; Eutychius, Ann. ii. 101; Theophanes, Chronogr. 95.
(268) Evagrius, H.E. iii. 4; Eutychius, Ann. ii. 105.
(269) Evagrius, H.E. iii. 12; Eutychius, Ann. ii. 108.
(270) Evagrius, H.E. iii. 23.
(271) Eutychius, Ann. ii. 132.
(272) Nonnosus, ap. Photium.
(273) Theophanes, Chronogr.; Paulus Diac. xvi. 471.
(274) Coptic life of Schnoudi, fol. 53 r.; Arabic life (in same vol. of Mémoires), p. 396.
(275) Coptic life of Schnoudi, fol. 47 v.; Arabic life, p. 380
(276) Codex Theodos. xiv. 262.

CHAPTER VII.

(277) Eutychius, ii. 152.
(278) *Ibid.* ii. 153.
(279) *Ibid.* ii. 161. See G. Lumbroso, Aneddoti di Archeologia Alessandrina, p. 12.
(280) Malala, xviii. p. 433; Paulus Diac. xvi. 461; John of Nikiou, 90.
(281) Procopius, de bello Persico, i. 20; Nonnosus (apud Photium). See also Beazley, Dawn of Modern Geography, pp. 184 and 208.
(282) Procopius de bello Persico, i. 20. See on this, Letronne, Materieux pour servir a l'histoire de l'Egypte, ii., and Revillout in R.E. iv. p. 156.
(283) C.I.G. iv. 8646.
(284) John of Nikiou, 95.
(285) John of Nikiou, 97.
(286) John of Nikiou, 107.
(287) John of Nikiou, 108.
(288) Eutychius, ii. 217.
(289) Paulus Diac. xviii. 579.
(290) John of Nikiou, 111, 112. See also E. W. Brooks, in Byzantinische Zeitschrift, iv. p. 435, on the chronology of the conquest of Egypt.
(291) John of Nikiou, 113. See Note XVII. App. IV.
(292) John of Nikiou, 114.
(293) John of Nikiou, 116–118.
(294) John of Nikiou, 119, 120.
(295) John of Nikiou, 120.
(296) Justinian, Edict XIII.
(297) See ch. I. § 30.
(298) John of Nikiou, 119.

CHAPTER VIII.

(299) C.I.G. iii. 4957; Dio Cass. lvii. 10.
(300) See ch. I. §§ 4, 7, 8, 10, 19.
(301) Pap. B.M. 267; B.G.U. 563.
(302) C.I.G. iii. 4957.
(303) See Note XVIII. App. IV.
(304) Pap. B.M. 267.
(305) See ch. I. § 19; and Kenyon, Catalogue of Greek Papyri in B.M. ii. p. 88.
(306) *E.g.* B.G.U. 64.
(307) B.G.U. 15; Pap. B.M. 295, 197.
(308) Pap. B.M. 256^{R}a; G.O.P. i. 63, 127^R, 142.
(309) C.I.G. iii. 4957.
(310) B.G.U. 414; Pap. B.M. 367a. See also Kenyon's note on the latter.
(311) See Note XIX. App. IV.
(312) See Viereck, Hermes, xxx. p. 107.

(313) B.G.U. 457; Pap. B.M. 193. See also Kenyon's note on the latter.
(314) B.G.U. 64, 534, 652; Pap. B.M. 347.
(315) B.G.U. 141.
(316) Pap. B.M. 119.
(317) B.G.U. 657.
(318) G.G.P. ii. 56.
(319) B.G.U. 572, 574, 662; Pap. B.M. 193, 380, 451; C.P.R. 1.
(320) Pap. B.M. 193; see also Kenyon's note.
(321) B.G.U. 563, 572, 573, 574; Pap. B.M. 451.
(322) B.G.U. 41, 216, 653.
(323) B.G.U. 236, 330, 342; Pap. B.M. 380, 451; C.P.R. 1.
(324) B.G.U. 25.
(325) B.G.U. 41, 63, 199, 292, 382; Pap. B.M. 255, 312.
(326) B.G.U. 41, 199^v, 219, 461, 521, 654; Pap. B.M. 319, 323, 468; G.G.P. ii. 48, 52.
(327) G.G.P. ii. 52.
(328) See Kenyon, Catalogue of Greek Papyri, ii. p. 79.
(329) B.G.U. 51, 52, 192, 266, 352, 353, 354, 355, 357, 358, 421; G.G.P. ii. 45, 45a (camels); B.G.U. 133 (sheep and goats).
(330) See Wilcken, Hermes, xxviii. p. 230; and Kenyon, Catalogue of Greek Papyri, ii. pp. 17, 20, 43.
(331) See examples in the ostraka published by S. Birch, P.S.B.A. v. pp. 84, 124, 158; also Pap. B.M. 170, 340. Compare, however, Kenyon, Catalogue of Greek Papyri, ii. p. 53.
(332) See Kenyon, *op. cit.* p. 18; Grenfell, G.G.P. ii. 55, note. Examples of census returns are, Pap. B.M. 476a (for year 103/4); B.G.U. 53, 420 (131/2), 95, 137 (145/6); G.G.P. ii. 55; B.G.U. 54, 58 (159/60); Pap. Gen. 18; B.G.U. 59 (173/4), 60, 115, 116 (187/8), 97, 129, 577 (201/2).
(333) B.G.U. 79, 110.
(334) Josephus, Bell. Jud. ii. 16.
(335) See Kenyon, Catalogue of Greek Papyri, ii. p. 44.
(336) Pap. B.M. 347.
(337) B.G.U. 62, 268, 362, 452, 458, 518, 535; Pap. B.M. 474, 477. See Note XX. App. IV.
(338) See the ostraka published by Birch, as above; also B.G.U. 220, 221, 277, 756 (ἁλιέων), 9, II. (βαφέων), 337 (γναφέων), 9 (γρυτοπωλῶν), 1; Pap. B.M. 255; (ξυτηρά) B.G.U. 10, 25, 199^v, 277, 652 (ζωγράφων), 485 (ἰχθυηράς), 617; G.G.P. ii. 60 (κοπῆς τριχός); B.G.U. 9, iv. (κορσάτων), 337 (λαχανοπωλῶν), 9, i. (μυροπωλῶν), 199^v, 212, 653 (πλοίων), 10, 337 (πλοίων ἁλιευτικῶν), 337, (ταριχευτῶν).
(339) Ostraka found at Syene, C.I.G. iii. 4863-4889 and elsewhere.
(340) Petrie, Koptos, c. vi.
(341) G.G.P. ii. 50; B.G.U. 724; Pap. B.M. 206 d, 307, 316 b. c., 469 a, b.
(342) Strabo, xvii. 1.
(343) *Ibid.*
(344) Published by D. G. Hogarth in Petrie, Koptos, c. v.

v—16

(345) G.G.P. ii. 58 ; Pap. B.M. 318, 320.
(346) G.G.P. ii. 50 a, b, f, g, h, i, m; Pap. B.M. 206 d, 307, 316 b, c.
(347) B.G.U. 724.
(348) G.G.P. ii. 50 c ; Pap. B.M. 469 a.
(349) See E.E.F. Report, 1896, p. 18.
(350) See Mommsen, Roman Provinces, ii. p. 299.
(351) G.O.P. i. 44.
(352) B.G.U. 748 II.; G.O.P. i. 96, 99 ; Pap. B.M. 297 b ; see also Kenyon's note on the last.
(353) B.G.U. 240, 326, 340.
(354) B.G.U. 96, 326, 338.
(355) B.G.U. 567, 568.
(356) B.G.U. 350, 542, 667 ; C.P.R. i. 4, 9, 10.
(357) C.I.G. iii. 4956.
(358) G.G.P. ii. 80, 81, 81 a, 82.
(359) G.O.P. i. 86.
(360) See ch. I. §§ 8, 19.
(361) C.I.G. iii. 4957.
(362) Pap. B.M. 306.
(363) C.I.G. iii. 4957.
(364) B.G.U. 194.
(365) B.G.U. 180.
(366) B.G.U. 658, 722, 733 ; G.G.P. ii. 53 a-g ; Pap. B.M. 139 b, 165, 166 b, 316 a, 321 a-c, 325.
(367) B.G.U. 99, 359, 391, 704 ; Pap. B.M. 296, 337.
(368) Pap. B.M. 113 ; G.O.P. i. 43, 60.
(369) G.O.P. i. 43.
(370) G.G.P. ii. 95.
(371) Codex Theodos. vii. 6.
(372) B.G.U. 362.
(373) B.G.U. 199, 292, 337 ; Pap. B.M. 460, 478.
(374) B.G.U. 199^v, 337 ; Pap. B.M. 347.
(375) Pap. B.M. 460.
(376) B.G.U. 383, 463, 718 ; Pap. B.M. 472.
(377) B.G.U. 337.
(378) B.G.U. 337, 471 ; Pap. B.M. 352.
(379) B.G.U. 707 ; and see Wilcken, Hermes, xxii. p. 142.
(380) B.G.U. 181, 234, 475.
(381) B.G.U. 156, 462 ; C.I.G. iii. 4957 ; Dio Cassius, lxvi. 8.
(382) B.G.U. 656.
(383) C.I.G. iii. 4713.

CHAPTER IX.

(384) See F. Krebs, Zeitschrift fur Æg. Sprache, xxxi. p. 31.
(385) B.G.U. i. 296 ; Pap. B.M. 353.
(386) App. III. No. 1.
(387) App. III. No. 5.
(388) B.G.U. 16, 149.

(389) B.G.U. 28.
(390) B.G.U. 16.
(391) E.g. B.G.U. 86.
(392) E.g. Pap. B.M. 258, ll. 206, 208.
(393) B.G.U. 16.
(394) B.G.U. 82.
(395) B.G.U. 1, 149; see ch. VIII. § 19.
(396) B.G.U. 194; App. III. No. 5.
(397) See ch. VIII. § 11.
(398) See ch. VIII. § 19.
(399) B.G.U. 229, 230.
(400) B.G.U. 296; Pap. B.M. 353.
(401) B.G.U. 337.
(402) See E.E.F. Report, 1896, p. 15; B.G.U. 124, 707.
(403) See E.E.F. Report, 1896, p. 18.
(404) B.G.U. 471.
(405) B.G.U. 488.
(406) B.G.U. 149, 248, 337, 362, 479, 748 II.; Pap. B.M. 262, 299, 345.
(407) Inscr. P.S.B.A. xi. 228.
(408) C.I.G. iii. 4711.
(409) C.I.G. iii. 4955.
(410) G.O.P. i. 43^v, 46, 47.
(411) C.I.G. iii. 5042-5070.
(412) C.I.G. iii. 5032, 5033.
(413) C.I.L. iii. 79; C.I.G. iii. 5074-5106.
(414) C.I.G. iii. 4714; Letronne, Recueil, DCXIV. seqq.; R.E.G. iv. p. 46, No. v. 1.
(415) C.I.G. iii. 4716.
(416) E.g. B.M. Catalogue of Greek Coins—Alexandria, 287, 572.
(417) C.I.L. iii. 75.
(418) See R. S. Poole, Introduction to B.M. Cat. of Greek Coins—Alexandria, p. xcix.
(419) C.I.G. iii. 4683.
(420) C.I.G. iii. 4713.
(421) B.M. Catalogue, 744, 1102, 1362.
(422) G.M. 301; G.G.P. ii. p. 85.
(423) B.M. Catalogue, 533.
(424) B.M. Catalogue, 126-131.
(425) C.I.L. iii. 75.
(426) B.M. Catalogue, 132-135.
(427) B.M. Catalogue, 929, 930, etc.; *ibid.* 427, 1041, etc.; App. III. No. 3.
(428) C.I.G. iii. 4839.
(429) Letronne, Recueil, No. DXLVII.; App. III. No. 6.
(430) B.C.H. 1896, p. 169.
(431) B.M. Catalogue, 936, 937.
(432) B.M. Catalogue, 141-144.
(433) E.g. B.M. Catalogue, 583, 1257.
(434) B.M. Catalogue, 586, 938.

(435) *E.g.* B.M. Catalogue, 585, 1404.
(436) B.M. Catalogue, 1191.
(437) B.M. Catalogue, pp. 353, 360.
(438) See R. S. Poole, Introduction to B.M. Catalogue, p. xlv.
(439) B.M. Catalogue, p. 354.
(440) B.M. Catalogue, 2173, 2313.
(441) B.M. Catalogue, 700.
(442) B.M. Catalogue, 1345.
(443) G.O.P. i. 114; B.C.H. 1896, p. 248; *ibid.* p. 167.
(444) B.G.U. 471.
(445) *E.g.* B.M. Catalogue, 138, 575.
(446) B.M. Catalogue, 69.
(447) B.M. Catalogue, 916.
(448) B.M. Catalogue, 407.
(449) B.M. Catalogue, 408, 582.
(450) B.M. Catalogue, 451.
(451) App. III. No. 4.
(452) B.G.U. 248.
(453) B.M. Catalogue, 2543.
(454) B.M. Catalogue, 1047-1057.
(455) Published by J. Baillet in R.A. 1889, p. 70.
(456) *E.g.* B.M. Catalogue, 703, 947, 1708.
(457) Tacitus, Hist. iv. 84.
(458) Tacitus, Hist. iv. 83; Plutarch, de Iside et Osiride, 28.
(459) B.M. Catalogue, 1193.
(460) B.M. Catalogue, 875.
(461) See Note XI.
(462) G.O.P. i. 43^v, 98, 99, 104, 110.
(463) C.I.G. iii. 4948.
(464) C.I.G. iii. 4839.
(465) B.G.U. 73, 136, 338, 362, 455; Pap. B.M. 445.
(466) B.G.U. 276, 332, 333, 384, 385, 449, 451, 623, 625, 714; as against B.G.U. 229, 230.
(467) B.M. Catalogue, 540, 879.
(468) *E.g.* B.M. Catalogue, 305, 750; see Introduction, p. lxiii.
(469) App. III. No. 10.
(470) B.M. Catalogue, 1121, 1339.
(471) C.I.G. iii. 4683 b.
(472) C.I.G. iii. 4713 b.
(473) Pap. B.M. 345.
(474) G.O.P. i. 34^v.
(475) B.G.U. i. 296; Pap. B.M. 353.
(476) B.G.U. 337.
(477) C.I.G. iii. 5115.
(478) C.I.G. iii. 4948, 4839.
(479) C.I.G. iii. 4715.
(480) App. III. Nos. 2, 3, 9, 11 (Apollinopolis); No. 7 (Pathyra).
(481) G.O.P. i. 43^v.
(482) Letronne, Recueil, cviii-clii.
(483) See ch. VI. § 10.

REFERENCES

(484) See Introduction to B.M. Catalogue, pp. lxiv-lxvi.
(485) M.A. inscription C.
(486) B.G.U. 1.
(487) B.G.U. 362.
(488) App. III. No. 2.
(489) Pap. B.M. 345.
(490) See Petrie, Religion and Conscience, p. 45.
(491) *E.g.* B.M. Catalogue, 625.
(492) *E.g.* B.M. Catalogue, 626.
(493) Petrie, Koptos, p. 22.
(494) See R. S. Poole, Introduction to B.M. Catalogue, p. lxviii.
(495) B.M. Catalogue, 1197.
(496) See R. S. Poole, Introduction to B.M. Catalogue, p. lxxi.
(497) B.M. Catalogue, 881.
(498) *E.g.* B.M. Catalogue, 639, 473, 647. The full number of sixteen cubits appear on a billon coin of Domitian in the Bodleian; but the specimen is too worn to give a good illustration.
(499) *E.g.* B.M. Catalogue, 28, 1161.
(500) *E.g.* B.M. Catalogue, 1158.
(501) B.G.U. 362.
(502) G.O.P. i. 43^v.
(503) Philo, leg. ad Gaium, 20, 43; Tacitus, Hist. iv. 81.
(504) C.I.G. iii. 4715.
(505) Lumbroso, Documenti Greci del R. Mus. Egiziano di Torino, App. II.
(506) C.I.G. iii. 4699.
(507) M.A. 108.
(508) Pap. B.M. 317; G.O.P. i. 43^v.
(509) C.I.G. iii. 5900.
(510) B.G.U. 82, 347.
(511) B.G.U. 362^5.
(512) Philo, de vita contemplativa.
(513) Eusebius, Hist. Eccl. ii. 16.
(514) Eusebius, Hist. Eccl. iv. 7.
(515) Eutychius, Ann. i.
(516) Eusebius, Hist. Eccl. vi. 6.
(517) Eusebius, Hist. Eccl. vi. 1.
(518) Eutychius, Ann. i.
(519) Eusebius, Hist. Eccl. vi. 40, vii. 11.
(520) Butler, Coptic Churches, i. p. 228.
(521) G.O.P. i. 43^v.
(522) Eusebius, Hist. Eccl. viii. 8.
(523) Socrates, Hist. Eccl. vii. 15.
(524) Mémoires d. l. Mission Archéologique, iv., Panegyric of Macarius, 130 f.
(525) Mémoires d. l. Miss. Arch. iv., Coptic Life of Schnoudi, foll. 50v, 65v; Arabic Life, pp. 385, 386, 425.
(526) *Ibid.* Arabic Life, p. 387; fragment, 5 B, col. 2.
(527) Zosimus, iv. 37.
(528) Priscus, fr. 21.

[529] See Petrie, Religion and Conscience, p. 46.
[530] Cod. Theod. v. 3.
[531] Cod. Theod. xii. 1. 63.
[532] See Butler, Coptic Churches, i. c. 4.
[533] Mém. d. l. Miss. Archéol. iv., Arabic Life of Schnoudi, p. 396.
[534] Eutychius, Ann. ii. 161.

CHAPTER X.

[535] G.O.P. i. 43.
[536] G.O.P. i. 42 (Grenfell and Hunt's translation).
[537] G.O.P. i. 59 (Grenfell and Hunt's translation).
[538] G.O.P. i. 138 (Grenfell and Hunt's translation).
[539] G.O.P. i. 152.
[540] G.O.P. i. 145.
[541] John of Nikiou, 119.
[542] G.G.P. ii. 67.
[543] G.O.P. i. 110 (Grenfell and Hunt's translation).
[544] G.O.P. i. 111 (Grenfell and Hunt's translation).
[545] G.O.P. i. 112 (Grenfell and Hunt's translation).
[546] E.E.F. Report, 1896, p. 17.
[547] Cecil Smith in Petrie, Hawara, ch. vi.
[548] See for example figs. 71, 73.
[549] See for examples fig. 56.
[550] See fig. 17.
[551] See fig. 87.
[552] B.G.U. 362, vii. There are several heads in the Museum at Alexandria.
[553] E.g. fig. 61.
[554] Fig. 63.
[555] G.O.P. i. 66.
[556] Hist. Aug. Saturninus, 8.
[557] See Mommsen, Rom. Prov. ii. p. 254.
[558] Hist. Aug. Aurel. 45.
[559] E.g. B.G.U. 426; Pap. B.M. 257.
[560] G.O.P. i. 84.
[561] G.O.P. i. 85 (Grenfell and Hunt's translation).
Prof. Petrie, however, remarks on this, "Either the denarius was a ridiculously small money of account, or else the 'pound' is misread. It should be either 600 pounds or else 10 denarii by value. Six pounds is a ridiculously small stock for a whole guild. I should emend it as 600 pounds or 6 talents."
[562] G.O.P. i. 83 (Grenfell and Hunt's translation)
[563] Pap. B.M. 131.
[564] B.G.U. 14.
[565] See B.G.U. 84.
[566] G.O.P. i. 102, 103.
[567] E.g. B.G.U. 166.
[568] See Note XXI. App. IV.

REFERENCES

(569) Pap. B.M. 131ᴿ.
(570) See ch. VIII. § 17.
(571) B.G.U. 362, viii.
(572) B.G.U. 14.
(573) See ch. I. § 3.
(574) B.G.U. 22.
(575) G.G.P. ii. 78.
(576) Mém. d. l. Miss. Archéol. iv., Arabic Life of Schnoudi, p. 356.
(577) *Ibid.* Coptic Life, fol. 26.

INDEX

ABRAHAM, ruler of Homeritæ, defeats Axumitæ, 109.
Abyssinia, embassy to, 109.
Adane, destruction of, 34.
Administration of justice, prefect at head of, 3.
,, dikaiodotes, assessor of prefect in, 4.
,, position of archidikastes in, 4.
,, local authority of epistrategos in, 5.
,, position of strategos in, 5.
,, duties of elders, 7.
,, entrusted to military officials, 9–13.
 v. Police.
Ælius Gallus, prefect, made expedition into Arabia, 20.
Æmilius Rectus, prefect, rebuked by Tiberius, 25.
Æthiopians, treaty of Gallus with, 19.
,, invaded Upper Egypt, 21.
,, defeated by Petronius, 21.
,, made terms with Rome, 23.
,, invasion proposed by Nero, 36.
Agoranomos, position and duties of, 8.

Agoranomos at Alexandria, 11.
Agriculture, irrigation, 164.
,, crops, 165.
,, terms of leases of lands, 165.
Agrippa, riots caused in Alexandria by visit of, 29.
,, secured restoration of Jewish privileges, 32.
Agrippa the younger, king of Chalkis, complained of by Alexandrian Greeks, 33.
Alexander Severus, reign of, 73.
,, ,, and Epagathus, 74.
Alexandria, local government of, 11.
,, privileges of citizenship at, 11.
,, position of, lowered by Augustus, 16.
,, senate at, restored by Severus, 11.
,, anti-Jewish riots at, under Caligula, 29.
,, riots provoked by Jews at, under Claudius, 31.
,, ,, under Nero, 35.
,, ,, under Trajan, 52.
,, buildings restored by Hadrian, 54.
,, riots at, 61.

INDEX

Alexandria, sacked by Caracalla, 71.
,, revolted against Gallienus, 77.
,, occupied by Palmyrenes, 80.
,, captured by Diocletian, 86.
,, and Arian controversy, 88 *et seq.*
,, patriarchs of, and civil government, 97, 107.
,, besieged by Arabs and evacuated by Romans, 116.
,, state of, at close of Roman rule, 117.
,, allowance of corn to, 119.
v. Annona.
Amen, associated with Zeus, etc., 133.
'Amr, Arab general, defeated Romans at Heliopolis, etc., 115.
,, took Babylon and Nikiou, 116
,, made terms with Cyrus, 116.
v. Note XVII., 224.
Anastasius, reign of, 103.
Annona, tax for allowance of corn made to Alexandria, 119.
v. Note XIX., 227.
Antinoopolis, senate at, 12.
,, founded by Hadrian in memory of Antinous, 59.
Antinous, death of, 59.
v. Note XIII., 220.
Antoninus Pius, reign of, 60.
,, visited Alexandria, 62.
Aphrodite, worship of, 137.
Apollinarius, made patriarch and prefect by Justinian, 107.
Apollo, worship of, 136.

Arabia, unsuccessfully invaded by Ælius Gallus, 20.
,, trade with, *v.* India, Homeritæ, Red Sea.
Arabs, and trade with India, 33.
,, revolt of, against Persians, 114.
,, under 'Amr defeat Romans at Heliopolis, 115, 116.
v. Note XVII., 224.
Arcadius, reign of, 97.
Archephodos, duties of, 8.
Archidikastes, position and duties of, 4.
,, local judge of Alexandria, 11.
v. Note I., 196.
Archives, in general charge of archidikastes, 6.
,, local, kept by bibliophylax, 7.
,, housing of, at Alexandria, 219.
Archon, of Thebes, 12.
v. Note VII., 214.
Ares, worship of, 137.
Aristomachus, defeated Nubians and Mauretanians, 111.
Arithmetikon, house-tax, 121.
Arius and Arian controversy, 88 *et seq.*, 154.
Arkarikarios, position of, 14.
Arsinoe, senate at, 12.
Art, revival of, under Hadrian, 56.
,, low level of style of, in Roman Egypt, 162.
Artemis, worship of, 136.
Artemius, condemned to death, 92.
Asklepios, worship of, 140.
Assessment of farm lands, 118.
Athanasius, and Arius, 88.
,, deposed and banished, 89.
,, returned, 90.
,, again deposed, 90.
,, and Constantius, 91.
,, and Julian, 92.

INDEX

Athanasius again patriarch, 93.
Athene, worship of, 137.
Augustus, reasons for organisation of Egypt by, 2.
,, senate at Alexandria abolished by, 11.
,, reign of, 15.
Aurelian, reign of, 80.
,, Palmyrenes expelled by, 80.
,, defeated Firmus, 80.
Aurelius, Marcus, reign of, 62.
,, ,, revolt of native Egyptians under Isidorus against, 63.
,, ,, and revolt of troops under Avidius Cassius, 63.
,, ,, visited the East, 64.
Aurelius Theocritus, v. Note XV., 222.
Avidius Cassius, revolt of, 63.
Avillius Flaccus, rule of, as prefect, 28.
,, ,, disgrace of, 30.
Axumitæ, treaties with, 94, 108.

BABYLON, fortress of, rebuilt by Turbo, 53.
,, taken by Amr, 116.
,, adapted for monastic purposes, 156.
,, station of a Roman legion, 169.
Balbinus, reign of, 75.
Basilicus, expelled Zeno, 102.
Basilides of Alexandria, Gnostic heresy, 152.
Baths, tax on, 10.
,, sign of Greek influence, 160.
Bes, worship of, 131.
Bibliophylax, position and duties of, 6.

Blemmyes, joined Palmyrenes and threatened frontier, 79.
,, dominated the Thebaid, 81.
,, driven back by Probus, 81.
,, subsidised by Diocletian, 86.
,, ravaged the Greek Oasis, 99.
,, defeated by Maximinus, 100.
,, treatment of, by Justinian, 110.
Bonakis, defeated imperial troops, 112.
,, defeated and slain by Bonosus, 112.
Bonosus, victory of, over Bonakis, 112.
,, defeated by Niketas, 113.
Bucolic troops, revolt amongst, 63.
v. Note XIV., 221.
Buddhism and Egyptian religions, 151.
Byzantine period, change in organisation during, 13.
,, ,, officials of, Note VIII., 215.

CÆSAREUM, sign of Roman influence, 160.
,, and emperor-worship, 149.
Caligula, reign of, 28.
,, worshipped by Alexandrians, 149.
Canals, care of, 19, 82, 126.
,, from Nile to Red Sea, 53.
Capitolium, sign of Roman influence, 160.
Caracalla, gives citizenship to all Egyptians, 11.
,, reign of, 70.

INDEX

Caracalla, massacres Alexandrians, 71.
Carinus, reign of, 82.
Carriers, receive allowance for transporting corn, 119.
Carus, reign of, 82.
Catholicus, position of, 13.
Cattle, taxes on, 121, 124.
Census, ordered by prefect, 3.
" received by strategoi, 6.
" royal scribe assisted in, 6.
" collected by village scribe, assisted by laographoi, 8.
" taken every fourteen years for purposes of taxation, 122.
Chalcedonian decrees, and the Egyptian Church, 103.
China, trade with, 65.
Christianity in Egypt, introduced by Mark, 151.
" decree of Theodosius for, 96.
" and Egyptian politics, 76, 87, 88, 96–107.
" liberty of religion granted to Christians, 156.
" and union of civil and religious powers, 153.
" and influence of Platonist and pagan ideas, 155.
v. Heresies, Monasticism, Persecutions, Patriarchs, etc.
Citizenship, Alexandrian, privileges of, 11.
" a step to Roman, 11.
Claudius, reign of, 31.
" and Jews, 32.
" Alexandrian mints under, 34.

Claudius, development of trade under, 38.
Claudius II., reign of, 78.
Coinage, reopening of Alexandrian mints under Claudius, and general state of coinage up to time of Nero, 34, 38.
" revival of artistic taste marked in, 56.
" drop in standard of, 66.
" further deterioration of, 82.
" reform in, introduced by Diocletian, 86.
" decrease in, 95.
v. Note IX., 217.
Coins, representations of deities on, 133 et seq.
Comes, and control of troops, 12.
Commodus, reign of, 65.
" Egyptian trade under, 65, 66.
Constans, supports Athanasius, 90.
" and Constantius, 91.
Constans II., reign of, 116.
Constantine, relieves Christians, 88.
" and Arian controversy, 89.
" relation of, with Christian Churches of Egypt, 89, 152.
Constantinus II., reign of, 115.
Constantius II., deposes Athanasius, 90.
" reign of, 90.
Convict labour in quarries and mines, 127.
Coptic remains, 111.
Copts, go over to Arabs, 115.
Cornelius Gallus, prefect, suppressed revolt, 17.

INDEX

Cornelius Gallus, recalled by Augustus, 19.
Corn tax, v. Taxes, and Note XVIII., 225.
Council, of prefect, 4.
Crops raised in Egypt, 165.
Curiales responsible for taxes, 95, 125.
Customs, collected by farmers, 10.
,, houses, 123.
,, rates, 124.
,, stations, 123, 124.
Cyril of Alexandria and Jews, 98.
,, ,, and Orestes, 99.
Cyrus, made peace with Arabs, 116.

DECIUS, reign of, 76.
,, persecuted Christians in Egypt, 76.
Deities, local, not identified with Greek gods, 131.
,, of Fayum, 129.
v. Chapter IX. generally.
Dekaprotos, position of, 10.
Demeter, worship of, 138.
Didius Julianus, reign of, 67.
Dikaiodotes, position and duties of, 4.
Diocletian, reorganised government, 12, 86.
,, reign of, 84.
,, and the Thebaid, 84.
,, besieges and sacks Alexandria, 86.
,, and coinage reform, 86.
,, and persecution of Christians, 87.
Dioiketes, position of, 11.
Dionysus, worship of, 137.
Dioscorus, patriarch of Alexandria, excommunicated, 100.
Dioskouroi, worship of, 139.
Dodekaschoinoi, occupied by Roman troops, 23.

Domain-lands, property of emperor, 89.
,, administration of, 11, 13, 127.
Domitian, reign of, 46.
,, recognition of local deities under, 47.
Domitius Domitianus, L. (Achilleus), revolted against Diocletian, 86.
Dux, position of, 12.
,, Ægypti and Byzantine officials, Note VIII., 215.
Dykes, repair of, 126, 165.

ECONOMIC conditions—
During first century of Roman rule, 38.
From Severus to Diocletian, 82, 83.
Improvement under Diocletian, 94, 95.
During last century of Roman occupation, 117.
Eirenarchs, duties of, 8.
Eirenophylax, duties of, 8.
Elagabalus, reign of, 73.
Elders, position and duties of, 7.
,, associated in police administration, 8.
,, in Byzantine period, 13.
Elesbaan, king of Axum, and Homeritæ, 109.
Embolator, position of, 14.
Embole, corn tax required from villages, 119.
Emperors, worship of, 149.
Ephor, position of, 13.
Epibole, corn tax (= Embole), 119.
Epimeletes, position of, 14.
Epistatikon, 126.
v. Taxes.
Epistrategos, position of, 4.
,, duties of, 5.
,, abolished by Diocletian, 12.
Epitropos, position of imperial, 11.
,, under Diocletian, 13.

Estate-duties, 124.
Ethnikos, position of, 14.
Euschemones, duties of, 8, 9.
Euthenia, consort of Nilus, worship of, 147.
Exactor, position of, 13.
Exegetes, position of, 9.
,, at Alexandria, 11.
Export and import duties, 122-125.

FAMINE, a signal for disturbances, 50.
Farmers, difficulties of, during second cent. A.D., 82.
,, v. Agriculture.
Farmers of taxes, position of, 10.
,, v. Taxes.
Faustina, wife of M. Aurelius, intrigue with Avidius Cassius, 63.
Fayum, deities of the, 129.
,, customs, dues, etc., in the, 124.
Firmus, defeated by Aurelian, as a "Tyrant"; v. Note XVI., 223.
Florus (Prefect), compelled Blemmyes to agree to peace, 100.

GALBA, accession of, 39.
,, murder of, 41.
Galerius, reign of, 88.
,, persecution of Christians by, 98.
Gallienus, reign of, 77.
,, granted liberty of religion to Christians, 152.
Gallus, reign of, 76.
Games, in Oxyrhynchos, 160.
,, privileges of victors in, 160.
,, "Blues" v. "Greens," 161.
,, the racecourse, 160.
,, village festivals, 161.
Garrison, Roman, reduced by Tiberius, 24.

Garrison, withdrawn for Jewish war, 44.
,, further reduced by Trajan, 49.
See App. I., 169.
Geometria, estate tax, 121.
George of Cappadocia, patriarch, 91.
,, murder of, 92.
George the Mukaukis, Note XVII., 224.
Germanicus, visited Egypt, 26.
Geta, reign of, 70.
Ghizeh Museum, inscriptions in, 183 et seq.
Gnostic heresy, 152.
Gods, worship of, 128 et seq.
,, joint (double) names, 133.
,, Greek and Egyptian, worshipped in same temple, 132, 133.
Goods, rates and duties on, 124.
Gordianus I., reign of, 75.
Gordianus II., reign of, 75.
Gordianus, III., reign of, 75.
Goths, brought into Egypt, 96.
Grapheion, contracts registered at, 8.
Greek deities, identification of, with Egyptian gods, 132.
,, v. Hellenic Theology.
Greeks, and Jews in Alexandria, 32, 33, 54.
,, influence of, in Egyptian religious systems, 128-132, 141.
Gregory and Athanasius, 90, 91.
Gymnasiarch, position of, 9.
,, at Alexandria, 11.
Gymnasium, sports, etc., 160.
,, supplanted by the racecourse, 160.

HADAD, king of Axum, and Romans, 108.
Hades, type of Sarapis, 140, 141.
Hadrian, reign of, 54.
,, and Alexandrian philosophers, 55.

INDEX

Hadrian, artistic revival under, 56.
,, and Antinous, 59.
,, visits Egypt second time, 59.
Hadrianeion at Alexandria, Note XII., 219.
Haroeris, identified with Herakles, 139.
Harpokrates, worship of, 145, 146.
Helios, worship of, 136.
Hellenic Theology—
and Egyptian religious systems, 128-132.
worship of Zeus (Ammon, etc.), 132-134.
Greek deities worshipped in Egypt, 132-141.
Henotikon, edict published, 103.
Hera, worship of, 135.
Heraclius I., reign of, 113.
,, drove Persians out of Egypt, 114.
Heraclonas, reign of, 116.
Herakleopolis, senate at, 12.
Heresies, Arian, 88 *et seq.*, 154.
,, Gnostic, 152.
Hermanubis, worship of, 147.
Hermes, worship of, 137.
,, Pautnuphis, temple to, at Pselkis, 133.
Hermopolis, senate at, 12.
,, custom-house at, 124.
,, temple of, 133.
Heroopolis, revolt of, 17.
Homeritæ, treaty with, 94.
,, asked by Anastasius to attack Persia, 103.
,, second embassy by Justinus, 104.
,, quarrel of, with Axumitæ, 108.
,, subdued by Axumitæ, 109.
Horus, worship of, 133, etc.
House property, taxes on, 121.
Hygieia, worship of, 140.

Hypatia, murder of, 99.
Hypomnematographos, clerk of city at Alexandria, 11.

IDIOLOGOS, position and duties of, 9.
,, abolished by Diocletian, 13.
Imperial lands, *v.* Domain Lands.
Imperial treasury, and revenue from Egypt, 118.
Import duties, 123, 124.
Income-tax, 122.
India, trade with, through Red Sea ports secured by Government, 33.
,, duties on goods from, through Arab ports, 34.
,, trade with, through Axumitæ, 108.
,, development of trade with, 38-65.
Industries and manufactures, 163.
Irrigation, system of, improved under Augustus, 19.
v. Agriculture and Canals.
Isidorus, revolt of native Egyptians under, 63.
Isis, worship of, 142 *et seq.*
,, in Rome, 47.
,, at Tentyra, 149.
,, temple of, at Philæ, destroyed by Justinian, 110.
,, at Oxyrhynchos, 159.
,, associated with Sarapis and Harpokrates at Alexandria, 140.
,, as Nepherses associated with Soknopaios, 129.

JEWS, in Alexandria, favoured by Augustus, 16.
,, governed by an ethnarch, 16.
,, rising of Greeks against, under Caligula, 29.
,, deprived of citizenship, 29.

INDEX

Jews, send embassy to Rome, 31.
," provoke riots, under Claudius, 31.
," privileges restored to, 32.
," Egyptian, and Palestine, 35.
," disturbances between Greeks and, 32, 33, 52.
," revolt of, suppressed by Turbo, 52.
," expelled by Cyril, 105.
," and religious matters, 151.
," Therapeutai, sect of, 151.
John, prefect of Alexandria, deposed and reinstated, 112.
," of Nikiou, and Arab conquest of Egypt, 225.
Jovian, reign of, 93.
Julian, reign of, 91.
," and Arian controversy, 91, 92.
Julius Æmilianus, nominated emperor by Alexandrians, 77.
," ," defeated, 78.
  v. Note XVI., 223.
Justinian, reign of, 106.
," and Monophysites, 107.
," appointed Apollinarius patriarch and prefect, 107.
," and monastic establishments, 107.
," destroyed temple of Isis at Philæ, 110.
," and Alexandrian school of philosophy, 110.
Justinus, reign of, 104.
," and Homeritæ, 104.
Justinus II., reign of, 110.

KANDAKE, queen of Æthiopians, 23.
Katoikoi, exempted from poll-tax, 122.

Khem, assimilated with Pan, 133.
Khnum, assimilated with Zeus, 133.
Komarch, position of, 13.
Koptos, custom-house at, 123, 124.
," worship of Osiris at, 147.
Kosmetes, position of, 9.
Kronos, worship of, 135.
Kybele, worship of, 135.
Kynopolis, war of, with Oxyrhynchos, 47.

LAOGRAPHOI, duties of, 8.
Legal contracts, fees on, 124.
Leo I., reign of, 101.
Leo II., reign of, 102.
Lestopiastes, position of, 8.
Library, public, of Alexandria, 141.
Licinius, reign of, 88.
," defeats Maximinus, 88.
," rival of Constantine, 90.
Liturgies, hereditary burden of, and exemptions from, 125.
," of repairing dykes, etc., 126.
," of collecting taxes, 10.
Local government, in villages, 7.
," ," comparison of ancient with modern, Note IX., 216.
Logistes, position of, 13.
Logos, doctrine of; Platonists of Alexandria and development of, 155.

MACRIANUS I., reign of, 77.
Macrianus II., reign of, 77.
Macrinus, reign of, 73.
Manumission of slaves, fine on, 124.
Marcianus, reign of, 100.
," and Alexandrian Church, 100.
," sacked Alexandria, 101.

INDEX

Mark, and introduction of Christianity into Egypt, 151.
Mary, Egyptian influence on development of worship of, 155.
Mauretanians, defeated by Aristomachus, 111.
Maurice, riots in reign of, 112.
Mavia, queen of Saracens, 94.
Maximinus, reign of, 75, 88.
,, persecution of Christians by, 88.
Maximinus (prefect), defeat of Blemmyes by, 100.
Min, Osiris worshipped as, 147.
Monasticism, influence of the desert on, 151.
,, and the Therapeutai, 155.
,, and the Christian Church of the Middle Ages, 158.
,, whole districts under monastic vows, 104.
,, monastic corporations, power of, 104, 105.
,, recognised by law, 155.
,, monasteries as refuges and forts, 93, 107, 156-158.
,, as refuges of overburdened officials, 95, 125.
,, troops quartered in, 126.
,, the Red M., 98.
,, the White M., 157, 158.
,, at Nitriotis destroyed, 97.
,, monks, military service and liturgies, 93, 155.
,, and robbery and expulsion of Alexandrian merchants, 99.

Monophysite controversy, 107, 155.

NAUBION, property-tax, 120.
Naukratis, senate at, 12.
Nero, reign of, 34.
,, and conquest of Eastern provinces, 36.
,, recalled legions, 39.
,, as "Agathos Daimon," 149.
Nerva, reign of, 48.
Nicæa, Council of, 89.
Niketas, defeated Bonosus, 113.
,, abandoned Egypt to the Persians, 114.
Nikiou, taken by 'Amr, 116.
Nikopolis, founded by Augustus, 16.
,, camp of Roman garrison, 17.
Nile, worship of, connected with Sarapis, 147.
,, rise of, and corn tax, 118.
,, trade, custom-house for, at Syene, 123.
Nit, Athene identified with, 137.
Nitriotis, monasteries of, destroyed by Theophilus, 97.
Nobatæ, invited to settle on frontier, 86.
,, made war on Blemmyes, 99.
,, punished by Maximinus, 100.
Nomarch, position and duties of, 6.
Nubians, defeated by Aristomachus, 111.

Octroi, customs and entrance dues, 123.
Odænathus, prince of Palmyra, and Romans, 78.
Offices, nominations to government and local, supervised by prefect, 3.
,, made by strategos, 5.

V—17

Offices, returns for, supplied by village scribe, 8.
Officials, difficulties of position of, 95, 125.
Ombos, quarrel of, with Tentyra, 47.
Orestes (prefect), and Cyril, 99.
Osiris, worship of, 147.
,, Apis (Sarapis), 140.
Ostraka, receipts of payments on, 122.
Otho, reign of, 40.
Oxyrhynchos, senate at, 12.
,, war of, with Kynopolis, 47.
,, life at, 156, 159 *et seq.*
,, papyri, 159.
,, churches, temples, public buildings, etc., at, 159.
,, festivals, etc., 160.

PAGARCH, position and duties of, 13.
,, house of Flavius Apion described as, 14.
Palestine, Egyptian Jews and, 35.
Palmyrenes, invaded Egypt, 78, 79.
,, and Blemmyes occupied Upper Egypt, and part of Alexandria, 80.
,, defeated by Aurelian, 80.
Pan, assimilated with Khem, 133.
Panopolis, temple to Pan-Khem at, 133.
Paralemptes, duties of, 10.
Patriarchs of Alexandria, and civil government, 97, 100, 106, 107.
Patronage, in villages, 95.
,, forbidden, 14.
,, patrons and village amusements, 161.

Persecutions by Galerius and Maximinus, 88.
,, by Diocletian, 87, 152.
,, by Decius and Valerian, 76, 152.
,, by Christians, 153.
Persephone, worship of, 139.
Persians, and Egyptian trade, 108, 109.
,, invaded the Delta, 103.
,, took possession of Egypt, 114.
,, expelled by Heraclius, 114.
,, revolt of Arabs against, 114.
Pertinax, reign and murder of, 67.
Pescennius Niger, declared emperor, 68.
,, defeated by Severus, 69.
Petesouchos, worship of, 131.
Petronius, C., suppressed rising of Alexandrians, 19.
,, cleared canals, 19.
,, again prefect, 21.
,, defeated Æthiopians, 21.
v. Note X., 217.
Phemnoeris, deity of Fayum, 131.
Philæ, temple of Trajan at, 50.
,, temple of Isis at, destroyed by Justinian, 110.
,, fortifications of, renewed by Theodorus, 110.
Philip, reign of, 75.
Philosophical school of Alexandria—
Hadrian and, 55, 56.
Justinian and, 110.
Influence of, on Jewish writings, 128.
and Christianity, 155.
Philumenus, plot of, 90.
Phocas, revolt against, by Heraclius, 112.

INDEX

Phylax, position and duties of, 8.
Pnepheros, deity of Fayum, 131.
Police, under prefect, 3.
,, duties of elders, 7.
,, local officers of, 8.
,, Note V., 209.
Poll-tax, collected by praktores, 9.
,, by farmers, 10, 121.
,, exemptions from, 122.
Poseidon, worship of, 135.
Posting rights, claimed by officials, 128.
Præpositus pagi, position of, 13.
Præses, position of, 12.
Praktor, position and duties of, 9.
,, superseded by exactor in Byzantine period, 13.
Prefect, position and duties of, 3.
,, changed position of, under Diocletian, 12.
,, list of prefects of Egypt, 176.
v. Delegation of Duties, Note III., 203.
Priesthood, Egyptian, privileges of, 129–131.
Probus, defeated by Palmyrenes, and committed suicide, 79.
Probus, drove back the Blemmyes, 81.
,, named emperor, 81.
Pronoetes, position of, 14.
Property, taxes on, 120.
Proterius, bishop of Alexandria, 100.
Pylons, occupied by monks, 156.

QUADRARIUS, position of, 13.
Quietus, reign of, 77.
Quintillus, reign of, 80.

RATES, charged on passengers, goods, etc., 124.
Red Sea, trade, 33.
,, suppression of piracy on, 34.
,, trade, customs, and dues on, 123, 124.
Red Sea, development of trade on, 38.
Register of lands under cultivation, 119.
Registry of deeds, etc., Note IV., 208.
Rents, land, Note XIX., 228.
Revenues, collection of, etc., 9.
v. Taxes.
Roman citizenship, attainable through Alexandrian, 11.
,, granted to all provincials, 111.
Roman influence, on Egyptian religious ideas, 148.
,, in worship of the Emperors, 149.
,, in control of religious affairs and temple treasures, 149.
Royal scribe, position and duties of, 6.
,, list of, in Herakleid division of Arsinoite nome, 202.

SABINA, wife of Hadrian, visits Egypt, 59.
Sahara, custom-house for goods from the, 124.
Saracens, incursion of, 94.
,, treaty with, 94.
Sarapis, temple at Alexandria destroyed, 97.
,, worship of, 140.
,, worshipped at Rome, 47.
,, Isis and Harpokrates, 140.
,, Hades and, 140, 141.
,, Isis and, 142.
,, temple of, at Oxyrhynchos, 159.
Saturninus, Note XVI., 223.
Schedia, customs station at, 124.
Schnoudi, information regarding monasteries in Life of, 104, 158.

Schmoudi, and pagan property, 153.
Scribe, royal, 6.
" village, 71.
Sebek, local forms of, 131.
" worship of, 133.
Seed-corn, supplied by the authorities, 120.
Selene, worship of, 136.
Senate, at Alexandria, abolished by Augustus, 11, 16.
" restored by Severus, 11.
" at Ptolemais, Naukratis, Antinoopolis, and nome capitals, 12.
" in Byzantine period, 13.
    v. Note VI., 212.
Severus, restored senate to Alexandria, 11, 70.
" defeated Pescennius Niger, 69.
Sinai, Mount, passes under, guarded by monastery, 158.
Sitologos, collection of corn tax by, 119.
Slaves, fine on manumission of, 124.
Social customs, 162.
Sokanobkonneus, deity of Fayum, 131.
Soknopaios, worship and temple of, 129.
" associated with Isis Nepherses, 129.
" priesthood of, 130.
Sokonpieios, deity of Fayum, 131.
Sothiac period, completed in first year of Antoninus, 62.
Souchos (Sebek), deity of Fayum, 131.
Stephanikon (tax), 10, 122.
    v. Note XX., 228.
Strategos, position and duties of, 5.

Strategos, superseded in Byzantine period, 13.
" of police at Alexandria, 11.
    v. Notes, 200, 203.
Sukatoimos, deity of Fayum, 131.
Syene, custom-house at, 123.

TACITUS, reign of, 80.
Talmis, temple of, 18.
Taxes, supervised by prefect, 3.
" strategoi responsible for local, 6.
" nomarchs local supervisors of, 6.
" elders intermediaries in, 7.
" based on returns of village scribe, 8.
" under special supervision of idiologos, 9.
" collected by praktores, 9.
" by epiteretai and paralemptai, 10.
" by farmers, 10.
" by exactores, 13.
" by ethnikos and embolator, 14.
" curiales responsible for, 95.
" annona, 119.
" bath tax, 10.
" corn tax, 10, 118, 119, 225.
" for charitable purposes, 120.
" naubion, and geometria, 120.
" on house property, arithmetikon, etc., 121.
" on cattle, 121, 124.
" poll-tax, 121.
" (exemptions), 122.
" stephanikon, 10, 122, 228.
" special, on temple property, offerings, etc., epistatikon, 126.

INDEX

Taxes, customs and indirect, 123, 124.
Temples, used as Christian churches, 97.
,, joint use of, by native and Greek worshippers, 132.
,, as public library at Alexandria, 141.
,, taxes on property of, 126.
Tentyra, quarrel of, with Ombos, 47.
,, gateway of Trajan at, 51.
,, temple of, 19.
Theatre, sign of Greek influence, 160.
Thebaid, revolt of, in time of Augustus, 18.
,, ruled by dux, 12.
,, invaded by Blemmyes, 81.
Thebes, archon at, 12.
 v. Note VII., 214.
Theodosius I., enforced Christianity, 96.
Theodosius II., reign of, 98.
Theophilus, of Alexandria, destroyed monasteries of Nitriotis, 97.
Therapeutai, Jewish sect, 151.
,, and monasticism, 155.
Thoeris, special deity of Oxyrhynchos, 159.
Tiberius, reign of, 24.
,, and unjust taxation, 25.
Tiberius II., reign of, 111.
Timagenes, invited Palmyrenes to enter Egypt, 79.
Titus, and Alexandrians, 44.
,, and nations of the Greek East, 46.
Town life in Oxyrhynchos, 159.
Trade guilds, 163.
Trade routes, 19, 123.
 v. Custom-houses.

Trade with East, developed under Claudius, 33.
,, extended to China, 65.
,, controlled by Axumitæ and Homeritæ, 94.
Trajan, reign of, 48.
,, reduced Roman garrison of Egypt, 49.
,, temple of, at Philæ, 50.
,, cut canal from Nile to Red Sea, 63.
Triad of Alexandrian deities, 140 *et seq.*
Triakontaschoinoi, under Roman protectorate, 19.
Trinity, doctrine of the, Egyptian influence on development of, 155.
Triptolemos, worship of, 139.
Troops, Roman, in Egypt, under control of prefect, 3.
, ,, reduced by Tiberius, 24.
,, ,, reduced by Trajan, 49.
, ,, withdrawn, 117.
,, ,, supplies for, 126.
Tyche, worship of, 149, 150.
Tyrants, Egyptian, *v.* Note XVI., 223.

VABALLATHOS, son of Zenobia, 80.
Valens, reign of, 93.
,, and monks, 93.
,,' edict of, regarding curates, 95.
Valerianus, reign of, 77.
Vespasian, proclaimed emperor at Alexandria, 41.
,, expedition of, against Vitellius, 41.
,, recognised at Rome, 42.

Village, council formed by elders, 7.
„ scribe, position and duties of, 7.
„ amusements, 161.
„ lands and corn tax, 225.
Vitellius, proclaimed emperor by German troops, 41.

WAGES of labourers, etc., 166.
Watchmen, assigned to temples and public buildings 159.

ZABDAS, commander of Palmyrene army invading Egypt, 79, 80.
Zeno, expelled by Basilicus, 102.
„ reign of, 102, 103.
„ and Henotikon, 103.
Zenobia, invasion of Egypt by armies of, 78 80.
Zeus, worship of, as Zeus-Ammon, etc., 132-134.

www.ingramcontent.com/pod-product-compliance
Lightning Source LLC
Chambersburg PA
CBHW031942230426
43672CB00010B/2013